Urte Undine Frömming, Steffen Köhn, Samantha Fox, Mike Terry (eds.)
Digital Environments

**Media Studies**

Urte Undine Frömming, Steffen Köhn,
Samantha Fox, Mike Terry (eds.)
# Digital Environments
**Ethnographic Perspectives across Global Online and Offline Spaces**

[transcript]

The printed version of this book is available thanks to the support of Freie Universität Berlin, Department of Political and Social Sciences, Reserach Area Visual and Media Anthropology.

 An electronic version of this book is freely available, thanks to the support of libraries working with Knowledge Unlatched. KU is a collaborative initiative designed to make high quality books Open Access for the public good. The Open Access ISBN for this book is 978-3-8394-3497-0

**Bibliographic information published by the Deutsche Nationalbibliothek**
The Deutsche Nationalbibliothek lists this publication in the Deutsche Nationalbibliografie; detailed bibliographic data are available in the Internet at http://dnb.d-nb.de

**© 2017 transcript Verlag, Bielefeld**
transcript Verlag | Hermannstraße 26 | D-33602 Bielefeld | live@transcript-verlag.de

All rights reserved. No part of this book may be reprinted or reproduced or utilized in any form or by any electronic, mechanical, or other means, now known or hereafter invented, including photocopying and recording, or in any information storage or retrieval system, without permission in writing from the publisher.

Cover layout: Mike Terry
Typeset by Francisco Bragança, Bielefeld
Printed in Germany
Print-ISBN 978-3-8376-3497-6
PDF-ISBN 978-3-8394-3497-0

# Content

**Foreword** | 9
Sarah Pink

**Digital Environments and the Future of Ethnography**
An Introduction | 13
Urte Undine Frömming, Steffen Köhn, Samantha Fox, Mike Terry

## PART 1
## DIGITAL COMMUNITIES AND THE RE-CREATION OF THE SELF AND SOCIAL RELATIONSHIPS ONLINE

**A Comment on East Greenland Online**
Media Commenting Systems as Spaces for Public Debate with a Focus on East Greenland in the Greenlandic Media | 25
Jóhanna Björk Sveinbjörnsdóttir

**Welcome Home**
An Ethnography on the Experiences of *Airbnb* Hosts
in Commodifying Their Homes | 39
Brigitte Borm

**How has the Internet Determined the Identity of Chilean Gay Men in the Last Twenty Years?** | 53
Juan Francisco Riumalló Grüzmacher

**Red Packets in the Real and Virtual Worlds**
How Multi-Function WeChat Influences Chinese
Virtual Relationships | 67
Xiaojing Ji

**Antifeminism Online**
MGTOW (Men Going Their Own Way) | 77
Jie Liang Lin

**Exploring the Potentials and Challenges of Virtual Distribution of Contemporary Art** | 97
Jonas Blume

**Blind and Online**
An Ethnographic Perspective on Everyday Participation Within Blind and Visually Impaired Online Communities | 117
Olivier Llouquet

**How Has Social Media Changed the Way We Grieve?** | 127
Ellen Lapper

**Watch Me, I'm Live**
*Periscope* and the "New-Individualistic" Need for Attention | 143
Dario Bosio

## PART 2
## POLITICAL DIGITAL ENVIRONMENTS AND ACTIVISM ONLINE

**Hair, Blood and the Nipple**
*Instagram* Censorship and the Female Body | 159
Gretchen Faust

**Berlin. Wie bitte?**
An Exploration of the Construction of Online Platforms for the Mutual Support of Young Spanish Immigrants in Berlin | 171
Teresa Tiburcio Jiménez

**An Exploration of the Role of *Twitter* in the Discourse Around Race in South Africa**
Using the #Feesmustfall Movement as a Pivot for Discussion | 195
Suzanne Beukes

**Migration, Political Art and Digitalization** | 211
Sara Wiederkehr Gonzáles

**"You're Not Left Thinking That You're The Only Gay in the Village"**
The Role of the *Facebook* Group *Seksualiti Merdeka* in the Malaysian LGBT Community | 227
Veera Helena Pitkänen

**Finding a Visual Voice**
The *#Euromaidan* Impact on Ukrainian Instagram Users | 239
Karly Domb Sadof

**Google A Religion**
Expanding Notions of Religion Online | 251
Joanna Sleigh

**Notes on Contributors** | 263

# Foreword

*Sarah Pink*

The title of this book—*Digital Environments*—signifies a significant step in the ways we experience and conceptualize the everyday worlds that we live and research in. That is, both anthropologists and the people who collaborate with us in our projects, inhabit and co-constitute environments in which digital technologies and media are inextricably entangled. This is continually evidenced by our everyday experience as researchers, as the people we meet in the course of our projects move through worlds that are at once on-line and off-line, and as we ourselves undertake research in ways that are never separated from the digital or material elements of life. As argued in two recent publications, the way that we understand our ethnographic practice needs to account for this (Pink, Horst et al 2016), and we also need new theoretical tools with which to understand the "digital materiality" of our environments, and ongoing changing processes and things through which they are configured (Pink, Ardevol and Lanzeni 2016). As this book of essays shows, this digital material world is infinitely extensive and continually unfolding in new ways. It can be encountered across many places and is integral to many research themes and questions. In fact, there may not be anywhere that it does not impinge, given that in a world where the digital has come to dominate, to be non digital is itself a state or status that is determined, relationally, to the digital.

*Digital Environments* is moreover published in an academic context where digital anthropology and ethnography are flourishing. Its chapters therefore capture an intellectual moment where we are beginning to make sense of the digital elements of the environments we share with research collaborators; not so much as an object of study in themselves, but as something that anthropologists and ethnographers of other disciplines need to account for when exploring other topics—including fields such as art, wellbeing and activism. In this case we might ask: what is special about this "turn" in anthropological practice and attention? The answer is not that we simply have a new research subject or a new theoretical perspective that we might apply old forms of enquiry to, but rather that digital technologies and media bring with them a body of theoretical, methodological and practical implications. Many of the themes and issues they raise are in fact already part of the subdisciplines of visual and media anthropology. It is therefore, in this sense, not at all surprising that such an interesting collection of essays should emerge from the Visual and Media Anthropology program at Freie Universität Berlin. Media anthropology scholars have been ready for this moment for a long time. Moreover, recent works in media anthropology demonstrate a strongly developed field of theoretical and empirical media research (cf. Postill and Bräuchler 2010). Likewise, visual anthropologists were amongst the first to explore the possibilities of the internet for unconventional ways to disseminate their work. These sub-disciplines of anthropology and their fields of theory and practice therefore offer an important starting point for the study of digital environments. This is, moreover, a different starting point from others which have emerged, for instance, in ways situated more closely theoretically to material culture studies (Horst and Miller 2012) or that put participant observation at the center of the ethnographic research (cf. Boellstorf et al 2012). Instead, an approach to digital environments that is more closely harnessed to media and visual anthropology, and that is also informed by a training in visual anthropology practice, has something different to offer anthropology which will inevitably be itself performed in a digital material environment. It invites us to engage with visual and sensory research techniques as part of digital ethnography practice, to use these technologies in ways that are experimental—while at the same time theoretically coherent—and attentive to seeking ways in which to get beyond the surface that is often only scratched at by standard qualitative interviewing methods. An approach rooted in visual anthropology invites us to engage with the potential of audio-visual media for enabling empathetic understandings, as well as a tradition of reflexive and collaborative ways of working with participants in research, which can be translated with digital technologies into new forms of collaboration online.

*Digital Environments* therefore is a book that has emerged from a new generation of anthropologists. What is exciting about it is that it also represents the work of new scholars whose practice focuses on a central issue for the discipline, but does so through the prism of visual and media anthropology, which has traditionally not been part of the concern of mainstream scholarship in anthropology. This, I believe is a good sign. It implies an exciting future for the discipline as these perspectives and projects develop in the next years.

## REFERENCES

Boellstorff, Tom/Nardi, Bonni/Pearce, Celia /Taylor, T.L. (eds.) (2012): Ethnography and Virtual Worlds: A Handbook of Method, Princeton: Princeton University Press.

Bräuchler, Birgit/Postill, John (eds.)(2010): Theorising Media and Practice, Oxford: Berghahn.

Horst, Heather./Miller, Daniel (eds.)(2012): Digital Anthropology, London: Bloomsbury.

Pink, Sarah/Horst, Heather/Postill, John/Hjorth, Larissa /Lewis, Tania/Tacchi, Jo (eds.) (2016): Digital Ethnography: Principles and Practice, London: Sage.

Pink, Sarah/Ardevol, Elisenda/Lanzeni, Debora (2016): "Digital Materiality: Configuring a Field of Anthropology/Design?" In: Sarah Pink/Elisenda Ardevol/Debora Lanzeni (eds.), Digital Materialities: Anthropology and Design, Oxford: Bloomsbury, pp. 1-26.

# Digital Environments and the Future of Ethnography
An Introduction

Urte Undine Frömming, Steffen Köhn, Samantha Fox, Mike Terry

With the notion of digital environments, we aim to propose a conceptual term that describes the mutual permeation of the virtual with the physical world. The digital environment encompasses phenomena such as wholly immersive and user-constructed virtual worlds—for example, *Second Life*—and Massively Multiplayer Online Role-Playing Games (MMORPGs)—such as *Minecraft*— as well as other three-dimensional online spaces. There are expansive digital social environments to be considered such as social networking sites and smartphone applications, together with the people and communities who engage with them. It is constituted and shaped by a wide range of internet technology—including devices like smartphones, tablets and "wearables"—and online venues such as virtual communities, blogs, forums and e-commerce. Digital environments hence are the conglomeration of technologies, events and realities that interpenetrate each other, sometimes co-constitute each other, and that have led to changed ways of being.

They have fostered new expressions of identity, new forms of collaborative working, new commercial and political strategies, new modes of producing and distributing art, and new configurations of sociality, exchange and intimacy. Digital environments are so closely entangled with the physical world that any opposition between the "virtual" and the "real" is fundamentally misleading in almost the same manner as a distinction between the "digital" and the "non-digital" (or "analog") is untenable. As Boellstorff (2016), Frömming (2013), Hine (2010) and Ginsburg et al. (2002) point out, such a dichotomy completely fails to acknowledge how the online is, indeed, real. If one falls in love in a virtual world or on an online dating site, these emotions have implications in the physical world (Gershon 2010; 2011). The same goes for what one learns in an online educational environment. Yet just as problematically, the constructed opposition between the digital and the real implies that everything physical necessarily is also real. Boellstorff engages with timely literature on the ontological turn within anthropology to complicate such widely held misrepresentations of the reality of the digital. Our concept of digital environments avoids such a problematic dualism and allows us to ask precisely when and how online and offline worlds intersect, how users experience them and what consequences this has for social formations within the physical world. The ERC funded research project "Why We Post" at the University College London (UCL) and led by Daniel Miller (2016), provides one answer to the existing research gap that exists, considering the digitalization process as having a deeper and much faster influence on societies than we initially considered.

The 16 contributions to this volume likewise explore how people in Greenland, the Netherlands, Chile, China, Spain, Germany, South Africa, Columbia, Malaysia, Ukraine and the USA actually engage with various digital environments and how this changes their feelings and ideas about intimacy, social interactions, geographic distance, political situations, art production, or their very bodies. The individual articles are concerned with issues such as people's creative use of social media platforms like *Instagram*, *WeChat*, *Reddit*, *Facebook* or *Twitter* in trans-local or transnational settings. They examine the emergence of new online communities around Greenlandic news blogs or Malaysian LGBT *Facebook* groups, and describe the rise of transnational migrant networks facilitated by digital media. They investigate health issues in digital worlds and assistive digital technologies for blind people, the representation of conflicts, and the proliferation of ideologies within online spaces. Our aim with this book is to present fresh and timely research by young scholars from the Research Area of Visual and Media Anthropology at the Freie Universität Berlin's Institute of Social and Cultural Anthropology to a wider academic. By eschewing the false dichotomy between the virtual and the real—as encouraged by other practitioners in this research field—these young scholars are able to forge new methodologies in the nascent field of digital anthropology, pursuing novel practices of entangled fieldwork in both online and offline contexts. As people enact their social lives through complex combinations of online and offline practice, the contributors to this publication accordingly construct their fieldsites out of intricate configurations of the (trans-)local, the digital and the global. Hence, they lead us to believe in both the physical and the digital as real and entangled entities. We strongly believe that such intertwined forms of research—online and offline—have the potential to innovate both ethnographic methodologies and anthropological theory.

As Pink et al. (2015) note, the digital unfolds as an indispensable part of the world that we, as well as our research participants, co-inhabit. A methodological perspective on the digital is thus becoming an essential aspect of all kinds of ethnographic fieldwork endeavors, even those centered on presumably non-mediated areas of investigation such as migration, politics, medicine, economy or religion. Human lifeworlds, practices and cultures, be it in European, North American, or so called "indigenous communities" are increasingly subtly shaped by digital technology (Budka 2015), while such recent technology also offers ethnographers new ways of engaging with their field (Coleman 2010). One might think here of digitally mediated "efieldnotes" (Sanjek 2016), interviews via *Skype* or *Messenger* software, the potential to record visual media with a smartphone, or simply the possibility to stay connected with interlocutors beyond the period of fieldwork via email or social networking sites. The younger generations of anthropologists, raised during the proliferation of the internet, are already using digital technologies as part of their research as accepted and valuable resources. Yet with the increasing amount of new digital gadgets, apps and software, they are tasked with constantly adapting and re-inventing their ethnographic approach and methodology.

Importantly, Pink et. al. argue that digital ethnography does not necessarily have to engage with digital technology in both its methodology and its research focus; they see "non-digital-centric-ness" as one of the key principles of digital ethnography. Our own notion of digital environments equally emphasizes the ways in which technologies have become inseparable from other materialities and human activities. Hence, instead of putting digital media at the center of analysis, our approach seeks to pay careful attention to the manifold and complex forms in which digital environments have become a ubiquitous aspect of contemporary life and cultures. Elderly Chinese, for example, who never learned how to use computers have rapidly become avid users of the smartphone app *WeChat*, allowing them to improve their relationship with their adult children (Yun 2015). Likewise, amateur athletes increasingly use wearable technology for tracking their movements and physical fitness (Howse 2015), while Filipina migrant mothers working in Great Britain have grown accustomed to taking part in the lives of their children back home via *Viber*, *Skype*, or *Facebook* (Madianou and Miller 2012). The seamless integration of digital social media into our everyday practice has rendered them almost invisible (Fuchs 2013; David 2010). Our conceptual term stresses just that: digital environments have become so embedded in various social practices that we move through them like fish in water. Yet while digital technologies now form a part of most human relationships, these relationships are never purely digital. They do not produce novel forms of human interaction but may rather bring about different qualities in human lives, relationships and activities. We therefore need ethnography to look beyond the digital to understand how these technologies are played out precisely in their entanglement with other norms, relations and things.

As Collins and Durrington (2015) and Cohen (2012) note, such an ethnography of the present and future is, almost by definition, networked. Networked anthropology acknowledges the fact that digital technology, particularly social media, permeates the social fields that contemporary anthropologists examine. Moreover, it explores how these media might foster collaboration with informant communities on the production of meaning. While classical anthropological modes of publishing, slowed down by peer review and a lengthy process of publication, tend to produce static representations of an ethnographic engagement, networked anthropology offers fresh new possibilities for feedback, immediacy and measurable interventions with our collaborative partners. The data produced within such networked research often simultaneously serves as material that may be appropriated, utilized and shared by the individuals and communities participating in the research. For example, Lola Abrera's *Virtual Balkbayan Box* (2015) is a collaborative ethnographic project to which female OFWs (overseas Filipino workers) contributed mobile phone video diaries, pictures, or artworks to share their stories on their own terms. Quite often, anthropologists today even find themselves assisting in the efforts of such communities to network with different publics.

In our relationships with the digital, we thus have to engage in new forms of collaboration and convey our ideas and findings to new sets of addressees. This demands a greater reflexivity from individual researchers who have to negotiate their individual projects in the face of re-conceptualized notions of the "anthropologist," the "fieldsite," the "research participant" and the "audience." In *Ethnography and Virtual Worlds: A Handbook of Method* (2012), Boellstorff et al. explore how the often uneven and messy forms of "participation" in virtual worlds—as players, users, or producers—and various types of ethnographic immersion across online and offline spaces might be framed and analyzed. The contributions to our volume give accounts of this blurring of roles that ethnographers experience when they conduct research into and within digital environments. As digital environments emphasize user-generated content, contribution and self-presentation this almost inevitably brings an auto-ethnographic dimension into the research design (Dalsgaard 2008). Social media demands a certain kind of reciprocity of their users: if one wishes to connect with and receive information from other users, one is also required to reveal something about themselves. Digital ethnographies therefore often become journeys into the self. Through them we can better understand the new forms of identity and community as well as the social digital activism (Gerbaudo 2012, Postill 2010) emerging within and via digital technologies. Through these new forms of ethnographic expression, digital ethnographies can be our digital mirrors.

**Jóhanna Björk Sveinbjörnsdóttir (Iceland)**, in her contribution with a case study about East Greenland, examines online media commenting systems as spaces for public debates. Sveinbjörnsdóttir conducted ethnographic fieldwork in East Greenland over several months, with a focus on the online version of the most important newspaper in Greenland, *Sermitsiaq.AG*. Her seven interview partners from Greenland all agreed on one point: that the image of East Greenland was trapped in repeated portrayals of its inhabitants as murderers, alcoholics with social problems, or barbaric hunters. The author analyzes the comments, posted in response to news in the online version of *Sermitsiag.AG*, about a polar bear that was shot in front of the house by the father of a family and goes on to discuss the online making of an "imagined community."

**Brigitte Borm (The Netherlands)** analyzes the experiences of people, especially hosts, using the online platform *Airbnb*, which allows hosts to rent out their homes to other members, in exchange for a set fee. Borm raises the question: As the homes of hosts are temporarily or partly commodified, does the perception, experience or meaning of the homes of so-called hosts change? Following Tom Boellstorff (2012) in the notion that virtual and offline spaces are becoming profoundly interconnected, this contribution explores the relation between virtual participation on the hosting platform of *Airbnb* and the changing offline experience of the intimate environment of hosts' homes.

**Juan Francisco Riumalló (Chile)** examines the role that the internet has played for gay men in Chile across generations. Tracing the development of digital media—from anonymous chat rooms accessed via dial-up internet in the 1990s to smartphone-based dating apps that are popular today—Riumalló asks what social effects different media have had for gay men. While Chile remains a conservative, predominantly Catholic country, the internet can often be a safe, anonymous space for young men seeking support before coming out to their families. At the same time, pornography and sexualized dating sites present a limiting image of what it means to be a gay man. Riumalló addresses these concerns, as well as others, as he examines how the many facets of online interaction have shaped, and continue to shape, the identity of gay men in Chile.

In her contribution: "Red Packets in Real and Virtual Worlds. How Multi-Function *WeChat* Influences Chinese Virtual Relationships" **Xiaojing Ji (China)** presents the results of her research about the *Red Packet* app function as part of the mobile social application *WeChat*, which is extremely popular in China, similar to *WhatsApp* in Europe. With recourse to Marcel Mauss' theory of *The Gift* and the forms and functions of exchange, the author manages to reveal the enormous influence of the *WeChat Red Packets* on the lives of people in China and their social relationships.

**Jie Liang Lin's (China)** paper explores some of the nastier sides of the internet: the articulation of "antifeminist" views and identity formations in online communities. Particularly, she investigates the MGTOW ("Men Going Their

Own Way") movement—an online group that is active on dedicated websites, *YouTube* channels, *Facebook* groups and subreddits. It consists of mostly straight, white, middle-class males who attempt to analyze what they perceive as a feminist conspiracy against proper manhood and male destinies. The author traces this internet phenomenon back to male liberation movements, masculinist groups and sex-role theories of the 1970s in order to discuss how such views now slowly seep into the mainstream.

**Jonas Blume's (Germany)** chapter explores the internet as a participatory space for artists with new roles and new artistic online practices. The author explores the history of art and computer technology and the history of virtual exhibitions. The chapter culminates in the attempt of the author to understand the "integrative post-medium practices of post-internet Art." Blume also formulates a critique on contemporary museums that are, according to the author, "still rooted in their 19th century heritage, and are presently not equipped to appropriately present new media work."

**Olivier Llouquet (France)** explores, with his contribution: "Blind and Online," the everyday life of blind and visually impaired people and their networks in online communities. Over a period of two months, Llouquet gathered technical information on assistive technologies and joined several *Facebook* groups run by, and for, visually impaired people. He found out that their problem is not necessarily what is accessible to visually impaired people, but rather ignorance of the existing support structures.

**Ellen Lapper's (Great Britain)** chapter explores how social media has changed the way we grieve. In a time in which the deaths of celebrities become much shared "trending topics" on *Twitter* or *Facebook*, we all have to face the question of what happens to our own digital afterlives, as well as those of our loved ones. Starting from a very personal note, Lapper describes how following her father's death, she clung to the digital traces that remained of him on various digital platforms. Her research investigates how we negotiate a physical absence in light of a persistent digital presence, integrating theories of mourning and loss.

**Dario Bosio (Italy)** appraises the relationship between the ephemeral aspects of the social media platform *Periscope* and motivations for self-broadcasting. *Periscope* differs from other social media platforms that allow users to watch and offer views breaching the private sphere, due to its real-time broadcasting. According to Bosio, the added risk inherent in live broadcasting and the mostly anonymous audiences that 'tune in' to a specific scoper's video feed reveal a more accelerated and dynamic set of motivations. These include loneliness, anxiety surrounding online stimulation, boredom, New

Individualism, and even a possible desire for 'teleportation.' Bosio draws attention to the failure of the intended use of *Periscope*, as asserted by its developers, by offering examples that call attention to serious ethical and legal concerns. These include students using the app to publicly ridicule others, and abusive and suggestive behavior towards underage, specifically female users, revealing the need to examine the social effects of social media operating with anonymous and real-time connectivity.

**Gretchen Faust (USA)** is concerned with the representation of the female body in digital social environments. She analyses the new forms of censorship occurring on online platforms such as *Facebook, Instagram* and *Twitter* with regards to body hair, (menstrual) blood and nipples. Faust explores how the ambiguous "community guidelines" of social media platforms effectively perpetuate double standards with regard to the representation of male and female bodies. She then discusses feminist artists' approaches to problematize these gendered forms of censorship and tackles their severe implications for women's status on the internet.

**Teresa Tiburcio Jiménez (Spain)**, in her article "Berlin. Wie bitte?" makes an exploration of the construction of online platforms for the mutual support of young Spanish immigrants in Berlin. The author shows the ways in which these diasporic groups use the internet as an alternative space for communication, experimentation and the creation of new ideas for social innovation. During her fieldwork amongst the Spanish diaspora in Berlin, Tiburcio Jiménez asked the questions: how do young Spanish immigrants embody social innovation, what are their reasons for migration and in what ways do they use different digital environments during their migration process? The author examined several online platforms and social networking sites constructed and run by Spanish immigrants—such as *15M Berlin* (a nonpartisan, horizontal, self-managed and feminist political group for Spanish immigrants in Berlin), *Oficina Precaria* or *GAS* (Groupo de Acción Sindical)—and participated in offline meetings of the groups. Her research demonstrates the ways in which the online sphere is meaningful for political organization and identity creation in the diaspora.

**Sue Beukes (South Africa)** investigates the heightened discourse around race and inequality in South Africa. In this context, the entrance of an unmediated platform such as *Twitter* creates a new dynamic in this conversation through the entrance of a large and vocal young black South African online community, unafraid of challenging liberal views and the traditional Rainbow Nation narrative. Some have described this as a "psychic purge" or "shift in consciousness" which has been taking place over the last two years or so. In late 2015, the *#FeesMustFall* movement was born. This became one of the largest civic engagements since democracy as well as one of the biggest events on *Twitter* that year. The public aim of this movement was to address the rising cost of university fees, which would ultimately exclude many students from families already struggling to pay tuition and living costs. In October 2015, mass protests took place in institutions across the country eventually forcing the government to freeze fee increases in 2016. As a spin-off of this action, movements and related campaigns emerged such as *#OutSourcingMustFall* and *#ColourBlind*. It became clear that *#FeesMustFall* was about much more than rising fees; it aimed to address issues of colonization, inequality, and racism. Beukes seeks to explore the role of *Twitter* in this evolving discourse around race. It uses *#FeesMustFall* as a pivot for discussion because the movement both represents and touches on so many of the pertinent issues facing young South Africans, including issues central to the broader society in a post-apartheid environment.

**Sara Wiederkehr González (Switzerland/Colombia)** produces an analysis of the online and offline lifeworlds of Colombian migrants in the German capital of Berlin. The Colombian expats that Wiederkehr González interviews are all virtually engaged—via social media, webcam or blogs—with the present social reality in their conflict-laden home country. Engaging with Deleuze's distinction between the actual and the virtual, the author explores how these migrants inhabit what Daniel Miller (2011) has called "a third place."

**Veera Helena Pitkänen (Finland)** explores the social media landscape advocating for the LGBT community in Malaysia. Homosexuality there is punishable by law, and social media users must balance their desires for connection and social justice with exposure to legal consequences. Focusing on the *Facebook* group "Seksualiti Merdeka" (which translates from the Malay as "Sexual Independence") Pitkänen examines the role the group plays in the lives of her informants, how *Facebook* can be utilized both socially and politically, and what role privacy and anonymity play in a country where identity politics carry great risk.

**Karly Domb Sadof (USA)**, a visual anthropologist working as photo editor for the Associated Press, demonstrates the enormous importance and meaning of the role of the smartphone application *Instagram*, during the Ukrainian protests (*#Euromaidan*) that began in November 2013, after the Ukrainian government declared that it would not sign the association contract with the European Union. Domb Sadof shows the ways in which way "Selfies" played a central role in first-person or citizen journalism during the Ukrainian protests, affecting a strong and visible impact within Ukraine and abroad.

**Joanna Sleigh (Australia)** approaches modern religiosity through the virtual doors of *The Church of Google*, a website created in 2011 by enthusiasts of the search engine and technology company. Confirming that even online religiosity is still mediated by activity in real life, Sleigh outlines the marked differences between—yet gives equal credence to—the enthusiasts of *Googlism*, revealing two major factions: 'believers' and those that take a more satirical approach. Whether *Googlism* engages its followers through its impressive and infallible data organization and retrieval capabilities, or as a proxy for a critique of organized religion itself, modern technology and digital communication is thoroughly inscribed throughout the experience.

## REFERENCES

Abrera, Lola (2015): "The Virtual Balikbayan Box." In: Journal of Visual and Media Anthropology 1/1.
Boellstorff, Tom/Nardi, Bonnie/Pearce, Celia/Taylor, T. L. (2012): Ethnography and Virtual Worlds: A Handbook of Method, Oxford and Princeton: Princeton University Press.
Boellstorff, Tom (2016): "For Whom the Ontology Turns: Theorizing the Digital Real." In: Current Anthropology 57/4, pp. 387-407.
Budka, Phillip (2015): "From marginalization to self-determined participation: Indigenous digital infrastructures and technology appropriation in Northwestern Ontario's remote communities". In: Journal des Anthropologues 142/143, pp. 127-153.
Cohen, Julie. E. (2012): Configuring the Networked Self: Law, Code, and the Play of Everyday Practice, New Haven, CT: Yale University Press.
Coleman, Gabriella (2010): "Ethnographic Approaches to Digital Media." In: Annual Review of Anthropology 39, pp. 487–505.
Collins, Samuel Gerald/Durrington, Matthew Slover (2015): Networked Anthropology. A Primer for Ethnographers, New York: Routledge.
Dalsgaard, S. (2008): "Facework on Facebook: The presentation of self in virtual life and its role in the US elections.' In: Anthropology Today 24/6, pp. 8–12.
David, Gaby (2010): "Camera phone images, videos and live streaming: a contemporary visual trend." In: Visual Studies 25/1, pp. 89–98.
Fuchs, Christian (2013): Social Media: A Critical Introduction, London: Sage.
Frömming, Urte Undine (2013): "Introduction: Entangled Realities in Virtuality". In: Urte Undine Frömming (ed.): Virtual Environments and Cultures, Frankfurt am Main/ New York: Peter Lang Verlag, pp. 23-34.
Gerbaudo, Paulo (2012): Tweets and the streets: Social media and contemporary activism, London: Pluto Press.

Gershon, Ilana (2010): Breakup 2.0: Disconnecting Over New Media. Ithaca, NY: Cornell University Press.

Gershon, Ilana (2011): "Un-Friend My Heart: Facebook, Promiscuity and Heartbreak in a Neoliberal Age." In: Anthropological Quarterly 84/4, pp. 865–94.

Ginsburg, Faye/Abu-Lughod, Leyla/Larkin, Brian (eds.) (2002): Media Worlds, Berkeley, CA: University of California Press.

Hine, Christine (2000): Virtual Ethnography, London: Sage.

Horst, Heather A. and Daniel Miller (eds.) (2012): Digital Anthropology, London/New York: Bloomsbury Publishing.

Howse, Melody (2015): "Real World Repercussions of Motivation and Interactions in a Virtual Space. Explored in Relation to the Body and Self." In: Online Journal of Visual and Media Anthropology 1/1, pp. 22-31.

Madianou, Mirca/Miller, Daniel (2012): Migration and New Media, London: Routledge.

Miller, Daniel/Costa, Elisabetta/Haynes, Nell/McDonald, Tom/Nicolescu, Razvan/Sinanan, Jolynna/Spyer, Juliano/Venkatraman, Shriram/Wang, Xinyuan (eds.) (2016): How The World Changed Social Media. London: UCL Press.

Miller, Daniel (2016): Social Media in an English Village. Or how to keep people at just the right distance, London: UCL Press.

Miller, Daniel (2011): Tales from Facebook, London: Polity Press.

Pink, Sarah/Horst, Heather/Postill, John/Hjorth, Larissa/Lewis, Tania/Tacchi, Jo (eds.) (2015): Digital Ethnography: Principles and Practice, London: Sage.

Postill, John (2010): "Researching the internet", In: Journal of the Royal Anthropological Institute 16/3, pp. 646–650.

Sanjek, Roger/Tratner, Susan (2016) eFieldnotes: The Makings of Anthropology in a Digital World, University of Pennsylvania Press.

Yun Ke (2015): "Ageing on WeChat. The Impact of Social Media on Elders in Urban China." In: Journal of Visual and Media Anthropology 1/1, pp. 8-21.

# Part 1

# Digital Communities and the Re-Creation of the Self and Social Relationships Online

# A Comment on East Greenland Online

Media Commenting Systems as Spaces for Public Debate with a Focus on East Greenland in the Greenlandic Media

Jóhanna Björk Sveinbjörnsdóttir

Image 1

The article that caught my attention: "Shot a polar bear in front of his house." The caption reads: "It was a full-grown he-bear that had come into Kulusuk settlement. Gedion Kúnak shot it in three meters distance from his house." (my translation from Danish)

"Shot a polar bear in front of his house," was the sentence that accompanied the above image (Image 1.). It appeared several times in my *Facebook* feed on January 24, 2014. This was a shared link from the Greenlandic newspaper *Sermitsiaq AG* regarding Gedion Kúnak, a hunter in Kulusuk who had shot a polar bear from his doorstep. His daughter Justine, then 22 years old, had spotted the bear that was standing in the same spot she had just stood with her friends moments earlier. According to East Greenlandic tradition, the first to see the bear is the official hunter. This was Justine, but Gedion was the shooter. As a licensed hunter, Gedion is allowed to shoot polar bears according to an established quota (currently set at 25 animals annually for the region). To hunt a polar bear is a sought after achievement in Greenland. Over his lifetime, Gedion has shot more than fifteen. Friends and family, as well as other readers of the online article, congratulated Gedion and Justine in the comments section below the article.

What struck me about the news, apart from relief that Justine and her friends were safe and the joy expressed over a friend's achievement, was that—unlike most of the occasional news from East Greenland, often about violence or negative social challenges—this news was neutral. It was a simple description of the event together with a few words from Gedion. Amongst the congratulatory comments, the killing of the bear was described as barbaric and unnecessary: "Why is nobody asking if Gedion has a license?" "STOP KILLING THEM!" In the comments of the following days, a lively debate ensued between supporters of polar bear hunting and those against it. Some East Greenlanders stood up for their culture against heavy accusations from Danes and West Greenlanders.

This instance provides an interesting lens through which to study Greenlandic media. The country's population is scattered and isolated. Internet access is still limited, and printed media travels slowly due to logistical cost and weather. Moreover, Greenlandic media is state-run. For the last three years, I have spent my summers in East Greenland. During the long months in between, I try to keep up with current affairs via the online news from *Sermitsiaq AG* and KNR. However, there is very little coverage of the East, so I depend on *Facebook* and e-mails from friends to receive news from the area. The story about Gedion is a good example of how these new online platforms have become official public spaces to hold debate, and thus a means of some sort of "commenting-activism," where readers can add the East Greenlandic point of view to the published article. To understand the phenomenon better, I engaged in ethnographic research, specifically participant observation, with readers of Greenlandic online news. Commenting systems are connected to *Facebook* and provide easy access to a selected number of diverse users for further interviews. Until now, most research on the subject of "commenting" has been for the benefit of the media and journalism outlets, with regard to providing information relating to revenues, falling readership and audience engagement. In this research, I focus on the user's point of view—that of the readers and those who have made comments—to gain ethnographic insight about East Greenland and changing cultural traditions within the media landscape.

The polar bear debate reflects some of East Greenland's under-representation and misrepresentation in the media. In this article I take a closer look at commenting systems in a wider context to see if it is common practice for East Greenlanders to use the open platform for debate. To give the required background, I sketch out the split between the east and west of Greenland. Both Appadurai's (1990) theory of the *mediascape* and *imagined worlds*, and Habermas's (1989, 1996, 2006) concept of public space and common opinion, help to frame this investigation. By drawing up the Greenlandic *mediascape*, I establish a base to discuss the potential of commenting systems as public space that exists across geographical boundaries.

## EAST GREENLAND AND THE "NATURE-PEOPLE"

There are two stories to be told about Greenland: there is a story about Greenland in general, and a more specific story of the east coast.

The largest segment of Greenland's population of 56,114 lives on the west coast. The majority are Inuit, mixed with a large community of several generations of Danish migrants. There exists a long history of international contact. For example, Nordic Vikings lived in the southwest between the 10$^{th}$ and 13$^{th}$ centuries, eventually dying from starvation because they did not adapt to their new conditions. Later, Dutch and Norwegian hunters came to set up whaling stations. Eventually Danish/Norwegian Hans Egede established a missionary station in Nuuk in 1721, which later became the colony. Although Greenland was granted home rule in 1979, and self-rule in 2009, the legacy of colonialism is still apparent; the Greenlandic language only became the official language in 2009, thus placing the Danish language second.

Specifically, in East Greenland today 3,266 people live in five small settlements and the capital of the area, Tasiilaq. The area is called Ammassalik, or Tunu in Greenlandic, which means "the back-side." Due to extreme geographical isolation, the people of the east coast were unknown to others. They lived as nomadic hunters until Danish merchant Gustav Holm discovered the area in 1885. Here, people speak East Greenlandic, also called Tunumiit, a distinct dialect of Greenlandic. Greenlandic is their second language and Danish their third. Tunumiit is traditionally a spoken language without official spelling, therefore very few books exist in the language. Rough weather, geographical isolation, high travel costs, and limited internet access, all serve to maintain the isolation of East Greenlanders for a large part of the year. Lately, East Greenland has been catching up to modernity with incredible speed; the oldest among the population who grew up living in turf houses in the winter and sealskin tents during the summer, now use smartphones and travel by helicopter. Nonetheless, nature continues to shape living conditions and the area remains fairly isolated for nine months of the year. As before, people depend on the surrounding environment, themselves, and each other. Agriculture is impossible in East Greenland, a granite archipelago largely covered in ice and snow year-round. Hunting and fishing make the most efficient use of resources. These practices are on a small scale—involving methods that use small motorboats, snow scooters, and dogsleds—to sustain the family. There is no bank, only two ATMs, both located in Tasiilaq. Internet is expensive and limited. There is no public transport; people hitch rides with the small boats. Healthcare, social services, education, religion, and police are gradually being centralized in Tasiilaq. There is one supermarket, the state-run Pilersuisoq, where bras and bullets sit next to each another on the shelf and wine is kept behind the counter. During the three summer months, Pilersuisoq is stocked with products imported from Denmark, when the cargo ships can gain access through the ocean ice. Everything must last from the last ship in October until the first ship that arrives in late June. Therefore, the staple diet for an East Greenlandic family still comes from the ocean; their large freezers are filled with fish, seal and whale, along with blueberries, crowberries, some edible local herbs ... and the occasional polar bear.

Many of these descriptions also apply to other rural areas of Greenland, but collectively they form a lifestyle unique to the East. The language barrier is in some ways indicative of the split between East and West: East Greenlanders understand Greenlandic and the culture of those who speak it, but not vice versa.

*Image 2*

Landscape photographs from a dog-sled hunting trip. Bilingual caption in Greenlandic and Danish: "Sled tour today :)" (my translation). Photographed and posted on *Facebook*, by Mads Poulsen.

Early history texts in West Greenlandic schools mention three types of wild people: "wild-wild," "precious-wild," and "our own wild". Too often East Greenlanders are still considered "wild nature-people"—translated from Danish: *vilde naturmennesker*—by Greenlanders and Danes. These ideas influence the whole of Greenlandic society. Robert Petersen, a Greenlandic anthropologist, analyzed the power structures and behaviors of his fellow citizens in relation to colonialism; he claims that too many Greenlanders adopted Danish mentality and power structures. Compounding this, Greenlanders are not used to speaking up; not for themselves, nor against any kind of power (Petersen 1995: 7). Through their colonial efforts, the Danish influenced Greenlanders into believing they were lucky; that they were the best colony in the world, free from violence. As a result, today a distinct majority of Greenlanders are fond of the Danish. Since they were granted home-rule in 1979, educated Greenlanders took on the role of the Danish colonizers. This led to an internal colonialism between the west and the east, and also between towns and settlements, replacing an external colonialism imposed by Denmark. The output of local media is just one representation of this. The few things reported from the east come mostly from the police and tend to focus on violence and crime. This fuels old ideas and presumptions, and results in East Greenland's constant under- and misrepresentation and exclusion from cultural and political spheres both within and outside of Greenland.

## PUBLIC SPHERE AND GEOGRAPHICAL BORDERS

Media becomes an important factor regarding the creation of a community in a place where the world's largest glacier, challenging arctic weather, and language differences create obstacles for Greenlanders to get together. The *mediascape*, borrowing from Appadurai's (1990) term, is composed of various means of production and distribution of news—magazines, television, films, and advertisements—and creates a certain media landscape for the individual who consumes it. A consumer world view is heavily dependent on the *mediascape*, complicated by the fact that it is composed of both fiction (such as films) and non-fictional (like documentary news reports and social posts). The lines between what is real and what is not are blurred (ibid: 298). Unlike the *"imagined communities"* Benedict Anderson (1983) believed the media that is capable of creating, "an imagined world" becomes more likely when the audience's imagination plays a significant role (Appadurai 1990: 298-299). For a large percentage of the Greenlandic population as a whole, the East Greenlandic culture is simultaneously exotic and traditional. This exoticism developed simply because, unlike most of Greenland, the East Greenlandic culture never lost its traditions. Through their situation of geographical isolation, they also became culturally remote thereby unable to counter narrow perceptions of their culture from the "outside." This limited view became the basis for an ill-informed imagined world of the place and its people. The interactive aspect of Web 2.0 invites the chance to change this view. News agents now depend to a larger extent on readers' letters, offering platforms for blogs, readers' images, and commenting systems to facilitate these. Readers add their point of view, interact with journalists and other readers and thus add another layer to the original news article. Readers are becoming producers, or *"produsers"* according to Axel Burns (2008a). Online newspapers increasingly become a public sphere, which, according to Jürgen Habermas (1989), is created when citizens come together to debate current affairs. Public opinion is created through the exchange of ideas and information, debate, and the discovery of a common opinion; it is a journalist's main purpose to foster these debates and exchanges. At times, commercial journalism may have eliminated some essential properties of the public sphere. Today interactivity and commenting systems are seen to be returning these properties to the table. Newspapers around the world are shifting toward more user-generated content (UGC) in response to decreased revenue and technological development. In a similar fashion, online newspapers are opening up to readers through commenting systems and links to social media platforms such as *Facebook* and *Twitter*. If used well, these spaces have the potential to form an online public sphere for discussion and debate, a place to criticize and be criticized, in order to reach a common consensus.

## THE GREENLANDIC *MEDIASCAPES*

### Newspapers

My main source for Greenland current affairs is *Sermitsiaq AG*, though there is rarely any news featured from where I live. *Sermitsiaq AG* is the major newspaper in Greenland and is based in Nuuk. It is comprised of three older newspapers, *Sermitsiaq*, *Atuagagdliutit* and *Grønlandsposten*. *Atuagagdliutit* is the oldest newspaper in Greenland, established by Danish geologist Hinrich Johannes Rink in 1861 in an attempt to reestablish Greenlandic identity after Danish colonization. Furthermore, Rink wanted to bring Greenlanders the main news from the "outside world" and for this reason, the paper was solely written in Greenlandic. Later, in 1952, *Atuagagdliutit* merged with the Danish language newspaper *Grønlandsposten* published since the Second World War. The new paper was called *AG*. *Sermitsiaq* had provided Greenlanders with news since 1958. Since 2010, *Sermitisaq* and *Atuagagdliutit/Grønlandsposten* have worked under this common name. The two printed newspapers are still separate, while their website merges the two. *Sermitsiaq AG* is published four times weekly, bilingually in Greenlandic and Danish. The content is descriptive news and event reports rather than investigative or analytical journalism; some material is simply press releases received from institutions, organizations and individuals around the country. The *Sermitsiaq AG* website is updated several times daily.

The relation between the online and printed newspaper is shaped by conditions in Greenland. The editorial board must take into consideration that the physical newspapers travel slowly, as flights are infrequent and weather dependent. In the East, for example, there is only one flight per week from Nuuk over the winter, two in the summer, weather permitting. The only newspaper I have ever seen there is the copy housed in the library. In such conditions, a printed newspaper quickly loses relevance. Internet opens up the newspaper's opportunity to achieve its reach potential. Online, each article has a link to related articles previously published in the newspaper. Through the website, readers are offered a domain for blogs, where everything from personal stories of everyday lives to theorizing about important political issues get equal space, and enrich the medium. The content is further enriched by the reader's opportunity to comment and share articles through their *Facebook* and *Twitter* accounts. *Sermitsiaq AG*'s commenting system is lively and provides a platform for personal opinions, debate or simply greetings to the person who the article is about. Those who comment are advised to follow a set of guidelines set by the editorial board. When readers comment via the website, the comments appear underneath the given article, and sometimes create a rich discussion—as in the news about Gedion and Justine's killing of the polar bear.

## Radio and Television

Every morning, my housekeeper connected his new smartphone to my portable speakers and turned on the radio, KNR, or Kalaallit Nunaata Radioa (Greenland's National Radio) being the only option. The program is mostly in Greenlandic, with the hourly news in Danish and an occasional inclusion of a Danish documentary program. News and weather is reported hourly throughout the day. There are church broadcasts, a children's program, talk and call-in programs—where East Greenlanders are frequent callers—and of course, there is music: Greenlandic choir music is a regular offering. Like radio, TV plays another large role in a Greenlandic household. The TV schedule is made up mostly of news and weather reports, children's TV and sporting events, sprinkled with a few documentary programs and talk and debate shows. Danish television from DR1, DR2 and DR3 are also available. The established technology leads radio and TV to be Greenlanders main source for news and information.

KNR is funded by self-rule government and has provided Greenlanders with radio and television broadcasting since the 1920s. The operation is bilingual— Greenlandic and Danish—but most of the material broadcast is in Greenlandic. KNR claims to have correspondents in each part of the country, and indeed there are several on the East Coast: one in Tasiilaq, one in Kulusuk, one in Isortoq and one in Illoqqortoormiut. These reporters, as well as other local reporters, report local news in their own languages and are given particular attention in the radio's morning program. Throughout the day, the most important news may be repeated in the national news and also on the website. KNR approximates that East Greenlanders do take part in interactive programs, such as call-in-shows, as much as other Greenlanders. To expand the interactive aspects of radio, KNR went online in 1996 and in 2012, introduced a live-stream "for the joy of all the Greenlanders that live outside of Greenland." As a result of audience demand, they recently set up a *Twitter* account and a commenting system through *Facebook*. As on *www.sermitisiaq.ag*, there are common guidelines to do with commenting but comments are not edited. However, KNR's commenting system is not as commonly used as that of *Sermitsiaq AG*.

**Internet**

TELE Greenland, the state-run telecommunication operator, has a monopoly-position on internet services. Private companies have made attempts at competition, but the high costs of maintaining physical infrastructure is quickly discouraging. In 2014, 66.7 percent of the nation had access to the internet compared to 98.2 percent in Iceland, and 86.2 percent in Germany. According to TELE Greenland's customer service department, Tasiilaq had something between 1,000–1,300 internet subscriptions. Smartphones and a 3G connection have provided more people with access to the internet, but smartphones are still a luxury. Although internet is particularly expensive in Greenland, and not accessible in most homes, there are alternatives. On the east coast, the school libraries offer computers and wireless internet two days a week for two hours. Unfortunately, this is only available to those who are 13 years and older. There is a small internet café in Tasiilaq, where an old computer opens up the world to those who need it.

These conditions limit the readers of the Greenlandic newspaper's online versions to those who can afford an internet connection and can read Greenlandic and/or Danish. This also determines who can take part in the debate offered by the online platform.

## A Comment on East Greenland

In a scattered and geographically divided country like Greenland, conditions prevent a physical public sphere in the Habermasian sense, and public opinion is therefore almost impossible to realize in real life. The internet opens up a previously unknown possibility. The article about Gedion and Justine's killing of the polar bear offers evidence that this online platform has potential to join the split nation in an accessible public place that Habermas (1989) believes is essential for a common opinion.

Using the online public space found within the commenting system is fairly simple for anyone familiar with reading the news online. The simplest and most used option is to "like" the articles; that is, to actively press the "like" button by the article on the medium's website—for example those found on *Facebook*, or *Twitter* sites. Additionally readers can share articles on their Walls, re-tweet from *Twitter*, or simply comment directly below the given article on the media's *Facebook* account, and also on their own Wall. There is a good balance between Greenlandic and Danish comments, but very few, if any, East Greenlandic comments. Unfortunately, my language abilities confined my observations to the Danish comments. Following a global tendency, most comments are short: anything from a word to a few lines. Sharing an article is more common among my *Facebook* contacts because the comments are not published on the official website, and therefore not bound by the commenting guidelines. Regardless, comments remain mostly civilized. In the cases where comments come below the article, they become a part of the article in a way. This can take the form of individual comments such as greetings, or reader's opinion, a critique on what is said—possibly a trigger for further debate. For the purpose of my research, this was the most important aspect because it is here that the shared official space is created.

My impression was that readers felt that East Greenland is too often forgotten, which leads to invisibility on a national level. When I consulted media officials they claimed that, per capita, they paid East Greenland as much attention as other parts of the country. Whatever the percentage may be, the area's unfair representation was another repeated point made among readers. They felt the few reports from the east centered on the people's barbaric nature, alcoholism, and other related social problems; such as violence or child-neglect. "Perhaps there are not so many newsworthy events in a small hunting community, but that does not mean the area should go unnoticed," says Massanti Riel. Riel, who works for Destination East Greenland, the official tourist bureau, is concerned with the area's reputation and manages the organization's social media accounts. Regarding news coverage, he comments:

It isn't so much what is missing, it's about what should NOT be there. Although those things do happen, there is no reason to feed the disputes that already exist between the east and the west. And when there finally is something [neutral or positive], there is someone that turns it around and makes it negative. (Interview with the author, March 2014).

Massanti refers specifically to the polar bear incident in Kulusuk and subsequent comments. Rather than being privy to the actual statistics regarding the percentage of the media's coverage in East Greenland, I focused on perceptions and difference of opinion between those in East Greenland and the media organizations. Based on my research, I divide reasons for commenting on East Greenland into a list of six categories:

- A reminder that East Greenland should be considered in nationwide discussions
- Gratitude for the rare attention
- Regret that news is predominantly negative
- East Greenlanders disagreement over specific news reports from the area
- Outsiders pointing out East Greenlander's barbaric behavior
- Justification for reported behavior

*Image 3*

An article from *Sermitsiaq AG* shared on a reader's timeline on *Facebook*. Comment: "Accessibility to good food products are very different between the east and the west, the prices aren't just different, they are CRAZY different. The normal health conditions will be impaired because of simple foods and more intake of western foods. More diseases, more instances of tuberculosis could be a consequence. I would think someone would want to do something about this?????" Heading: More poverty in East Greenland: As something new in the population's research, we have asked the question if there is food shortage in the house. The answers are different between East and West Greenland. http://sermitsiaq.ag/node/182695 Accessed: March 5, 2016. (My translation)

What I noticed is that most of the comments on the media's website are from Danish-born East Greenlanders or Danes who live, or have lived, in the area. These are individuals who, like me, have gotten to know the culture, respect it and have subsequently formed a strong bond with it. East Greenlanders do not speak out to the same extent, and I believe the reasons are deep-rooted and complicated.

On the most basic level, they are still in the process of keeping up with modern ideologies and technology. As I mentioned earlier, it has only been about 130 years since they first came into contact with the "outside world," and the adjustment is understandably gradual. Related to this fact, there is a certain class divide in the East between the locals and the Danish. Because of their higher level of education and their familiarity with "modern", "western" ways of working, Danes occupy many of the well-paid jobs in the area while many natives are unemployed or work in low-paid jobs. This means that Danes, more than locals, are more likely to have access to a computer and regularly use the internet. Yet the full truth is not so simple.

I believe that limited participation from the locals relates largely to the online language. In other words, Danish and Greenlandic language is of utmost importance when it comes to the Greenlandic media, and not all Greenlanders share a native tongue. All schoolbooks are written in Greenlandic and Danish; none are in East Greenlandic. From an early age, children study in their second and third language. This has its benefits, but it mostly results in a high number of students who struggle throughout their entire school life, many of whom drop out (Lynge 2015). Erna, who has worked closely with the East Greenlandic youth as a social worker, sees this as a severe discrimination against the inhabitants of the country. If West Greenlandic children are struggling with further education because Danish is their first language, one can only imagine how difficult it must be for their counterparts in the east. The question of language also leads to the fact that written language is a relatively new phenomenon for East Greenlanders. This is a deep-rooted challenge for media to overcome. Only when the first foreigners came to the area in 1885 were East Greenlanders introduced to the idea of written language in the form of the Bible. Writing came even later. Aanaa Kirsten, a Danish sociologist who also worked in Tasiilaq for many years, believes that this historic fact could be a reason that local people do not comment on the news. Writing is still not a part of everyday life. She expressed a difficulty in getting her East Greenlandic colleagues to write meeting notes when working in Tasiilaq. She realized this problem was not limited to work meetings, but that they were not used to writing in general. Still today, there are no official East Greenlandic spelling rules; the spelling of a word is based on phonetics and therefore different depending on who writes. Surprisingly, this applies to even the most educated. The headmaster at the school where I worked was shy to reply to my e-mails for a long time because her Danish was not good enough. I only got a reply when I returned to Greenland again, months later, and she told me in person what she would have written. Within these linguistic challenges, there exists the risk that, because an individual's Greenlandic or Danish language skills are insufficient, one would rather not write to avoid embarrassment. This may also explain why East Greenlanders prefer radio.

With the rise of social media, East Greenlanders are starting to write more, even in their own language. This is an important development that could lead to increased participation in online and offline debates. Massanti believes that, "to be able to correct misrepresentation, East Greenlanders must learn to document positive events, not just with short updates via *Instagram*, *Facebook* and *Twitter*, but also just to send good news to *Sermitsiaq* that they can publish." To date, there have been several journalism courses, none of which have had lasting effect. Until East Greenlanders have regular access to the internet and the confidence to engage in online media in meaningful ways, they cannot speak-up for themselves and take part in a nationwide debate about matters related to their area. I believe that depending on others to stand up for them maintains some of the post-colonial circumstances.

## CONCLUSION: AN ONLINE PLATFORM AS PUBLIC SPACE

Debating different opinions is a fruitful path to knowledge and should be encouraged. According to Habermas (1996), the exchange of views and knowledge, as well as criticism are essential characteristics of the public sphere (Blanning 1998: 27). The news about the polar bear incident, a simple and neutral report, turned out to be a very sensitive political issue. The comments section allowed a greater story to be told, far beyond one man shooting a polar bear. It shed light on people's pride in a way of life that others consider barbaric. In line with what Robert Petersen suggested, it made clear that a considerable number of Greenlanders are drifting away from their hunting heritage and instead adopting the mentality of the colonizer, but in a global context, rather than directed towards the Danes. The commenting system on the *Sermitsiaq AG* became a public sphere to discuss a major cultural matter. Although no common opinion was reached, nor a conclusion as such, the comments brought together different views and stirred debate that otherwise would not have taken place.

For a scattered nation like Greenland, the online commenting system has enabled dialogue and an exchange of viewpoints. By opening up for participation from their readers, they are increasing the chance that each point of view will be raised, and a common opinion can be reached. Readers can harness the power of the media to create an imagined world and a represented identity that is fair. This option brings East Greenlanders great potential to compensate a deep rooted under- and misrepresentation, yet it seems that they have handed the responsibility over to those more familiar with modern technology and western ideologies. Through news publication, *Sermitsiaq AG* originally set out to create a common identity as Greenlanders, set apart from Danes. The Greenlandic language was instrumental in the effort. However, they now have a new challenge: to unite Greenlanders across language barriers, isolated locations and differing levels of familiarity with "modern" and globalized mindsets.

## REFERENCES

Anderson, Benedict (1986 [1983]): Imagined Communities. Reflections on the Origin and Spread of Nationalism, London: Verso Editions and NLB.

Andersson, Ulrika (2013): "Maintaining Power by Guarding the Gates: Journalists. Perceptions of Audience Participation in Online Newspapers." In: Journalism and Mass Communication, 3/1 Pp. 1-13.

Appadurai, Arjun (1990): "Disjuncture and Difference in the Global Cultural Economy". In: Theory, Culture & Society, vol.7.,pp. 295-310.

Blanning, T. C. W. (1998 [1987]: The French Revolution Class War or Culture Clash?, New York: St. Martin's Press.

Burns, Axel (2008a): Blogs, Wikipedia, Second Life and Beyond. From Production to Produsage, New York: Peter Lang.

Burns, Axel (2008b): "The Active Audience: Transforming Journalism from Gatekeeping to Gatewatching." In: Chris Paterson/David Domingo (eds.) Making Online News: The Ethnography of New Media Production, New York: Peter Lang, pp.171-184.

Egede Lynge, Aviâja (2015): Interview https://www.youtube.com/watch?v=r9 U2PV88fwc&feature=youtu.be Accessed: September 3, 2015.

Habermas, Jürgen (1989): The Structural Transformation of the Public Sphere: An Inquiry into a Category of Bourgeois Society. Translated from German by T. Burger, Cambridge, MA: MIT Press.

Habermas, Jürgen (1996): Between Facts and Norms: Contributions to a Discourse Theory of Law and Democracy. Translated from German by W. Rehg, Cambridge, MA: MIT Press.

Habermas, Jürgen (2006): "Political Communication in Media Society: Does Democracy Still Enjoy an Epistemic Dimension? The Impact of Normative Theory on Empirical Research." In: Communication Theory 16/4: 411-426.

KNR official website, Danish version http://www.knr.gl/da Accessed: March 6, 2016.

KNR's Guidelines http://www.knr.gl/da/guidelines Accessed: March 6, 2016.

Naalakkersuisut, The Government of Greenland http://naalakkersuisut.gl/da/ Naalakkersuisut/Nyheder/2013/12/Fordeling-af-kvoter-paa-isbjoerne-i-2014 Accessed: March 24, 2016.

Payrow Shabani, Omid A. (2003): Democracy, Power and Legitimacy: The Critical Theory of Jürgen Habermas, Toronto: University of Toronto Press.

Petersen, Robert (1995): "Colonialism as Seen From a Former Colonized Area." In: Arctic Anthropology 32/2, pp. 118-126.

"Population in East Greenland, July 2015" Greenland Statistics http://bank.stat.gl/pxweb/da/Greenland/Greenland__BE__BE01__BE0120/BEXST3.PX?rxid=BEXST306-03-2016%2012:16:42 Accessed: March 6, 2016.

"Population in Greenland, July 2015" Greenland Statistics (http://www.stat.gl/dialog/main.asp?lang=en&sc=BE&version=201503 Accessed: January 14, 2016.

Sermitsiaq AG official Website, Danish version http://sermitsiaq.ag/da Accessed: March 6, 2016.

Sermitsiaq AG's Guidelines http://sermitsiaq.ag/node/155630 Accessed: March 6, 2016.

"Shot a Polar Bear", In: Sermitsiaq.AG, January 24, 2014. http://sermitsiaq.ag/skoed-isbjoern-foran-hus Accessed: March 6, 2016.

World Bank http://databank.worldbank.org/data/home.aspx Accessed: April 5, 2016.

# Welcome Home

An Ethnography on the Experiences of *Airbnb* Hosts in Commodifying Their Homes

Brigitte Borm

Image 1

Home(page) *Airbnb*. www.airbnb.com Accessed: April 15, 2015.

> Most serious thought in our time struggles with the feeling of homelessness.
> -Susan Sontag, "The Anthropologist as Hero"[1]

The online platform of *Airbnb* allows users to rent out their house to other members of this community. As a host, you need to create a "profile" and a "listing" in which you describe your house and set a nightly price, basically turning your place or a part of it, into a hotel for specific dates. The city of Amsterdam has become one of *Airbnb*'s top destinations worldwide and for a long time the municipality of Amsterdam struggled with how to respond to this sudden increase of private renting. Much public discussion has taken place

---

1 | Sontag in Jackson (1995: 27).

with regard to the impact on the city center, which indeed on busy days can feel more like a tourist attraction than anything else.

Whilst initially *Airbnb* was almost uniformly prohibited, in 2014 Amsterdam passed an *"Airbnb*-friendly law," making it the first example of a European city hospitable to this new hosting platform.[2] Although *Airbnb* is now permitted, conditions are strict. Renting out through *Airbnb* is only allowed for 60 days a year; one has to pay taxes and not more than four guests are allowed at any one time. Social housing projects are not eligible, since they often do not permit subleasing. Because of this, *Airbnb* has become mostly a privilege for private house owners who have permission from their VvE (*Vereniging van Eigenaren*; translated from Dutch as: Association of House Owners).

Central to this research was the hosts' own experiences, rather than the social impact on the scale of the city and its neighborhoods. Turning one's home into a hotel, on the positive side, offers an alternative income for people in precarious financial situations. On a more critical note however, *Airbnb* makes the personal and private space of the home into a commodity. Does the concept of "home" still refer to one's private and intimate place when it is made available as a temporary space for strangers? Most importantly, how does the perception, meaning, and experience of "home" change for people who participate as hosts in the virtual community of *Airbnb*? Tom Boellstorff (2012), the well-known anthropologist specializing in emerging online and offline worlds, states that anthropological research of online communities should explore the relationship between the virtual and the actual space, arguing that the border between these two is not blurring, but the spaces are becoming intertwined and interconnected in more profound ways (ibid: 40). Previous research on *Airbnb* and other hosting sites has mostly focused on the largely financial interaction around hospitality, mainly from the perspective of guests. For other interesting examples, see the research on racial discrimination against hosts (cf. Edelman/Luca 2014), on network sociality (cf. Molz 2014) and the monetizing of hospitality networks from hosts' perspectives (cf. Ikkala/Lampinen 2015). No research has been done, however, on the possible change in the experience or the meaning of home for hosts.

The conceptualization of home has been contested in anthropological literature. As Irene Cieraad (2012) notes, the term "home"—often taken for granted—is ultimately a problematic, culturally constructed and multi-layered concept. For her, the concept of home refers to a "strong emotional bonding with a place and a material environment, ranging in scale from a room, a dwelling, or a residential institution to a street, a neighborhood, a village, a town, a region or even a country" (ibid: 68). Cieraad states the concept of home is so hard to define precisely because it is engrained in societal organization, since Western

---

**2** | http://www.theguardian.com/travel/2014/jul/08/airbnb-legal-troubles-what-are-the-issues Accessed: May 5, 2016.

society thrives on the "emotional, social, and spatial opposition between the domains of home and work." (ibid.). In the case of *Airbnb*, financial interactions are placed *inside* the home, in conflict with this societal construct of home and work as spatially opposite domains. As previous research has indicated, the act of performing paid work inside the home influences people's experience of their home (Phizacklea/Wolkowitz 1995; Massey 1996; Duncan 1996). Therefore, does hosting through *Airbnb* then change the meaning of the home?

As with any other place, a home's identity and meaning must be constructed and negotiated. Hence, the particular meaning of a home is flexible and changes over time. The home is constructed through its lived experience and is simultaneously an ideological construct, more so than a particular space. In the discursive construction of the meaning of home, affective emotions are of great importance. Somerville (1992) argues that, crucial to research on the topic is an understanding of "what home means to different people and to attempt to explain the range of different meanings that we find" (ibid: 115). In understanding the ascribing of identity to a particular space, the work of French anthropologist Marc Augé is essential. Augé (2008) describes the terms of anthropological place and non-place as vital to the contemporary age. The former, according to Augé, carries within it history, identity and relations; whereas the latter—instead of merely being defined as the negative of a place—is to be seen as a space that carries instructive, prohibitive and informative words, texts or symbols (ibid: 52, 96). According to Augé, the traveler's spaces—typically roads, airports or hotel rooms—may be seen as the archetype of non-places (ibid: 86).

In the case of *Airbnb*, hosting can be understood as a constant redefinition of the home as either a place, a non-place, or somewhere in between. Augé writes that indeed neither of these places ever exist in a pure form, and that "place and non-place are not opposites but opposed polarities: the first is never completely erased, the second never totally completed" (ibid: 79). Whereas a home, to the host, can indeed be an anthropological place, by offering to rent it could thus be argued that it is (temporarily) transformed into a non-place. This transformation would occur by stripping the place of its history, its identity, its relations and unformulated rules of know-how; and replacing them with informative, prohibitive and instructive signs or texts.

Thus, the hosts' private place becomes the archetypical non-place of the traveler. A possible transition from something being a place to being a non-place, can be found in the conceptualization of the home through the "social life of things"; a concept most famously described by Arjun Appadurai (1988). According to this renowned anthropologist, whilst humans attribute significance to things, precisely the 'thing-in-motion" can give insight into its social contexts (ibid: 5). Appadurai proposes that when a "thing" is being exchanged it turns into a commodity. He distinguishes three modes of commodification of things: commodities by *destination* (originally intended as primarily for exchange), by *metamorphosis* (firstly intended for other use, then turned into a commodity) and by *diversion* (something originally protected from this, then turned into a commodity) (ibid: 16). Hosting through *Airbnb* can mostly be seen as commodification by *metamorphosis*. How then does the perception, meaning, and experience of "home" change for people who choose to participate as hosts in the virtual community of *Airbnb*?

## METHODOLOGY AND RESEARCH DESIGN

In order to answer this main research question, a multi-site ethnography and five in-depth interviews were carried out. Fieldwork was conducted in the virtual space of *Airbnb*, as well as in hosts' homes. In this offline space, the virtual space—"profile" and "listing"— of *Airbnb* was visited together with the hosts. The hosts were asked to show their homes themselves: through *Skype* or offline. For the in-depth interviewing, semi-structured and open interview techniques were used following Bernard (1995). During the open part of the recorded interviews, respondents were asked about their meaning of home—by using the terms *home histories* and *homelessness*—hoping to grasp individual meanings of home. Notes were jotted down and extended directly after the interview and fieldwork. The aim here was to grasp whether, and if so how, the individual's meaning of the home changed through these renting practices.

No representative sample was conducted since, in this research, an in-depth understanding of personal experience mattered more than a general representation of all *Airbnb* users. However, a diverse scope of gender, age and class was maintained where possible in the selection of participants. Only one of the participants was male, though this seemed to have relation to the group studied, a point that will be touched upon later.

Two of the participating hosts rented out their complete house; the other three intended to share their home with guests. Noteworthy here is that all of the hosts normally lived in the property and were not merely commercially exploiting the space. Three of the five participants were currently not hosting—this might indicate that people mostly host temporarily. Reasons for refraining from hosting provide important insights to the problems hosts encounter in their involvement with this platform. Two of the three hosts had stopped hosting—one temporarily and one permanently—because they felt the risks were too high. The third host, Magda, had an ongoing struggle with her association of house owners throughout the fieldwork up until this writing, in her attempt to get permission for renting out her house. In a few cases in Amsterdam, people have been evicted from their houses after hosting through *Airbnb*. This also raises ethical issues in carrying out research on *Airbnb* hosts, concerning the importance of safeguarding the identity of hosts. These points were discussed with all participants and as a consequence most names have been changed. For the same reasons, limited information on the houses or their locations is disclosed.

## Becoming Part of the Global Community

According to the introductory movie on the *Airbnb* homepage,[3] BELONG ANYWHERE, "being an *Airbnb* host is to be part of a global community." *Airbnb*'s website features people of different backgrounds, and uses the symbol of the earth to signify its global community.

For all of the hosts, financial reasons were deemed as more important to start hosting than joining a global community. Reasons varied from paying the mortgage after a divorce (Ton, 54), earning money as a freelancer with a burnout (Annie, 60), to providing extra funding for travel, nice things, or studies (Eva, 27; Isa, 26 and Magda, 34). However, this financial need did not mean the hosts were merely victims of their financial situation, forced to open up their homes. Common was the idea that hosting had to be something they enjoyed. Equally common however, was the discussion about the risks involved. In Isa's case, her talk of risk concerned the possibility of people finding out about her unofficial hosting and the rise of anti-tourism/*Airbnb* movements in the city center. In the end, these were her main reasons to stop offering her home on *Airbnb*, she was afraid she would lose her home if her housing association would notice. With regard to another risk, Eva stated that she had experienced hosting on *Airbnb* as quite addictive because it was so easy to make money. If someone wants to make a booking, she says, *Airbnb* displays the amount you can earn with this offer and "as a student, you are not used to making that kind of money when you are just sleeping". On the other hand, for Ton, an actual decrease of risk was his motivation to become part of *Airbnb*: to be able to pay the mortgage after his divorce, he had initially planned on growing cannabis. We walked down the stairs and he showed me a special wall he had built to this end. Eventually, he felt renting out through *Airbnb* was less risky in a legal sense; and the extra wall came in handy now.

For all the hosts interviewed, performing the role of a host was generally a pleasant experience. Eva says she experienced being a host as a playful way of making money, comparing it to young kids selling lemonade. She used to leave a bottle of wine on the table for people and fold the towels in a nice way. Isa and Annie expressed the fact that they did the same. Annie states that in her previous jobs, freelancing and working in advertising companies, she continuously felt she needed to sell herself. With hosting, Annie finally felt that she could just be herself, in the natural role of what she calls "mother hen." In

3 | www.airbnb.com.

this sense, the performative role of the host seems to be connected to what Butler (1990) describes as the performativity of gender roles. Identifying as female the behavior of taking care of people in a private space seemed to resonate with the hosts, regardless of their own gender. As the only male respondent, Ton stated that, maybe atypically for a man, he himself very much liked to receive people in his home and take care of them. He added that he felt most of the *Airbnb* guests were female too, or at least he noticed that mostly women are in charge of booking the rooms. Although this is not a quantitative study, the majority of hosts and active participants in host groups were female. In the online ethnography, more commercialized apartments more often seemed to be hosted by men. This points at possibly gendered aspects in the experience of the home and the performance of the role of the *Airbnb* host.

*Image 2*

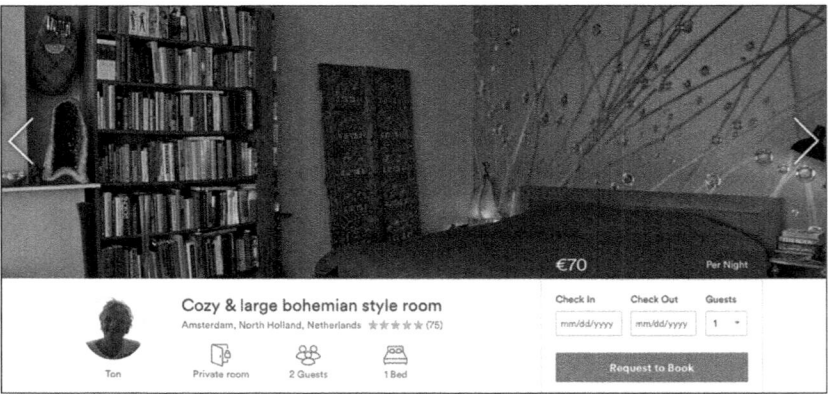

Ton's listing, welcoming guests to his hometown www.airbnb.com Accessed: April 24, 2015.

## COMMODIFYING THE HOME

*Airbnb* hosting in these cases can be understood as a commodification of *metamorphoses* as conceptualized by Appadurai (1988): a thing originally intended for another use is turned into a commodity. This process of commodification arose in three ways: firstly, by ripping a place of its personal identity particularly that contained in personal objects; secondly, by offering prescriptive and informative texts on how to use the place; and thirdly, by creating an idealized home. Isa offers the best illustration of this first aspect. Extensive cleaning was, for her, the biggest component of what might best be understood as a ritual, eliminating any evidence of her identity from her home in order to construct it as a neutral apartment:

When you are cleaning your house like that and removing all of your personal things, it becomes more of a distant house ... So you tidy ... And you clean ... And that is a kind of process through which you're putting your most important things in the basement so they are gone, so to say. And then it becomes more of an apartment, just like any random apartment, instead of when your personal things are still there.

The personal things Isa removed were mostly objects that reminded her of her travels or of her parents' home; random things she liked and personal pictures. She said these would also be the objects she'd want to retrieve in the case of a fire. When asked for an example she points to a painting of birds, hanging on the wall. She made it for her dad when she was seven years old; it used to hang in the house where she grew up. Last June, when her parents moved, they gave it to her. She says that she likes the drawing because of its innocence, and it reminds her of the house she grew up in.

This process of transforming her home into a neutral apartment could be seen as a kind of commodifying or depersonalizing ritual. After guests had left, she would perform the same process in reverse order to retransform the random apartment back into her own again. Even if the place was clean already she would clean extensively before placing back her own things:

Because ... then some part of me somehow returned ... Now it is becoming mine again but then first I have to go over it myself before ... before my personal things are allowed back into the house ...Without it being obsessive but just because ... well because yes, OK, now I'm back and now the place is mine again.

She contemplated that, because of this switch of mindset—from the place being hers to a neutral apartment—she had never really thought about what happened while she was hosting. For almost all hosts the feeling of home, amongst other aspects, lay in objects and their memories. When asked about feelings of homelessness, Annie recounts a burglary that occurred in her home where all her gold and silver items had been stolen:

Yes, that really pissed me off to be honest. But on the other hand, it did get me thinking, maybe it is better not to collect so many things. A while ago someone in my choir; her whole house had burned down, so once you've experienced that, nothing is important anymore ... A fire destroys everything and where does your luck then lie? And in what does your home then remain?

Instead of a home being a dwelling, in Annie's articulation, the home is supposed to be *in something*: objects with particular memories. When asked about experiences of homelessness, stories of fires or burglaries (destroying personal things) were more common than stories of actually being without a dwelling. As Isa states:

I think I can live in many different places. But in the end, a home is being made or shaped—it becomes your own—through the presence of your personal things, or things you have certain memories attached too. In general, I see a house as something functional. But it becomes personal through my personal things.

These are objects you are attached to; the objects you would take out of your home in the event of a fire. Magda too says the collecting of objects is a way of making her feel at home, just like her mom used to do. The kitchen is an area of the house that she "had really let herself go" and "decorated, I guess, the room that I would have wanted when I was a small girl."

The only exception in this stated connection with objects to the feeling of "home" is Ton. For him, above all, the city of Amsterdam is his home. On his *Airbnb* profile, Ton wrote about himself: "I love the city of Amsterdam and like to share its cosmopolitan and peaceful vibe." Ton's different perspective might relate to his personal history of living in squats; as Tom explains, he became quite used to sharing everything with other inhabitants. This different conceptualization recalls the diverse scales of Cieraad (2012), where the home can range from the large (a city) to the small scale (personal objects), although Cieraad does not mention the importance of objects in her definition of the home.

*Image 3*

Magda's kitchen: home as a place for your childhood dreams.

Commodification through metamorphosis and a switching mindset is also evident in Eva's case. It was the issue of noticing that strangers had lived in her home that Eva considers as her most uncomfortable experience with *Airbnb*. In her case, she had offered an informative text—in the form of house rules—on how her place was supposed to be treated. A violation around this in December had felt very uncomfortable. At that time, she had really needed the money and accepted a booking against her intuition. When she got back, the place had been trashed: cigarette butts were lying scattered all over the apartment, there was a bloodied tissue on the floor and she also noticed that the guests had been moving and touching her personal belongings. Striking in Eva's account the repetition of the reference to a burglary, as signifying something disgraceful had happened:

Normally you just don't see what happens. Now I did and it was uncomfortable. If there had been a burglary, you know that someone who wasn't allowed to entered your house. Here the problem is that you gave them permission to enter your house, and it was their home for that period of time.

*Image 4*

"Unlisted": Eva's living room on her *Airbnb* profile.

Even though Eva hired a cleaner and everything was back to normal within a day, she still felt uneasy after seeing what had happened in her home while she was away. Following this negative experience, for now, she was refraining from hosting. Normally, in conversations with guests, Eva avoids emphasizing that it is her home since, "You don't really want to think about it either, what people do to your home, what happened in your bed." In her document of house rules, however, she explicitly states that it *is* her home, with the first rule stating: "Please take good care of the apartment, it is our home." The rest of the text referred to descriptions of how to use specific aspects of the house. Like Eva, Annie also provided a similar list of house rules for guests. These documents can be seen as providing descriptive texts, pointing to the creation of a non-place as described by Augé (2008) in the commodification of the home. In these non-places people are reminded of a contract on how the non-place is supposed to be used by texts and symbols, defining its occupant as an individualized user (99-101).

All participants articulated the creation of an idealized home was important to their hosting. Performing the role of a good host was a crucial part in maintaining this ideal. As Magda states, in *CouchSurfing*[4] people just have to

---

**4** | Couchsurfing is another online community for hosting where, in contrast to Airbnb, no fees or other payments for the accommodation are involved. https://www.couch-surfing.com.

take or leave your place the way it is; with *Airbnb*, she expressed a wish to offer people value for their money. When I called by, she had a handyman coming over to work on a list of chores she felt were necessary before her home was suitable for hosting. She felt that the kitchen needed more attention, looking worried at the thought of how much work it would entail. Annie adopted a different approach, maintaining a spatial division: one part was for guests and another part was for herself, with a lock separating the two areas. In the hallway, she positioned a dresser for guests to put their dirty dishes so as not to enter her section of the house. Ton had bought new furniture, a fridge and a coffeemaker; and tidied up the place to make it as comfortable as possible for his guests.

*Image 5*

Proof of damage: picture for *Airbnb* customer service.

## CONCLUDING REFLECTIONS

For all of the hosts, the meaning of their home had not drastically changed through their participation with *Airbnb*. Metamorphosis was only temporary or partial.

Paradoxically, *Airbnb* gave Ton the possibility to keep his house instead of having to sell it after his divorce. For Annie, her house had become empty when her two daughters had moved out; as a consequence of her hosting activities there was, once again, more social life in her house, through which she experienced her home to be more complete. Isa and Eva both mostly realized, how lucky they are to have their homes—so many people wanted to stay there.

At the time of this writing, I spoke with Eva again. She said that she had taken her first booking since January: "I feel like I can do it again." Magda, still in dispute with her VvE, decided not to start renting until she had more certainty on what she was allowed to do.

A few issues arose from the data that deserve further theoretical attention and exploration. The point that personal objects or belongings can create a feeling of home—or at least a sense of belonging—is an issue that is worthy of more extensive focus in anthropological perspectives of the home. In this essay, it is suggested that the importance of objects might be added to the definition of home offered by Cieraad (2012). The reason for this is that most hosts articulated feelings of being "at home" through objects and their respective related memories. When asked about homelessness and home histories, stories about burglaries or fires destroying or disgracing the meaning of home and its objects, were more common than stories of actually being without a dwelling. References to homelessness during the periods hosts were renting out were absent. The lack of such reference can be explained by the partial renting out of the home or else a temporary distance made from the home. Commodification through metamorphosis, as formulated by Appadurai (1988), is thus partial or temporary in these cases; enacted through a cleaning ritual, the providence of instructive texts, a spatial division, or the creation of an idealized home.

Following from this research, two orientations seem to offer fruitful perspectives for future research on hosting experiences and the meaning of home. Firstly, there seems to be a gendered aspect in the experience of the home and the performance of being a host. In exactly what way gender and participation in *Airbnb* relate, needs to be explored in more detail. Secondly, the main motivation for hosting was money. Through this platform people found a solution for their precarious financial situations. The regulations and rules regarding *Airbnb*, set by jurisdiction and housing associations, juxtaposed with the tightening of availability of the state's social benefits, is a topic that might be interesting to explore to larger extent.

Finally, conducting research on *Airbnb* gives opportunity to be involved in participant observation in the more normally inaccessible sites of private spaces of the home; also to make exploration into the meanings of the home. As Appadurai (1988: 5) states, the significance humans attribute to things can best be explored precisely when these meanings are "shifting, renegotiated and redefined," such as in the case of homes being hosted through *Airbnb*.

## REFERENCES

Appadurai, Arjun (1988): The Social Life of Things: Commodities in Cultural Perspective, Cambridge: Cambridge University Press.
Augé, Marc (2008 [1995]): Non-Places: An Introduction to Supermodernity, translation by John Howe, London and New York: Verso.
Bernard, H. R. (2006): Research Methods in Anthropology: Qualitative and Quantitative Approaches Fourth Edition. Lanham: Rowman Altamira.
Boellstorff, Tom (2012): "Rethinking Digital Anthropology", in: Heather Horst/Daniel Miller (eds.), Digital Anthropology, London: Berg, pp. 39-59.
Butler, Judith (1990): Gender Trouble: Feminism and the Subversion of Identity, New York: Routledge.
Cieraad, Irene (2012): "Anthropological Perspectives on Home", in: Susan Smith (ed.), International Encyclopedia of Housing and Home, Oxford: Elsevier, pp. 65-69.
Duncan, Nancy (1996): "Renegotiating Gender and Sexuality in Public and Private Spaces", in: Nancy Duncan (ed.), Body Space: Destabilizing Geographies of Gender and Sexuality, London: Routledge, pp. 127 - 145.
Edelman, Benjamin/Luca, Michael (2014) "Digital Discrimination: The Case of Airbnb.com", in: Harvard Business School NOM Unit Working Paper 14/054.
Hareven, Tamara (1991): "The Home and the Family in Historical Perspective", in: Social Research 58/1, pp. 253-285.
Ikkala, Tapio/Lampinen, Airi (2015): "Monetizing Network Hospitality: Hospitality and Sociability in the Context of Airbnb", in: Proceedings of the 18th ACM Conference on Computer Supported Cooperative Work & Social Computing, pp.1033-1044.
Jackson, Michael (1995): At Home in the World, Sydney: Harper Perennial.
Massey, Doreen (1994): "Double Articulation: A Place in the World", in Angelika Bammer (ed.), Displacements: Cultural Identities in Question, Bloomington: Indiana University Press, pp. 110-122.
Molz, Jennie (2014): "Toward a Network Hospitality." In: First Monday 19/3. http://firstmonday.org/ ojs/index. php/fm/article/view/4824
Phizacklea, Annie/Wolkowitz, Carol (1995): Home-Working Women, Gender, Racism and Class at Work, London: Sage.
Somerville, Peter (1992): "Homelessness and the Meaning of Home: Rooflessness or Rootlessness?", in: International Journal of Urban and Regional Research 16/4, pp. 529-539.
Sontag, Susan (1966): "The Anthropologist as Hero", in: Susan Sontag. Against Interpretation and Other Essays, New York: Farrar, Straus and Giroux, pp. 3-14.

Tucker, Aviezer (1994): "In Search of a Home." In: Journal of Applied Philosophy 11/2, pp. 181-187.

Wardaugh, Julia (1999): "The Unaccommodated Woman: Home, Homelessness and Identity", in: Sociological Review 47/1, pp. 91-109.

"Zo Hard Groeit Airbnb in Nederland", August 26, 2015. http://www.z24.nl/ondernemen/airbnb-nederland-amsterdam-verspreiding-appartement-582139

# How has the Internet Determined the Identity of Chilean Gay Men in the Last Twenty Years?

Juan Francisco Riumalló Grüzmacher

## INTRODUCTION

Through this project, I explore the changing relationship between Chilean gay men and online communication over the last 20 years. I interviewed ten gay men between the ages of 24 and 55 years of age, from Santiago de Chile, via Skype and *Scruff*—a gay dating app.

In this paper, I describe the experience of using Chilean gay websites for men of different ages and social backgrounds, and how useful such sites were found to be in the process of assuming their own homosexual identities. I then discuss different ways of communication among Chilean gay men during the pre-internet times, the first gay chat rooms and the newest apps for smartphones. Finally, I concentrate the discussion about how important the internet has been in creating a sense of Chilean gay community, not only in the virtual world but also in the real world. Overall, my goal is to figure out how Chilean gay men have used the internet during the two last decades, and how the internet has affected the process of creating a sexual identity in these people.

## LEAVING THE ISLAND

Every one of my informants told me that the first time he looked at pornography was through the internet. This then became a habit and each spent a significant portion of his time online looking for these kinds of websites. Felipe is 36 years old and remembers that he was 16 when he used the internet for the first time. His aunt was the first member of the family with a connection in her house. To have access to the internet was not cheap in Chile in the 1990s and as a result, Felipe could not use the internet very often.

Every two weeks he used to take a bus after school to go to his aunt´s house on the east side of Santiago. At that hour of the day, around 3:00 p.m., he had to settle for simply viewing photos online because chat rooms were completely empty. The best time to meet people was at night, however it would have been considered strange to visit his aunt by night as a teenager. Then his parents got an internet connection. The first chat that he joined was called *mIRC* (Microsoft internet Relay Chat).[1] He remembers that there were people from many different countries, and with various interests. In the Chilean room there were around 200 people—this in a country with a population of around 16 million. Every night he found they were almost always the same 200 men. On the screen you could see only letters and codes, something unimaginable now in the age of *Grindr* and *Scruff*.

While Felipe was starting to discover his first gay experiences on the screen, Mateo was only six years old. Now he is 26, ten years younger than Felipe. He did not have to take a bus to access the internet, because it has been a part of his life from the very beginning. For him, the experience was completely different. "In my case it wouldn't have been so different to come out without internet. At least for me, it wasn't a deciding factor." Mateo came out in Chile ten years after Felipe. According to him, "It wasn't an aid to meet people. I had the luck of meeting real people by chance, in my daily life. I know that internet opened a world to a lot of people. But that hasn't been my reality."

Francisco is 23 years old and also started watching pornography online. He was brought up in a very Catholic context; an upbringing that caused him tremendous guilt. The first gay man that he met was not in a chat room, but in the metro. That was four years ago. He not only considers the internet irrelevant to his process of coming out and meeting other gay people, he would have preferred not to use it. For him, the internet is a highly eroticized and sexualized space, rather than a useful tool that might help him meet people who could become his friends, or help him find information and support for coming out.

Francisco's comments remind me of Delia Dumitrica and Georgia Gaden's (2008) work on the problematic potential of virtual space. They write, "as virtual spaces have been popularized, they have been both celebrated as an opportunity for liberation from conventional gender roles and criticized as white-male shaped spaces, filled with pornography, sexualization, and increased commodifications" (Dumitrica/Gaden 2008: 6-7). This view, that the internet can be both a space of liberation and one reinforcing existing norms and conventions, was confirmed in my interviews with informants whom I met through a dating app called *Scruff*.

---

1 | mIRC: www.mirc.com.

Balázs is the profile name of a 25-year-old man. According to him, dating apps are a double-edged sword. Balázsis thinks that he would have been healthier without the internet because, online, pornography opens an endless world for you. He told me, "I saw things and I said: 'What is this?'! It was something disgusting. It starts to idealize sexuality. It idealizes it so much that it's impossible to find it in real life. It would have been healthier to find out [about sexuality] on my own." He also thinks that the lack of information about sexual education, on websites or apps that promote sex dates, makes it much easier to engage in unsafe sexual practices.

Luis is of the same generation as Felipe. He is 35, and came out twelve years ago when he was 23. Nowadays, he is the President of "Iguales,"[2] one of the biggest and most important foundations in Chile for sexual diversity. He spent around four years looking at photos of gay pornography before entering a chat room to meet people. Luis explained, "On one hand I was not mature enough to realize that I had to talk about being gay with someone. But the internet wasn't helping much because when you searched, the only things available were pornographic photos. There wasn't a concept of community online, even less so in Chile."

In 2010, he decided to create a website called *Joven Confundido*[3] ("the Confused Young") on which young people could find answers to their questions during the process of coming out. After Luis came out, many other young gay men approached him to ask questions about how they could do the same. He tells me that he created the website so that people can find answers and interact with each other. Luis explains that in spite of the fact that being gay is so common, the internet did not offer any tools or support for coming out. "Existing sites were for people who were already out. But what happens with those who hadn't assumed their identity yet?" Luis asked.

He believes that adolescence is a very lonely stage in life for gay teens, because neither schools nor the Chilean government, nor the health public system provide young people any help. There is a lack of support among many families as well, due to the fact the parents are "straight." For the same reason, he believes that gay people use the internet to increase their exposure to a greater number of others like themselves as opposed to straight people. The feeling of being a minority pushes them to look for more people like themselves. Luis tells me: "A heterosexual goes to school and 90 per cent of his classmates are heterosexual as well. But for a gay man it's the opposite. In every working space, family space, educational space, he finds himself in a minority position. And therefore, as social beings, the internet constitutes a platform to search for pairs."

---

2 | *Fundación Iguales*: www.iguales.cl.
3 | *Joven Confundido*: www.jovenconfundido.com.

On Luis's website, aimed at the young, it is possible to find many important answers to common questions. A nurse and midwife, and two psychologists—all of them homosexuals—moderate the website. Notably, the site offers users the option to delete any trace of their visit in their computer history. Privacy is very important here.

*Image 1*

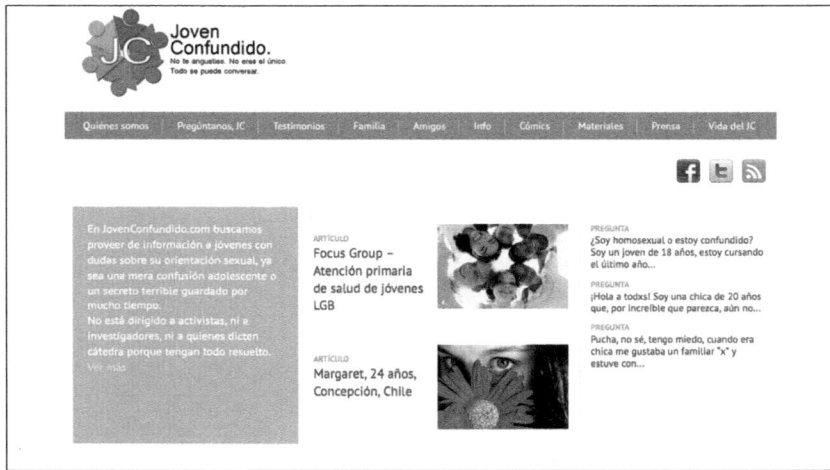

The Chilean website: www.jovenconfundido.com

## Like a Cow

On March 25, 2009, a new dating app for gay men called *Grindr* was launched. According to my participants, *Grindr* is the most popular dating app among their friends in Chile. The company says that they have more than five million users from 192 countries. It works with the GPS on a users' smartphone and shows other users who are close by. The app is free but if you want to see more profiles, you have to pay. *Scruff* is its most direct competitor in the gay scene, with five million users around the world (see also Phillips 2015). The main difference from *Grindr* is that you can see who has visited your profile and you are able to search in other locations by typing in an address or the name of a neighborhood.

*Image 2*

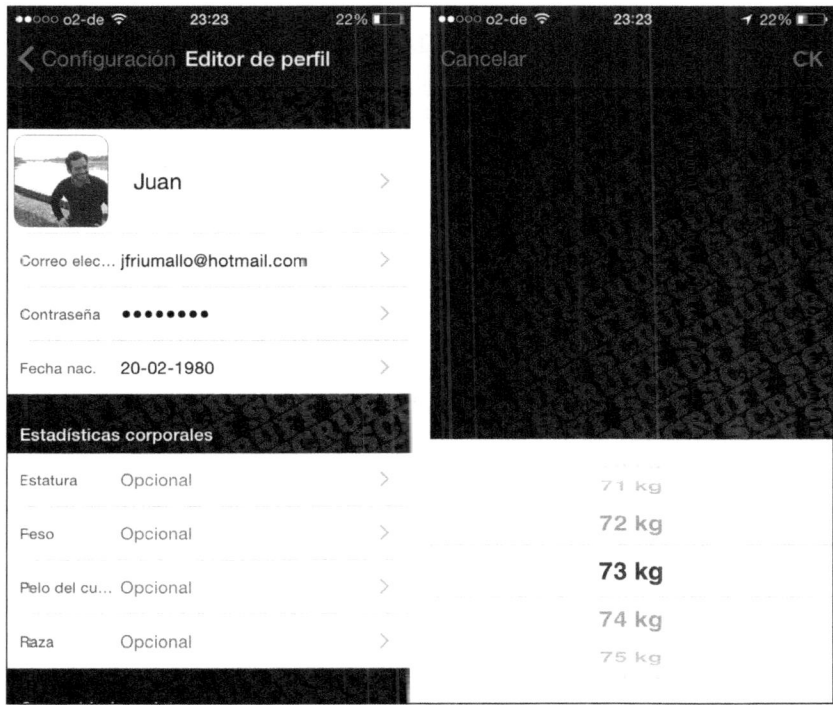

These screen shots were taken during the process of creating my own profile in *Scruff* I wrote, as a part of my data, that I am a student of the Freie Universität Berlin.

I decided to create a profile in *Scruff* because it allowed me to talk with men in Chile while I was living in Berlin. The app recommends one to choose a good profile photo and write a short biography. I included my age at that moment, 35, and my profession as "Universitario" (Student), along with my weight and height. In my profile I wrote about my program of study, Visual and Media Anthropology, and made my role as a researcher explicit.

"El ReY DeL MaMBO" sends me a message. I am in.

Amongst the profiles, I recognize the face of the friend of a friend. The following day I sent him a message via *WhatsApp*. I thought it would be too intrusive to appear suddenly on *Scruff* asking questions; maybe that is symptomatic of being a new user.

Gonzalo is 37 years old and a user of *Scruff*. He gives me an introduction to the app through *Skype*. He explains that *Scruff* is about making dates and unlike *Grindr*, it facilitates many types of interactions—from short chats to meeting the love of your life—and features many types of users—not necessarily "models." Gonzalo tells me that he always has felt very different from the other Chilean gay men, because of his way of speaking, his body type and his interests, but here he feels very comfortable. "It's not the perfect physique, but a more masculine one. It's not to be extremely hot, the perfect body. But on the other hand, I think that's very popular nowadays. The manlier, hairier man. Which wasn't very common ten years ago, now it is. And *Scruff* aims for that," explains Gonzalo.

I met some people in *Scruff*. I decided not to ask about age if this did not appear in the profile. Hermann does not show his age; he is simply described as "Hispano/Latino, 1,82m, 77kg." He tells me that he has not met anyone special through *Scruff* so far. In general, he uses these kinds of apps exclusively for sex. However, he also finds these types of apps useful when he is traveling, at least to go out and have dinner with someone. "But in general, people are here only to have sex. Very few people are looking for something else," he explains.

Oz is 43 years old and single: "White, 1,84m, 72kg, some body hair." I ask him how he feels using this app. He answers that he feels comfortable, but he uses it more for watching people rather than meeting them. "Sometimes I lose interest, sometimes the other person does; or, being more practical, I'm not coming out of my house at 3:00 a.m. because I got turned on with a chat." He thinks the younger one is, the more time one spends in these apps.

Balázs is 24 years old and also single: "Mixed, 1,80m, 76kg, hairy." He is almost 20 years younger than Oz. He disagrees with the idea that youth is indicative of better skills for using the app, at least on *Scruff*. He tells me that, through *Scruff*, you can find people of all ages and if you have a specific preference, you can use filters. He feels comfortable using the app but has had some bad experiences. "The local users on this app describe and demand a specific style of men, using aggression, segregation of subjects or their conditions. To my judgment, that's not healthy. It's ok to have our own tastes, but there are other ways," says Balázs.

*Image 3*

User profiles on *Scruff*,
in Providencia, Santiago de Chile.

I sent a good number of messages on *Scruff*, but I did not have much success. When I typed in "Providencia, Santiago de Chile,"—my former neighborhood in Santiago— 45 profiles out of 100 appeared semi-nude. Of course, as researcher, that was not the case with my own profile. In general, the photos were more suggestive than mine. Particularly in this app, the photo seems to be everything.

I ask more questions of Gonzalo, this time through *Scruff*. I want to know more about the significance of the photo in the profile. "I think it's important because it's a visual app, where you sell your image and the image that you sell has to be as good as possible to achieve your goal, which in this case is to be liked by the other person that you might be interested in," Gonzalo said. For him, it is like fishing, "You pick the best hook or you keep trying until you figure out which one to stay with."

After my first experience on this app, I got an e-mail from the *Scruff* team, signed by a man called Johnny Skandros, the founder of the app. He welcomes me and explains what I can find within the app. At the close of the e-mail, he says goodbye with a "Woof!"

Nowadays, it seems to be much easier to meet gay men in Chile than 15 or 20 years ago. Felipe explains that, before the explosion in access to the internet and smartphones, it was very difficult to find people to flirt with. There were some specific places in Santiago where closeted gay men went to hook up. Felipe tells me: "You drove there in your car, first of all you had to have a car, and then you got into a precise circuit of streets. Everyone was doing the same thing. You placed yourself at the side of the other car, you looked at the other person's face and if you liked him you pulled over a little further on. For many years this was all there was." He feels that kind of circuit was much less safe than being behind a screen.

Tomás is 43 years old and had his first experience in a gay chat room 14 years ago. "Is there someone out there? With that question I went into a gay chat room for the first time." In spite of his age, 29 years old at the time, he did not have any gay friends. He remembers that these chats were based on words, nicknames and codes. There were no photos. He says that everything was very unreal and frustrating; it took many months to meet someone. You could be talking with someone and suddenly that person disappeared—you did not know if it was because his internet connection had failed or because he just didn't like you. Also the risks were higher. He remembers talking for a long time with the same person, idealizing him in spite of not knowing him. The guy sent him a picture. Then they talked on the phone over many months. However, when they met, he was a different person to the one Tomás had expected. The guy had sent Tomás a fake picture.

According to Tomás, the process now of meeting people through the internet is much faster and people lie much less. Despite this, four months ago he decided to close his *Grindr* profile because he used to spend too much time viewing profiles and waiting for something that never happened. "It's like a cattle fair. You put your age, your height, your qualities. And I felt like a cow. Also I reduced my age, because I feel I look younger. I'd say: I'll put the age I represent [32]. I started to get very annoyed with people who, instead of saying 'hi,' would say 'age?'."

When Luis went to a virtual gay chat room for the first time, he felt that his life had changed. Luis says, "I got to talk virtually and then live for the first time with someone who was living a process that was similar to mine. Neither of the two of us would call ourselves gay at the time. But I feel that it helped me to start a process, to discover my sexuality, to talk about the processes we were going through."

In 2003, Luis went to Berlin for a period of six months to study. Suddenly his context changed dramatically, and also the way he approached other gay men. In Berlin, he left the chat rooms for a while and instead felt encouraged to actually go to a gay club to meet people; then, those people introduced him to their friends.

For Felipe, it was also very useful to start chatting with people through the internet but he also had bad experiences. At the end of the 1990s it was possible to send photos online but it took more than five minutes to send or receive such an image; downloading happened slowly, one line of the picture at a time and was viewed in a separate window. A digital camera or a scanner was also required. Most of the times he sent fake photos because of the fear of being discovered. Felipe tells me, "One time, we exchanged pictures with a guy. And while the picture was downloading I figured out that we were both sending the same fake picture. When I realized this, I just ended the chat."

In spite of the disadvantages of the early chat rooms, Luis, Felipe and Tomás agree that the internet contributed to the idea of feeling like a part of something; it was like a common new place where you were able to find more people like yourself—a weak sense of community, but one that was transforming with the passing of the years.

However, for my two youngest informants, the situation is different. Francisco feels that he was lucky, because immediately after coming out he was able to meet people face to face. Although he used *Grindr* and another website called *Manhunt*,[4] he told me that he had been able to make only one friend through the apps. "They were, in general, older people. It was the first time that I was in contact with so many Chilean gays and I thought: "What the fuck am I getting into?! If these are the gays from Chile, I'd rather not come out of the closet because it was all very explicit," explains Francisco. The experience was very shocking for him. He thought that he was never going to be able to introduce his family to one of "these people that show their penises on the internet."

He assumes that even for his generation—he is 23—to be seen on *Grindr* can be complicated, as it is still relatively taboo. He thinks that in Chile, sex is still considered something bad because of the Judeo-Christian culture. He closes the door of his room and tells me that if his mother hears him, she is going to collapse. "That they see you looking for sex on the internet is like, wow. What are they going to think, that I'm looking for sex all day long or that I'm not capable of doing it in person?" explained Francisco.

Mateo neither trusts the virtual world, nor feels particularly part of a community: "I think it's a double-edged sword. Someone who's 14 who is now coming out of the closet has an easier time meeting people. At the same time, I think it's a social insulator. You have access to everything but at the same time it's very easy to hide yourself in it. To have access to everything can be either a good thing or something to keep you in the dark, hidden."

But what happened with people who had to come out and meet other gay people before the internet era? Alfredo is 55 years old and started the process to

---

4 | Manhunt: www.manhunt.com.

assume his homosexuality when he was 18. He had some sense of community in some bars during the 1980s, which were the places where he sought to identify with others and started to discover that there were others like him who were in a similar situation. He tells me, "But it was a physical thing [in person] because you couldn´t get to know them if you hadn´t seen them physically before, in any friend´s house, or any bar or places like that. There were not any other ways." For this reason, when the internet appeared as a social tool at the end of the 1990s, Alfredo and other gay men of his generation did not use it to find out answers about how to come out or make friends. "Those of us who identified ourselves [as homosexuals] in our twenties, 25 years ago, approached the internet with a different attitude. And at the beginning we used it a lot to find sex rather than to form groups," explains Alfredo.

## SENSE OF COMMUNITY

As mentioned, Luis—the President of *Fundación Iguales*—believes that Chilean gay people use the internet more than Chilean heterosexual people, mainly because of the difficulty in meeting other gay people in a country where the Catholic Church still exerts so much influence. "The notion of minority makes you look for mechanisms to make contact with others like you," explains Luis. At Iguales they also use the internet, through their website and social networks, as a way to inform, educate, raise money and recruit volunteers.

Alfredo believes that the internet has been crucial in affecting changes in Chilean society. According to him, social networks such as *Facebook* or *Twitter* are much more able to capture peoples' feelings and express changes in mentality about topics, such as LGBT[5] rights. When those changes are reflected on these networks, it is much easier to point to a social basis for modifying or creating new legislation in parliament with regard to issues such as civil unions. Alfredo is a lawyer and also is involved with Iguales. "The internet provides you with the input to improve laws, in the long term," he said.

According to Felipe, the internet was enabling in creating a sense of Chilean gay community twenty years ago, when he used the first chat rooms to share his experiences and doubts with others unknown guys. He commented that when you have a good group of friends in real life, the internet becomes more dispensable. During 2014 he moved to Berlin for six months for work. Through the process of relocation to a strange city, he was reminded of a similar feeling that he had experienced a long time ago. In moving to Berlin, the internet was very determinant in his ability to find his way; it took on the same importance that it had in the past, largely because he was in a place where he did not belong

---

5 | Lesbian, Gay, Bisexual and Transgender.

and also where he did not know anyone. "I didn't have work mates because I worked alone, and I had a sense of urgency because I was certainly not going to spend two months talking to a wall. And that is when the internet makes you feel part of a space, of a group. The smaller the circle, the more important the internet is."

On the other hand, Felipe says that today you can find several small communities online on *Facebook* or other websites specifically for gay people. However, while there is still not a large online Chilean gay community, there are different smaller groups around several topics or interests, like the fetish scene. "There's still a community being created there and you go back a little bit to the past because these things are more of a taboo. What yesterday was to be gay, today could be sado-masochism. And the internet protects you, it gives you a safe place to interact with other people," Felipe told me. In this sense, Gonzalo said something similar when he described *Scruff* as an app for people with more specific characteristics or tastes.

Tomás also does not feel like he belongs to an online Chilean gay community. He feels more comfortable meeting people through wider apps and social networks like *Instagram* or *Facebook*, which are for gay and straight people alike. A few weeks ago, he met someone via *Instagram*. He sent him a message and then they started talking. "Today I'm interested in showing my context and having access to others. More than just knowing if the person is gay. It's amusing to know who his friends are, because it enriches the relationship. His tastes, the way he takes pictures." According to Tomás, these things are much more important than height, age, or if he is a "top" or a "bottom."

In spite of their 20 years of difference, Francisco also prefers to use apps like *Tinder*, which is for both homosexual and heterosexual people, rather than *Grindr*. "*Tinder* is more like a community. It's healthier because pictures from *Facebook* are being used. Pictures that everybody sees. You're no longer who you want to be, but who you really are online." *Tinder* allows you to know if you have more friends in common. Also it will not let you send extra pictures, so you have to move to *WhatsApp* quickly if you are really interested in one person. Francisco feels that the internet has not directly contributed to generating a Chilean gay community. For him, the websites and social networks for gay men, in most instances, alienate people rather than help them due to the extreme sexualization of the interactions that such sites foster.

## Conclusion

In spite of it being quite difficult to generalize, based on 10 interviews, I think it is possible to compare these different points of view, and so discover some aspects of how the internet has determined and modified relationships among Chilean gay men.

In general, it seems that the initial interaction between these gay men and the internet was through pornography. The first time that they saw pornography was on the Web, and that factor seems to have determined the ensuing relation between my participants and the internet. The second notable aspect was the search for other gay people as a way to leave their place of isolation and loneliness. While the first step has not seen big changes in 20 years—with the exception of the fact that today access to the internet is far more widespread and relatively inexpensive —the second one has changed dramatically.

Nowadays, younger Chilean gay men seem to have more opportunities to meet other people like them in real life, rather than just through online apps. It is also evident that for those who are younger, most apps and sites that are geared only to gay men do not have a good reputation among their friends; they do not feel comfortable being seen using those apps. However, almost one year after doing these interviews, my participants are still frequently using *Grindr* and *Scruff*. Apparently, apps have become part of everyday life as a way to meet or observe other gay men.

However, many of my informants agree that after the first boom of the gay sites and apps such as *Grindr*, they now prefer to use less targeted social networks such as *Facebook*, *Instagram* and *Tinder*. These tools provide more context about people—such as photos, interests, information about friends, studies and work—while also allowing users to get to know new people. Either way, the internet seems to be less important and useful when gay men already have a circle of friends and relationships in real life.

Yet, the virtual world can be considered of more vital use to Chilean gay people than heterosexual people, because of the stark necessity to safely find more people with the same sexual identity but remain behind a screen; this in the context of a country that still is perceived as very conservative. The virtual world still seems to be the public square for gay people to meet and share experiences.

## References

Dumitrica, Delia/Gaden, Georgia (2008): "Knee-High Boots and Six-Pack Abs: Autoethnographic Reflections on Gender and Technology in Second Life. In: Journal of Virtual Worlds Research 1/3.

Phillips, Christian (2015): Self-Pornographic Representations with Grindr. In: Journal of Visual and Media Anthropology. Vol 1, No.1. pp. 65-79
*Facebook* official website. Accessed: June 2016. https://www.facebook.com/
*Fundación Iguales.* Accessed: June 2016. https://www.iguales.cl/
*Grindr* official website. Accessed: April 2015. http://grindr.com/learn-more
*Instagram* official website. Accessed: June 2016. https://www.instagram.com/
*Scruff* official website. Accessed: April 2015. http://www.scruff.com/en/
*Tinder* official website. Accessed: June 2016. https://www.gotinder.com/
*WhatsApp* official website. Accessed: June 2016. https://www.whatsapp.com/?l=en&

# Red Packets in the Real and Virtual Worlds
## How Multi-Function WeChat Influences Chinese Virtual Relationships

Xiaojing Ji

The Gift: Forms and Functions of Exchange in Archaic Societies, a classical book by French sociologist Marcel Mauss (1966), details how the early exchange systems center around the obligations to give, to receive and to reciprocate.
    There is a series of rights and duties about consuming and repaying existing side by side with rights and duties about giving and receiving. The pattern of symmetrical and reciprocal rights is not difficult to understand if we realize that it is first and foremost a pattern of spiritual bonds between things which are to some extent parts of persons, and persons and groups that behave in some measure as if they were things (Mauss 1966: 11). This essay states primarily that the most popular mobile social application in China, WeChat has changed Chinese social relationships—between family, friends, colleagues, strangers— via the "Red Packet" app function. With the goal of exposing how *WeChat Red Packets* impact and influence people's lives, I have collected examples both from groups and individuals, together with stories from my family and friends, and additionally from some *WeChat* group members previously unknown to me. Further, I interviewed some Western friends of mine who live and work in Berlin, who use *WeChat* to communicate with Chinese people. I asked them about their reaction to *WeChat Red Packets*, as they are quite familiar with *WeChat*. However, because *WeChat* requires a Chinese bank account to use this function, they had never actually used *Red Packets* themselves.
    These examples and stories illustrate why and how *Red Packets* could deeply influence Chinese social relationships and how they could indeed take the lead in developing new personal relationships. All the interviewees were very open to sharing their own stories, however, some of them were not interested in sharing the financial aspects of their *Red Packet* usage. This data does not reflect all segments of Chinese society. Exclusions of note are residents of western China and Chinese people over sixty-five years.

## What is WeChat?

WeChat began as a project at the Tencent Guangzhou Research and Project Center in October 2010. The original version of the app, *Weixin*, was invented by Xiaolong Zhang, and named by Ma Huateng, CEO of Tencent. In April 2012, *Weixin* was re-branded as *WeChat* for the international market. On 12 August 2015, Tencent revealed *WeChat's* Monthly Active Users (MAU) metric[1] to be 600 million, a rapid increase over the previously released figure of 549 million MAUs released only five months previously.[2] *WeChat* is a social application that combines a communication function similar to *WhatsApp* or *Messenger*, a digital payment function—which connects to the customer's private bank account (similar to *Paypal* or *Alipay*)—and also information posting via *Moments* (like *Facebook*). With this multi-functional application, each smartphone owner uses one or two accounts (one for work and a second one for his or her personal life).

According to the GSMA Intelligence 2016 research report[3] there are 1.3 billion people in China who have mobile device connections, 62 percent of whom were using a smartphone by the end of 2015, exceeding the Europe average of 55 percent. Concurrent to the rapid increase in mobile device usage, *WeChat* has become the number one social application in China with 600 million active users, which represents 93 percent of the Chinese social app market. *WeChat* is not only a social messaging app, with multiple functions such as Moment, Contact Card, Share Location, Real Time Location, Wallet, Red Packet and Transfer; *WeChat* also has a *WhatsApp*-like messaging function, which has a practical use in daily life.

---

**1** | Monthly Active Users is one of the ways to measure the success rate of online social games and social networking services. The metric is defined by counting the number of unique users during a specific measurement period.

**2** | Steven, Millward. "WeChat now has 500 million monthly active users" Accessed April 30, 2016. https://www.techinasia.com/wechat-500-million-active-users-q4-2014

**3** | Data sources from: GSMA Intelligence. https://www.gsmaintelligence.com/markets/623/dashboard/

## What Are "Red Packets"?

In China, a *Red Packet* is a monetary gift, given during holidays or special occasions such as weddings, graduation or the birth of a baby.[4] *Red Packets* are given by older people to younger ones, by married people to unmarried ones, or by employed people to unemployed ones. During the Chinese New Year, the older generation traditionally put money in a red envelope and give it to the younger generation with best wishes for the coming new year; they also prepare *Red Packets* with small amount of cash for neighborhood kids. In the streets, all the flowerpots are decorated with lots of red packets.

*Image 1*

A red packet given to my nephews this year, bearing the word of my family name: JI

When I was little, the most exciting thing about New Year was waiting for midnight on New Year's Eve when my parents took out *Red Packets* to give to me—inside was brand new money. However, before they gave them to me, I had to say "gong xi fa cai, hong bao na lai", which means: "I wish you a good fortune,

---

**4** | "Red packet: Sign of prosperity" Accessed: May 1, 2016. http://www.char4u.com/content/red-packet-sign-of-prosperity/

give me a red packet!" Since going to work, after graduation from university, I no longer receive red packets from my family or relatives. Instead, I now have to prepare them for my twin nephews who are the sons of my elder sister.

I still remember the night before my elder sister's wedding, when my mother and I prepared a small amount of red packets for her big day. My mother was actually very sad about the fact that, in traditional Chinese culture, when a daughter gets married this means that she will go to her husband's home; henceforth she will belong to her husband's home. My mother was not looking forward to the day that her daughter would go to her husband's home because she feared that this change might mean her daughter would have a less caring relationship with her mother than before. The next day, my new brother-in-law came to my house to pick up my sister. He and his best man first needed to complete all of the bridesmaids' tasks while remaining outside the front door. According to Chinese tradition, the bridesmaids are responsible for protecting the door until all tasks are completed. The tasks could include, for instance, performing fifty push-ups or singing a technically challenging love song to the bride. In practice, most of these tasks remain uncompleted. To compensate for such uncompleted tasks, they must send *Red Packets* through the door to the bridesmaids, then after at least 30 minutes, the bridesmaids may finally grant them entry in order to take the bride away. Another traditional Chinese ritual involves the newly married couple serving tea together with green tea leaves, red dates and lotus. After serving tea for the third time, the couple must formally address each other's new in-laws as "father" and "mother" for the first time. Following this, the new couple receives a large number of red packets from the older generation. Nowadays, in the virtual social world, things have changed. Virtual consumption leads to a change in people's values, and this affects their patterns of consumer behavior. *WeChat* launched *Digital Wallet* in 2013. Since then, people have used the *WeChat Wallet* payment system for consumer activity in daily life—for instance, shopping in convenience stores, restaurants and even buying street food. In early 2014 just before Chinese New Year, WeChat launched a new product; it became possible to digitally "send" *Red Packets*. Each *Red Packet* can be 'filled' with any amount from 200 RMB[5]; there is no upper limit on the amount that can be sent but there is a single bank account limit of 50.000 RMB each day. People send *Red Packets* via WeChat without rituals or red-envelope objects and without meeting face-to-face; they only need to click on their smartphone for 5 seconds, after which everything is taken care of.

---

5 | RMB Chinese Yuan Renminbi—the official currency of the People's Republic of China.

*Image 2*

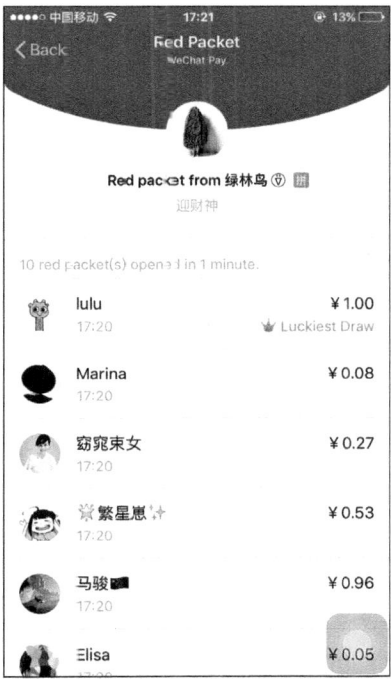

Red Packet WeChat screenshot.

In 2015, WeChat cooperated with other major Chinese companies to launch "Yao Yi Yao."[6] Five hundred million RMB were sent in *Red Packets* whilst playing the game during Chinese New Year 2015.

According to *WeChat* official data, people sent 51,94 billion *Red Packets* (equivalent to 37 *Red Packets* per person) via *WeChat* over six days during Chinese New Year 2016. This was a 16-fold increase in comparison to the same six days of the last Chinese New Year, which saw 3,27 billion *Red Packets* sent via *WeChat*. However, *WeChat* did not publish the total amount of money of the *Red Packets* sent during 2016 Chinese New Year.

Divided by generation, the predominant user group are people born in the 1980s who sent 10,2 billion Red Packets; people who were born during the 1960s-1980s sent more than 0,8 billion *Red Packets*; people who were born before the 1960s only sent in total 0,4 billion.

---

6 | "Yao Yi Yao" is a commercial entertainment game during the Chinese New Year eve gala, which involves shaking a random amount of *Red Packets*. When the event hosts announced "action", people who have *WeChat* accounts keep shaking their cellphones for about 30 seconds, could get a random amount of *Red Packets*.

## How Do *WeChat Red Packets* Impact on Real and Virtual Relationships?

Prior to the emergence of *WeChat Red Packets*, the giving of *Red Packets* was normally confined to happy occasions. Today, *Red Packets* are also used in other situations. For example: HuiJuan is a graduate student at the Humboldt University in Berlin who, while researching her thesis, needed to find some Chinese academic information. She posted on *WeChat Moment* asking for help from her friends living in China who could offer her a user account in order to access the Chinese National Knowledge Infrastructure website—she added the comment: "despite lots of love, will offer a *Red Packet* in return for your help." Examples such as that of HuiJuan, illustrated to me how *Red Packets* are now being sent between friends who provide help. Last year in May, I injured my ankle in an accident. The consequence of the injury meant I could not walk anywhere so I stayed at home for nearly two months. After posting about this incident in a *WeChat Moment*, I received kind greeting messages from more than one hundred friends—some of them came to see me, bringing me gifts such as packages of fruit or flowers. Amongst those who could not come in person, some instead sent me Red Packets via *WeChat*. With the fast-growing urbanization of China, people often move away from their hometown to big cities; families no longer live close, or they are too busy with their work and personal life. More and more, people are choosing to send red packets with greeting messages via *WeChat* instead of spending the time to go shopping for gifts and visiting in person, because it takes too much time and also might interrupt the recipient's daily schedule. In a company *WeChat* group, however, things could be just the opposite; to give an example, a senior manager or a team leader sends a *Red Packet* to the group. Group members who are at a lower level in the company are usually quite cautious and hence they hesitate to open the packet at all.

In my former colleague's *WeChat* group, I once saw a *Red Packet* sent by a general manager. Curiosity drove me to click and see whether or not the other group members had opened the *Red Packet*. For those group members who had opened them, I was able to see the details of the sent status, while I was forced to keep waiting to see whether the remaining group members would open their *Red Packets* or not. I simply could not understand the psychology of those users who had not yet opened their gifts. Later, one co-worker told me that she always opens her Red Packets the minute she sees them, while other colleagues joked with her, asking "Why is your internet connection always so much faster than ours?" In the end, in order to save face, she ended up having to send a larger amount of *Red Packet* money back to the group than she had received from the group in the first place. In the case of another colleague who rushed to open her *Red Packets*, her colleagues asked her to buy lunch for everyone in the office and no one turned her offer down. In order to avoid this political office game, less and less people tend to scrape for *Red Packets*, resulting in the *Red Packets* being returned to the sender unopened after twenty-four hours. However, younger colleagues are still very addicted to this game mode, so they continue to scrape for *Red Packets*.

## How Do *Red Packets* Become Addictive?

*Red Packets* become addictive, particularly in *WeChat* groups, which are limited to a maximum of five hundred members. *WeChat* groups are set up by one person who invites his or her *WeChat* friends to join his group. Group members normally do not know each other, as they usually only know the person who invited them to join the group. The group typically has a specific subtitle—for example, among my *WeChat* groups there are traditional cultural, travel, classical-music and virtual-reality sub-groups. Members either talk about the topic and events in the subtitle or they post advertisements and relevant links. Often I have received about 1000 messages from just one group, forcing me to mute such notifications. Once you send a *Red Packet* for a random amount, people in the group will scramble for it, as otherwise they will be too late and go empty-handed, receiving the notification, "better luck next time." In addition, when the amount is set to "random," the person who opens the packet containing the largest amount will be marked as having received the "luckiest draw." The game model of the group *WeChat Red Packet* stimulates people's enthusiasm and initiative, at the same time exposed among the users a lack of independent personality, criticism, savvy, self-reflection or creativity (Saunders 2002).

Mr. Mao had a big family reunion on the Chinese New Year's Eve. His family set a specific *WeChat* group named "Family group only for red packet scramble." In this game model, a portion of the amount a person receives from the group needs to be sent back as a courtesy to those with whom one maintains an interpersonal relationship.

He and his relatives—even their kids—are in this game war. They teach kids how to send and open *Red Packets* via *WeChat* when they do not have time to check their own cellphones, thus their kids help to scramble for *Red Packets* from the group. This reciprocity of sending and receiving, results, in a subtle way, in the relationship becoming closer and stronger. Nels is a girl from Shanghai who lives in America, with her husband. She migrated there and started her own business as a purchasing agent. She knows how urban Chinese girls are fond of purchasing luxury goods from USA because the prices for these goods are much lower overseas than in China. Nels would go to shopping malls or outlet stores to search for goods on sales for her customers. She took nearly fifty pictures and videos of luxury-brand products and posted nearly fifty of them every day to *WeChat Moments*. Her friends shared her contact card with others, or posted her QR code on *Moments*, and also shared their own experience of purchasing products from Nels. This led to an expansion of her business. She receives about 15-20 friend requests every day, and even though she doesn't know all of her customers, it apparently does not affect her business. All her customers send her product price fee via *WeChat Red Packets*, and in return she sends a package containing the products to them. She told me that her daily order income is nearly 10.000 RMB—her family dedicates an entire room to the storage of her goods for sale.

In fact, there are many such small internet businesses that are similar to Nels'. They pay no income tax or extra fees and they don't need to start a company. They do everything with their smartphones and process all deals via WeChat[7].

## WeChat Red Packets *are Occasionally Used Illegally*

According to a Jie Fang daily newspaper report, a group of people used the *WeChat Red Packet* platform to gamble. The Shanghai Xuhui district court, in the first Chinese *WeChat* gambling case, sentenced the leaders of the *WeChat* gambling group to ten months in prison. The *WeChat* gambling group had two hundred members. The rule of their gambling was for each one to send a random-amount *Red Packet* worth 288 RMB. After that, the group member who drew the lowest amount due was required to send a next round of Red Packets and so on, while the group leader got a 28 RMB commission fee from each transaction. The group sent about 500 *Red Packets* with a total value of 100.000 RMB. Members of this group averaged twenty-six years of age. One police officer said that the four main criminals didn't realize that what they were doing is illegal until the police got involved. Although this case differs from a traditional gambling case, the main features of the two are essentially the same, the only difference being that one is in the virtual world while the other is in a real life. Since 2014, instances of *WeChat Red Packets* sent with intent to defraud are becoming more common. Fraudsters send *Red Packets* carrying links with viruses designed to get personal information, the weakness of humanity helping them to acquire illegal wealth.

---

7 | After moving to Berlin, I never spoke with friends about becoming a purchase agent as I am not at all interested in doing that. However, when a friend asked me to buy milk powder for her baby, knowing of the food-safety concerns in China especially regarding milk powder for babies, I did her a personal—not a commercial—favor for her. She sent me the money to pay for the products via *WeChat Red Packets*. As far as I know, nearly every Chinese student in Berlin uses *WeChat* in this way, either for their own business like Nels', or for their family and friends.

## Conclusion

*Westerners are cautious with wealth conversation, but Chinese are very fond of this, especially after experiencing a rapid economic growth period; people are exciting with the small amount of unexpected fortune* (Interview with Craig, an American who works in China, March 2016).

While a red packet is a monetary gift, it symbolizes a transfer of emotions during interpersonal communication; it serves to strengthen otherwise weak virtual interpersonal relationships. The problem arises over habit: if someone served you a cup of coffee every morning and a glass of wine every night, and so in a similar way you received red packets regularly on each festival, you would subsequently consider it to be an essential part of your life. People who are addicted to *Red Packets* always say, "don't speak of *Red Packets* as being a solution", or "if one *Red Packet* is not enough, then send two". *WeChat Red Packets* have become a public mechanism to deal with certain situations: one sends a *Red Packet* as a new *WeChat* group member, or as a departing *WeChat* group member who wishes to say goodbye. One sends a *Red Packet* in order to ask a favor of someone—to forward something or to ask that they vote for a post, etc. In the social world, people tend to persist in the sending and the scraping of *Red Packets* until eventually their thumbs get tired. Mankind is so interesting and complicated! A *Red Packet* sent through *WeChat* is not simply a payment or a monetary gift, it has also become a social mechanism. The expansion of *WeChat Red Packets* is not only about how the corporations execute their strategy, it is also about people who we would never expect to participate in the *Red Packets* scraping war. For example, people from Hong Kong and Taiwan try to find a way to open a Chinese bank account in order to register with *WeChat* so that they can use *Red Packets*. A well-known quotation reads, "no red packets, no social.[8]" This radically new phenomenon of *Red Packets*, combined with the highly complex social application *WeChat* is fast becoming a completely new form of gaming and entertainment in China.

---

8 | Tech Tencent. "Big data reading: The secret of Chinese netizen scrambling red packets". (《大数据解读：中国网民抢红包的秘密》). Last accessed 1st May, 2016. http://tech.qq.com/a/20160229/008778.htm

## References

Char4u "Red Packet: Sign of Prosperity". Last accessed 1st May, 2016. http://www.char4u.com/content/red-packet-sign-of-prosperity/

Ke Yun (2015): "Aging on WeChat. A study of Social Media Impact Elderly in Urban China." In: Journal of Visual and Media Anthropology 1, no.1, pp.8-21. http://www.visual-anthropology.fu-berlin.de/journal/Vol_1_1_2015/Aging-on-WeChat/index.html

Mauss, Marcel (1966): The Gift: Forms and Functions of Exchange in Archaic Societies, Cunnison, Ian (trans.), London: Cohen & West.

Saunders, Ian (2004): "10 Virtual Cultures," in The Year's Work in Critical and Cultural Theory 12/1, pp.130-142.

Steven, Millward. "Wechat now has 500 million monthly active user". Last accessed 30th April, 2016. https://www.techinasia.com/wechat-500-million-active-users-q4-2014

# Antifeminism Online
## MGTOW (Men Going Their Own Way)

Jie Liang Lin

## INTRODUCTION

Reactionary politics encompass various ideological strands within the online antifeminist community. In the mass media, events such as the 2014 Isla Vista killings[1] or #gamergate,[2] have brought more visibility to the phenomenon. Although antifeminism online is most commonly associated with middle-class white males, the community extends as far as female students and professionals. It is associated with terms such as: "Men's Rights Movement" (MRM),[3] "Meninism,"[4] the "Red Pill,"[5] the "Pick-Up Artist" (PUA),[6] #gamergate, and "Men Going Their Own Way" (MGTOW)—the group on which I focused my study.

I was interested in how MGTOW, an exclusively male, antifeminist group related to past feminist movements in theory, activism and community structure. I sought to understand how the internet affects "antifeminist" identity formation and articulation of views. Like many other antifeminist

---

1 | On May 23, 2014 Elliot Rodger, a 22-year old, killed six and injured 14 people in Isla Vista—near the University of California, Santa Barbara campus—as an act of retribution toward women who didn't give him attention, and men who took those women away from him. Rodger kept a diary for three years in anticipation of his "endgame," and subscribed to antifeminist "Pick-Up Artist" videos. http://edition.cnn.com/2014/05/26/justice/california-elliot-rodger-timeline/ Accessed: March 28, 2016.
2 | #gamergate refers to a campaign of intimidation of female game programmers: Zoë Quinn, Brianna Wu and feminist critic Anita Sarkeesian, from 2014 to 2015. http://time.com/3510381/gamergate-faq/ Accessed: March 28, 2016.
3 | cf. https://fightingfeminism.wordpress.com/
4 | cf. http://www.bbc.com/news/magazine-25462758
5 | A term appropriated from the popular film *The Matrix* (1999). I will discuss this later.
6 | cf. http://www.returnofkings.com/

groups, MGTOW comprises of mostly straight, white, middle-class men from North America and Europe. Unlike other antifeminist groups, MGTOW espouse the abandonment of women and a Western society that has been corrupted by feminism. The existing system, to them, is impossible to amend, so MGTOWs are "going their own way."

MGTOW believe that they are victims of "gynocentrism," that the male gender role entraps men as silent breadwinners. Through technological advancement, men as a "race," have essentially dug their own graves by creating technological advances leading to public spheres and digital phenomena such as "selfie-culture," wherein females are privileged and rewarded for their "narcissistic tendencies," while rendering "the average guy" inconsequential. Convinced that feminism will ultimately bring about societal demise, MGTOW vow to expunge themselves of gynocentric influences, and to nurse their besieged masculinities with the support of other men online. At the core of their philosophy is a neo-individualistic dogma to live on one's own terms at all costs. There is discussion of "actualized" masculinity, and nostalgia for American vistas and the old frontiers. The MGTOW community has its own figures, video feeds, websites, *Facebook* groups and *subreddit*[7]. In his video "Double Standards," Sandman, a prominent MGTOW *YouTube* content creator airs:

Double standards, cock-blocking and pecking order all go in hand in hand, and it's human nature and there's nothing we can do about. All we can do is accept it and realize its a bunch of bullshit, plain and simple...The evolutionary and scientific arguments for MGTOW has been laid. The theoretical framework has been laid down for MGTOW for the most part. The new world has been discovered and explored, but it hasn't been settled and colonized. The first MGTOW's were like Christopher Columbus, who discovered the new world, or James Cook, who provided the first map of the Pacific Ocean, or even like Lewis and Clark who explored the interior of the North American Continent. But now it's time to settle that landscape, and tell our own stories, make MGTOW about our personal journeys. If any of you have driven down I-95, the busiest highway in the East coast of the United States, you'll know you can drive all the way down from Canada all the down to Florida in about 24 hours. And along the way you'll see a lot of fast food joints and motels to stop along the way[...]

---

7 | A classified area of interest on *Reddit*. cf. https://www.reddit.com/reddits/

## LITERATURE REVIEW

In his "Lectures in Ethics," Immanuel Kant (1920[1997]) defined objectification as the use of a person as a thing. Kant provides the example of concubinage, wherein the female concubine gives herself over fully to the man, while the man, who has multiple concubines, does not fully submit to her. This unequal relationship sets the basis for the man to use his concubine as a thing in a dehumanizing way. For Kant, marriage was the only moral *commercium sexuale* in which both parties can morally yield to their sexual impulses.

(I)f a person allows himself to be used, for profit, as an object to satisfy the sexual impulse of another, if he makes himself the object of another's desire, then he is disposing over himself, as if over a thing, and thereby makes himself into a thing...Now since the other's impulse is directed to sex and not to humanity, it is obvious that the person is in part surrendering his humanty, and is thereby at risk in regard to the ends of morality. (Kant 1997: 157)

Following Kant's line of argument, objectification is immoral because the body cannot rightfully be separated from the self.

Second-wave feminist Catharine McKinnon built on Kant's link between sex and objectification for an anti-pornography campaign. In "Feminism Unmodified," she charges that pornography educates men to view women on objectifying and violent terms.

Gender emerges as the congealed form of the sexualization of inequality between men and women [...] Aggression against those with less power is experienced as sexual pleasure, an entitlement of masculinity For the female, subordination is sexualized, in the way that dominance is for the male, as pleasure as well as gender identity, as femininity. Sexism will be a political inequality that is sexually enjoyed, if unequally so. (McKinnon 1987: 7)

In "Gender Movements," Cynthia Felak, Verta Taylor and Nancy Whittier (1999) designate the popularized perception of rape—as being more than just a sexual act, but actually as an act of violence—as a success of the Feminist movement (ibid: 159).

Second-wave feminists promoted two types of organizational structures: first was the bureaucratic, democratic structure of larger organizations—such as the National Organization for Women (NOW)[8]; second was the smaller, collective structure led by feminist radicals. Bookstores, theater groups, music collectives, poetry groups, art collectives, publishing and recording companies,

---

8 | cf. http://now.org

spirituality groups, vacation resorts, and self-help groups were largely maintained by feminist lesbians and nurtured a feminist collective identity in the 1980s and 1990s (Pelak et al. 1999: 158-159). Feminist collectives organized themselves in a way that reflected or prefigured their values. Feminists strove to construct a women's culture "valorized by egalitarianism, the expression of emotion and the sharing of personal experience" (ibid.). They made decisions by consensus, rotated leadership and other tasks among members and shared skills to avoid hierarchy and specialization. The attempt to form a women's culture also furthered a larger social movement community outside formal organizations (ibid.).

Within the climate of re-emergent feminist activity, it also became possible to conceive of a "men's liberation." Men's liberation rhetoric and literature "optimistically posited men's liberation as the logical flip side of women's liberation" (Messner 1998). In the 1970s, men in colleges and universities across America organized male consciousness and collectivity workshops, groups and newsletters for men, which were sometimes included in women's liberation gatherings. Tensions and limitations in men's liberation discourse soon split the men's liberation movement into divided camps: antifeminists and pro-feminists. Problematically, men's liberation groups attempted to criticize male dominance and power over women in society, while at the same time professing to be oppressed by that same line of power (Messner 1998).

By the late 1970s and 1980s, the career woman became a popularized image and a feminine ideal in mass media. The implication was that feminism had achieved its ideals, and that women no longer needed a protest movement. Scholars declared the 1980s and 1990s a "post-feminist" era. In the early 1980s, the number of feminist organizations rapidly decreased. Funding for women's organizations such as rape crisis centers, shelters for battered women, abortion clinics and job training programs were cut and forced to close. Roe vs. Wade (1973) was curtailed in 1989 by the Supreme Court's decision Webster v. Reproductive Services.[9] Consequently, limits were set on abortion rights, such as "informed consent laws", 'parental consent laws' of under-age women, and outright bans of an abortion unless the woman's life was in danger. Simultaneously, under the Reagan administration, women's studies programs came under attack by conservatives in a backlash against "multiculturalism"

---

9 | The statute contained a preamble interpreting life to begin at conception. Thus, the foetus had protected rights. Doctors were required to perform tests to see if a foetus was "viable" at five months old, before conducting an abortion. The use of public facilities for abortion, as well as using public funds or employees to counsel on abortion, was prohibited unless the mother's life was in danger. https://www.law.cornell.edu/supremecourt/text/492/490

and "political correctness;" academic institutions sought to reestablish focus on the "great thinkers" of Western European history (Pelak et al, 1999: 158-159).

According to Messner (1998) in "The Limits of the 'Male Sex Role': An Analysis of the Men's Liberation and Men's Rights Movements' Discourse," men's liberation groups employed sex role theory, a functionalist analysis of family structures developed after World War II. Sex role theory posits that the socialization process puts men into instrumental roles and women into expressive roles in society. Ruth E. Hartley was a pioneer of sex role theory and examined the "costs" of the male sex role to boys and men.[10] Messner writes,

The ideas that socially created symmetrical (but unequal) sex roles trapped men into alienating, unhealthy and unfulfilling lives, and that the devaluation of 'the feminine' was the main way through which boys and men learned to discipline themselves to stay within the confines of this narrow sex role, became a foundation in men's liberation discourse and practice. (Messner 1998 in Farrell 1974; Fasteau 1974; Nichols 1975)

According to psychologist Joseph Pleck (1974, 1976, 1982), the paradoxical male reality was that despite institutionalized male privilege, most men do not feel powerful. Fulfilling the scripted male sex role to succeed in public life left them "emotionally and psychologically impoverished, leading men to feel that women had 'expressive power' and 'masculinity-validating power' over them" (Messner 1998). Sex role theory was radical in the pre-feminist context of the 1950s and 1960s, because it broke partially from biological essentialism, and suggested a correlation between identity formation and social structure.

Men's liberation, seeking to align itself with the women's movement and eager to resolve any contradictions, packaged sex role theory as an argument of the symmetrical oppression of men and women in a sexist society According to Warren Farrell, a public men's liberation figure and—for a while—a feminist, men are trapped in a "masculine mystique," compounded by women's economic dependency on them. "The unliberated woman [...] living vicariously has become a two-sex problem" (Messner 1998, in Farrell 1974, 73). Thus, men's liberation, coalescing with the women's movement, sought to undo sexist forms of oppression to the equal benefit of both genders.

A pointed feminist critique was that the men's liberation platform decontextualized institutionalized relations of power and the inaccessibility of women to male, institutionalized privilege. Sex role theory problematically posited a false symmetry between women's and men's liberation, and assumed white, male, middle-class and heterosexual identity to be normative. Furthermore, gender analysis often fell back on essentialist dichotomizations of men and women. Pro-feminist men and feminist scholars abandoned sex role

---

**10** | cf. Hartley, R. E. ([1959] 1974).

theory in favor of a discourse exploring gender relations and power, in which constructions of gender are studied alongside historical dynamics of race and class. However, Messner believes, "the language of sex role symmetry is still flourishing in men's rights organizations and is very common currency in the general public and the media. It tends, for instance, to be used to discuss and inform debates about affirmative action and can be employed to fuel backlash against 'special treatment' for women" (Messner 1998). Messner encouraged the use of sex role theory for the study of men's rights ideology.

In "Men's Responses to Feminism at the Turn of the Century," Michael S. Kimmel (1987) delineates three responses to the feminist movement:

The *antifeminist* reaction relies on natural law and religious theories to demand woman's return to the private sphere. Kimmel defines *antifeminism* as the direct opposition to the women's rights movement and women's participation in the public sphere. Antifeminists' arguments often rest on the distinction between natural right and civil right, claiming that feminism is a war against nature. Antifeminists use the argument of natural law to oppose women's education, arguing that education pushes women beyond their physical limits. Medical texts treated women's equality and newly found sexual autonomy as threatening, and deride the feminist rejection of femininity (ibid: 268).

The *masculinist* response opposed the feminization of culture—less than the advancement of women as a group—which masculinists believed had devalued male identity. Masculinists sought to create *homosocial spaces*, or islands of untainted masculinity (ibid: 261), to socialize young men to the hardiness appropriate to their gender. They did not oppose women's participation in the public sphere, so much as they sought to counteract women's monopoly of the private sphere and the feminizing influences of childrearing. Masculinism espoused anti-modernist and anti-urbanist sensibilities to reassert traditional values.[11] In the 1980s, masculinist men's rights groups and father support groups, perceived male supremacy to be an illusion and denounced female institutionalized privileges—such as exemptions from the draft, advantages in alimony and child custody and child support (ibid: 269-272). Kimmel quotes Messner:

Men they [masculinists] say, are emotionally and sexually manipulated by women, forced into provider roles where they work themselves to death for their gold-digger wives, kept from equal participation and power in the family and finally dumped by

---

11 | Thompson Seton, founder of "Boy Scouts of America," believed that in the cities "robust manly, self-reliant boyhood [turns into] cigarette smokers with shaky nerves and doubtful vitality" (Kimmel 1987: 271).

wives only to have courts and lawyers give all the property, money and child custody to the woman. (Kimmel 1987: 270, cited from Messner 1986: 32)

Finally, the *pro-feminists* embraced feminist views and supported feminist methods of social reconstruction as correctives for oppressive, patriarchal structures. In Kimmel's survey, pro-feminist texts constituted a minority of reactions to feminism. Contrary to masculinists, pro-feminists believed in the liberating potential of modernity. Men's support to feminism consistently came from the argument of scientific advancement and societal progress. Pro-feminists acknowledged the oppressive qualities of the marital institution and championed women's suffrage, education, equality in the workplace together with sexual freedom, divorce and birth control (ibid: 272-276). According to Messner, pro-feminists began to diverge from the men's liberation movement due to feminist critiques: "These men tended to be less impressed by the liberal, middle-class feminism of [men's liberation than] the student anti-war movement, the Black power movement, and especially by radical feminism and the fledgling gay and lesbian liberation movement" (Messner 1998). Pro-feminist rhetoric changed from that of sex role symmetry and equal oppression, to one in which they de-emphasized the costs of masculinity and emphasized men's derived benefits of patriarchy (Messner 1998, cited from Snodgrass 1977: 137). However, some pro-feminists outside the campus settings were also reverends and rabbis and others linked to patriarchal institutional power that held onto misogynistic beliefs and divisions of sex, while still furthering women's issues—such as suffrage, divorce and birth control—in the name of egalitarianism (Kimmel 1987: 272).

## Methodology

Initially, the antifeminist presence online caught my attention as a reactionary meme against the "Slutwalks" protests in Toronto, Canada. According to the Slutwalk Toronto website[12], Slutwalks began in 2011 "as a direct response to a Toronto Police Services officer perpetuating rape myths by stating 'women should avoid dressing like sluts in order not to be victimized'." Since then, Slutwalks have developed into an international movement. Antifeminist women wanted to distance themselves from Slutwalk protesters ostentatiously parading their sexualities, while still staking a claim in notions of (female)

---

12 | http://www.slutwalktoronto.com Accessed: March 15, 2016.

empowerment[13]. I grew aware that the internet hosts a large network community of antifeminists, both female and male.

From the beginning of my study, I knew my access—as a female researcher—would at least partly be hindered to male, antifeminist circles. I began with a remote approach—as set out by US anthropologists: Margaret Mead, Bateson and Benedict—designed to study Japanese, German and other "cultures at a distance" in the 1940s. As John Postill (in press) writes, "with the explosive growth of networked technologies in recent years, the remote study of social practices is once again on the agenda." Postill posits one of the advantageous facets of remote ethnography to be an extra element of safety (Postill in press). His concept of "safe distance" refers enmity and hostility on the "ground" or a single locale, but in context of #gamergate and the general phenomena of cyberbullying, the initial invisibility of my own "remoteness" cushioned antagonistic sentiments that may have been directed towards me as I sifted through a plethora of online material.

I identified different platforms that antifeminists frequent and use to communicate with each other. *Google* searches gleaned a variety of search results including *Tumblr* pages by young antifeminist women aged 15 to 25, a digital manifesto by a Men's Rights Activist, and a website for "Pick-Up Artists." I moved on to *Facebook* groups such as "Meninism" and other antifeminist groups for both males and females, inclusively and exclusively. This initial survey gave me a general idea of the rhetorical framework of online antifeminism.

I learned of MGTOW on *Facebook* and began to follow the MGTOW *YouTube* content creator, Sandman. I searched the MGTOW website and read MGTOW posts on *Reddit*. I became interested in what MGTOW was to various men, cross-platform. For example, how did Sandman's high visibility on *YouTube* as a MGTOW "star" reflect in the expression of his ideas of MGTOW, versus the "regular" MGTOWs on *Reddit?* One of the main challenges was to discern the ways in which the online and offline worlds informed each other. In "Social Media Ethnography: The Digital Researcher in a Messy Web," John Postill and Sarah Pink's study of Barcelona Free Culture social media and activism departs from models of "network and community to focus on routines, mobilities and socialities" (Postill/Pink 2012: 2). As MGTOWs conservatively numbered between 20,000-30,000 at the time of the study, my intention was not to map out this immense network and community or to define MGTOW by "bounded" (Postill/Pink 2012: 2) terms, but rather to understand different types of MGTOW socialities and how online and offline worlds create "intensities" (Postill/Pink 2012: 2) through participation and routines.

---

**13** | cf. https://twitter.com/WomAgainstFem and http://womenagainstfeminism.tumblr.com/

Researching MGTOW across platforms entailed,

flexibly adapting and developing new methods [...] yet retaining reflexive awareness of the nature of the knowledge produced and of its limits and strengths [...] This approach neither replaces long-term immersion in a society or culture, nor aims to produce 'classic" ethnographic knowledge but, rather creates deep contextual and contingent understandings produced through intensive and collaborative sensory, embodied engagements often involving digital technologies in co-producing knowledge. (Postill/Pink 2012: 4)

I was aware that when I finally did reach out to MGTOWs to ask questions, it would likely be viewed as an encroachment. This prediction was confirmed on April 29, 2015 when "thick_knees" chastised his fellow MGTOWs for responding to my questions on *Reddit*, "Congrats all. You've essentially written this chicks paper for her." As of April 29, 2015, "thick_knees' received one point for his comment, as did "Orbital Thrownaway" who chimed in: "Seems like old habits die hard." My response on April 30, 2015 also received one point: "I understand your concern thick_knees. Interviews and questions are only part of the research process. Those who respond help me represent MGTOW more correctly in writing." In submitting questions and comments via *Reddit* and *Facebook*, I was leaving "digital traces" of the ethnographic process, "thus weaving a digital ethnographic place that is inextricable from both the materiality of being online and the offline encounters that are intertwined in its narratives" (Postill/Pink 2012: 14). My very presence may have compromised MGTOWs conceptions of "exclusiveness" and the status of their "safe space." However, I was pleasantly surprised to receive multiple answers from MGTOWs on *Reddit* immediately. Sandman did not respond to the questions I submitted to him via *Facebook*, although he had agreed to it when I initially made contact. Restricted access also informed me of possible disparities of MGTOW identity formations across platforms.

## Findings

Meanodeano, on the MGTOW *subreddit*[14], informs me on April 28, 2015:

The MRM is the 'change' wing [...] they are seeking legal and social avenues to redress [men's] issues [...] MGTOW is the 'abandon' wing: seeing that men are disenfranchised in numerous very real and potentially lethal ways, MGTOWs are opting out of those aspects

---

**14** | http://www.reddit.com/r/MGTOW/comments/34fc80/some_questions_about_mgtow/

of life which are statistically most likely to result in extremely negative consequences for men: sex [false rape accusations], marriage [divorce/family court bias], traditional male jobs [high mortality rate due to assumed male disposability], etc. (Brackets in original)

Some men went through a bad divorce and scoured the internet for answers amidst bouts of depression. Others realized their financial assets were the target of "gold-digging women." Many came by way of other antifeminist groups such as MRM and *Red Pill*. Like many other MGTOW, Nigelh—a diver, caver and glider—lived his life according to MGTOW values for 14 years before even hearing of the term. He first heard of it after the Isla Vista massacre last year, when the mainstream media blamed online groups like MGTOW. Though many MGTOWs have had bad dating or divorces experiences, MGTOWs are careful to not cast themselves neither as unattractive, impotent, emasculated nor too nerdy. In the comments section of his "Double Standards" video Sandman elaborates that, in high school, he was more like "a physically-fit outsider." "Self-glorification" can be used to sum up MGTOWs neo-liberal and neo-individualistic values.

The internet is the only route of access to the community for MGTOWs. They feel unable to express their opinions openly in offline interactions, fearing that they will be shunned or judged in a gynocentric society and workplace. Some express their views to select family members, without mentioning the label MGTOW. Although one of the guiding rules of the MGTOW *subreddit* precludes it from being "safe space," the anonymity of the internet allows MGTOWs to create an all-male "safe space" on their own terms. Members may exchange ideas and personal experiences without fear of backlash. However, insularity and anonymity have its consequences. Meanodeano writes, "When we already have to hide our identities in order not to be seen as vicious misogynist neckbeards by wide society, we end up being defined by our more vocal and most shameless members."

MGTOWs post and exchange videos and articles exposing the "true" nature of society, feminists, "gold-diggers" and female (sex) criminals; there are discussions around the usefulness of pornography and prostitution to circumvent commitment and marriage. Fellow MGTOW members are commonly alerted to various salient cases and potential dangers—for example, one thread on the MGTOW *subreddit* is devoted to the *façade* of subservient Asian women. MGTOW share personal testimonials of instances where they have been "burned." Across platforms, MGTOWs consistently display pent up emotion, cynicism and resentment towards women. They deliberate over just how a man should go his own way, and whether men and women are *meant* to work together or not.

MGTOWs agree to disagree, and disagreements do not necessarily disrupt the greater sense of camaraderie. Responding to one of my questions, Ancap-biochemist writes, "MGTOW has probably been one of the most enriching parts of my life and I value the thoughts and insights of my fellow men [as well as my own insights]." Ancap-biochemist, like many of my informants, chose to write additional comments under their answers, which spoke of their willingness to come forth and discuss the group; MGTOW is a mantra, the means and the end, the individual and the collective. The popular films *The Matrix* (1999) and *Fight Club* (1999) are also sometimes referenced. Nigelh writes, 'It may sound contradictory, but like the Buddhist enlightenment once a person has embraced MGTOW they no longer need MGTOW."

The origins of MGTOW are unclear, though it seems to have emerged from the RP (*Red Pill*) phenomenon. "Red Pill" is a term appropriated from the 1999 film *The Matrix* that provides antifeminists with the metaphor for waking up to society's (gynocentric) evils. Its antithesis, the "Blue Pill," is blissful or willful ignorance. The MGTOW neologism: "Purple Pill," is between Blue Pill and Red Pill. Purple Pill is a Level 1 MGTOW: a man who is aware of that there may be conspiring gynocentric forces, but goes through the motions of a being Blue Piller[15] anyway. The media has spoon fed the Blue Piller false conceptions of love and romance from birth.

However, some MGTOWs also distance themselves from RP because, on *Reddit*, RP has become equated with PUA (*Pick Up Artists*). PUA are men who tailor their maneuvers to maximize on sexual encounters with different women ("game"), having become aware of what they perceive as women's dominance in the dating sphere—especially given the current popularity of social media and dating apps. ShitfacedBatman came to MGTOW via the RP *subreddit*. On April 28, 2015, he wrote:

I was already into *Seddit*[16] and RP and was trying to figure out what possible use I would have for MGTOW once I learned about it. I landed in MGTOW once I burned out on RP and all other pill metaphors. There was really nowhere else I was going to run with it. If you go to the Red Pill sub, a lot of it is really impatient men trying to burn through women in short order. They're not very relaxed or chill. One thing that happened to me [I don't know if it happens to other guys] is I was 'ex-RP' for a while, or thought maybe I was "Purple Pill." It's that your wheels are still spinning and they feel like they need to spin. But for me, after the wheels normalized I was still Red Pill, just not keyed up or losing sleep over it. If RP and MGTOW were a form of "game," RP is fast and MGTOW is slow. (Brackets in original).

---

15 | Neologism.
16 | A *subreddit* for "seduction, self-improvement, and pick-up." (https://www.reddit.com/r/seduction)

Such is the ambiguity of MGTOW's origins that some of my *Reddit* informants deny outright any correlation between MGTOW and RP. Still, another of my informants, oldredder, maintained this:

[U]ntrue. The true red pill which is the core of going your own way has been so since 1999. Truth is the bizarre version of "red pill" on *Reddit* isn't the real actual red pill at all. *Reddit* has a bad way of pretending it's the authority on something when in fact the subreddit "theredpill" is literally the least accurate source on what the red pill is on the face of this earth.

This led me to hypothesize that MGTOW, though diffuse across sites and platforms on the internet, also has specific identity formations on specific sites. According to the MGTOW website[17]:

*Men Going Their Own Way* is a statement of self-ownership, where the modern man preserves and protects his own sovereignty above all else. It is the manifestation of one word: *No*. Ejecting silly preconceptions and cultural definitions of what a "man" is. Looking to no one else for social cues. Refusing to bow, serve and kneel for the opportunity to be treated like a disposable utility. And, living according to his own best interests in a world which would rather he didn't.

The manifesto also provides a definition for *sovereignty*: "Supreme power or authority. Autonomy, independence, self-government, self-rule, self-determination, freedom. Self-governing." Exactly how the MGTOW philosophy should be applied to one's daily life varies from man to man, pointing again to the core tenet that men should live their lives however they want. Modern man must "unlearn himself" and return to a more primal, "actualized" state of manhood.

A common MGTOW claim mentioned in other "antifeminist" online circles, is that men are powerless and invisible in the society that they themselves have built up through industrialization and technology. While men have served society and their female partners dutifully, reality has painfully backfired on them. Many MGTOWs feel betrayed. According to MGTOW, women use the rhetoric of objectification to their own benefit—playing the victim card—while at the same time posting fetishized and sexualized selfies in order to solicit as many male admirers on social media as possible. MGTOW members believe that women's higher visibility on the internet, especially within the online dating sphere, promotes a mentality of narcissism within women. According to Sandman, women get "male attention on tap," and engage in *hypergamy*—a lifestyle of heightened sexual activity with multiple partners. Men, seeking to

---

17 | www.mgtow.com Accessed: April 15, 2016.

meet or simply chat with women online, must compete with a few thousand other "liking" admirers.

MGTOW believe modern women have been "brainwashed" by feminism to believe "they are right no matter what." She will "ride the cock carousel" with as many men as possible, most of whom will mistreat her and valorize her feminist claims of victimhood. When women do decide to settle for a man, he will be a passive "beta-type," whom she will boss around and target for his "utility value"—financial assets and stability. The "beta" may be a Purple Piller[18] who is aware of the risks of marriage, but tries to hold out for a "Disney-ending." However, divorce proceedings will inevitably sway in a woman's favor, due to institutionalized female privilege.

According to Sandman in his video: *College Girl Debt Bubble—MGTOW*, women who use their looks to get free favors from men, demonstrate the notion of female privilege. Sandman grew up in Florida and later in Canada. He went to a school for art, photography and design, and lives in Toronto. Growing up, he was the intellectual-type but instead of being the nerdy guy who helps girls with homework, he worked out and slept with them instead. He says, he felt like his body and his mind were in direct competition, because girls didn't seem to care about his thoughts. Nowadays, Sandman is working freelance about 40 hours a week. Often, he works with women to create start-up packages. He believes female-led start-ups often fail because women resort to paying others for their skills instead of learning those skills for themselves. In any case, he insists, most women are miserable having careers, because female instinct revolves around "manipulating men to build a home." Men, on the other hand, are "hard-wired" to be productive. Sandman muses that he himself earns more than he "could *possibly* know what to do with" but he keeps on pushing himself to work hard and to be productive anyway. His innuendo contains some irony: tragically it is the same productivity that has landed men in their current, dire situation.

Further, according to Sandman, men invent, while women 'manage and redistribute the wealth." Men do the "dirty work" and are responsible for "maintaining roads," while women are "city planners, working comfortably from behind the computer." Women are more likely to invest in higher education, but their degrees are "dumb" and "useless," as they "find themselves working at Starbucks, and leaning on their fathers and husbands for support to get out of debt." Although discrimination in the workplace may occur, Sandman states: "Perhaps companies are paying their workers based on productivity versus position" (Paraphrased from *Double Standards—MGTOW, College Girl Debt Bubble—MGTOW* and *The Ideal Woman*).

---

**18** | Neologism.

Sandman often rehashes that women might *seem* beautiful, innocent and harmless on the outside. He dated a "hippy girl" for a year and a half in his early twenties, with whom he was deeply connected. Since then, he hasn't been able to find that same kind of connection. Reflecting on the ephemeral nature of things, he concludes, "the notion of an *ideal* mate is childish." His ex-girlfriend only *appeared* like the ideal:

a soft-spoken, quiet hippy woman, but she was covertly feminist and manipulative, as her mother had taught her to be. MGTOW is the idea that men will use their faculties of reason and rationality to discern female mind games that enshroud day-to-day reality. (Paraphrased from *The Ideal Woman*)

With regards to actress Emma Watson's "HeforShe" speech at the United Nations,[19] Sandman remarks it is clearly a "feminist, utility campaign masked as gender equality." Feminists are trying to re-brand themselves as egalitarians, when feminist ideology is clearly aimed at female superiority. Men have never had the supposed benefits "male superiority," let alone equality. Men have only had "the burden and responsibility" of building up infrastructure. "Patriarchy" is just a term to take power away from men, but MGTOW is about "rebuilding the self-esteem of a ghost nation of men." Sandman attended and filmed the Toronto Slutwalk last year (for the video "Slutwalk Toronto 2014"). He, himself, was there to protest against the outlawing of prostitution by the government. Women and transgenders paraded the streets in bras and denim-cutoffs. Maybe, like feminists, Sandman muses, MGTOW needs "a smart, gay guy" to broaden its appeal.

A MGTOW has four levels to his journey; as paraphrased from Sandman's "Introduction to MGTOW," they are:

- Level 1: A man is aware that women use "the government, courts and men's desire to reproduce" as devices to manipulate him psychologically, but believes marriage is worth the risk. This man is referred to as the Purple Pill.
- Level 2: A man only believes in short-term relationships, but abstains from marriage, long-term relationships and cohabitation.
- Level 3: A man abstains from dating and limits his interactions with women.
- Level 4: A man limits his interactions with the state and society. It also means working as little as possible—"going ghost."

---

**19** | "HeforShe" is a gender equality and solidarity campaign initiated by UN Women to engage men and boys to fight for gender equality and women's rights. cf. http://www.heforshe.org/en

However, not all MGTOW delineate the community by Sandman's terms. According to one thread entitled: "Are MGTOW's completely against the idea of being in a relationship with a woman?"[20] vtsobnf writes,

Tradcons [Traditional Conservatives] claim its about self-actualization and being your own man. These "MGTOW" claim that even married men can be MGTOW. The original phrase "Men Going Their Own Way" came from a letter that went viral a decade or so ago that was basically a tradcon screed so tradcons do have a claim on what defines MGTOW.
Another "MGTOW" faction, let's call them Anti-Gynocentrists, would say that any man can be MGTOW so long as they avoid marriage.
Finally, the "MGTOW Monk" faction [according to Sandy] would say that MGTOW should avoid all relationships with women. They probably shouldn't fap[21] either. Also, they should live off the grid. Also, real MGTOW are child-free. Also, real MGTOW should get vasectomies, Also, the government is responsible for 9/11, and Grey Aliens, and the Illuminati, etc.
[...] MGTOW is a poorly defined philosophy with a few different factions trying to push their agenda.

In Vtsobnf's view, the MGTOW community is clustered into horizontally distributed subgroups, rather than divided by hierarchy based on fame and visibility.

In reviewing Sandman's *YouTube* content, I found that he makes concessions to "Level 1" MGTOW who date women, while staking most of his arguments in radicalized claims. Like radical feminist collectives, MGTOW disavows hierarchies, and similarly, hierarchies inadvertently crop up. Most of my informants on *Reddit* adamantly deny MGTOW as a movement, and fashion it more as a like-minded internet collective. Sergeant Dickhead writes:

Keep in mind MGTOW isn't a movement or something that can be penetrated or stopped. It's a personal choice that is shared in the Commons of like-minded. In fact, there is no winning or losing MGTOW is straight up just opting out completely [...] many undercover people come around here asking the same questions like you did trying to unearth and get under our skin and see the inner workings of what we believe in trying to debunk it as well as manipulate It. This can not happen because we are not a group we are individuals who believe in our own personal choices and "get together" to offer help and advice to others who share our common thought. In fact, a logical perception such as MGTOW can

---

**20** | http://www.reddit.com/r/MGTOW/comments/33fdwk/are_mgtows_completely_against_the_idea_of_being/ Accessed: April 15, 2016.
**21** | An onomatopoeic slang term for male masturbation. http://www.urbandictionary.com/define.php?term=fap Accessed: March 28, 2016.

only work when there is no hierarchy. When everyone is their own belief system. Now tell me, how does one change the choices of others when those others have all different choices? You cannot.

In the more radicalized directives of Sandman, and other *YouTube* content creators such as Barbarossaaa and Stardusk, MGTOW resembles an anarcho-masculinist movement, using the internet as an expansionist tool for MGTOW agenda and for plotting against "gynocentric forces." Unlike Men's Rights Activists (MRA), who advocate for changes in legislature concerning Men's Rights issues, *YouTube* content creators present the withdrawal from society as a subversive tactic, and the rejection of traditional standards, or gynocentric indicators of male success—such as being married or having a family—as the only recourse against society that has already failed.

In the last year, these MGTOW *YouTube* personalities have begun taking donations for their videos, a move that has been met by some MGTOWs with suspicion. Hard_Cold_Truth posted under Sandman's *Double Standards* video:

I didn't whole heartedly agree with your slandering video but what I and others like to know is if you're homeless or jobless cuz [s.i.c.] why should you be capitalizing on our pain, misery and fear while this is supposed to be brothers helping others out.

ProLifeVegan Aryan also commented:

Barb[22] is full of shit. Ever since he stated that he couldn't continue making video content since it cost him too much time, and thus money, he asked for people to donate. Funnily enough, since that time, the amount of content he has produced has dropped to the point of where he is supposedly retired. but is capable of both simultaneously moaning about other men "stealing" the spotlight, and that upsets his overinflated ego [...].

Sandman responded in a post to ProlifeVegan Aryan:

Between this and my full time gig I'm working 60+ hours a week [...] All I wanted to do was make enough "mobile" income so I could afford to travel around the USA and Canada and make these videos and do nothing but that! Make it my lifestyle.

---

22 | Barbarossaaa

## Conclusion

MGTOW is primarily a masculinist reaction to feminism that finds its conclusions in antifeminism, radicalism and anarchism. The internet provides MGTOW an anonymous, homosocial-type space, where men can resurrect lost notions of masculinity. MGTOW adheres to men's liberation's appropriation of sex role theory symmetry and parallels its "slippage [...] to angry antifeminist men's rights language of nude victimization" (Messner, 1998). Messner writes, "First is the claim of having been an early and ardent supporter of [liberal] feminism in hopes that it would free women and men from the shackles of sexism." At the beginning, a MGTOW is either Blue Pill or Purple Pill. Beginner MGTOWs buy into the gynocentric system. "Second is the use of the language of sex role theory that equates sexist thoughts and attitudes without discussing gendered institutional arrangements and intergroup relations." (ibid.). A MGTOW had alienating experiences, which consequently made them realize double standards exist that do not work in their favor. They realize they have been taught to buy into this unequal system by seeking validation in women. "[...] and last is a sense of hurt and outrage when women do not agree that men's issues are symmetrical with those faced by women, coupled with an enthusiastic embrace of an angry and aggressive antifeminist men's rights discourse and practice." (ibid.). MGTOW, unlike MRM, believe in breaking communication with women, divisively re-inserting male sovereignty into discourse and the re-inscription of essentialist divisions of sex.

Inverting Kant's notion of marriage as the only moral *commercium sexuale*, marriage is instead, an oppressive institution to be avoided, just as for many second-wave feminists. In keeping with sex role theory symmetry, men are not objectified by their sexuality like women, but by their success. Again echoing the men's liberation platform of the 1970s, the husbands' success is the woman's source of power in marriage. MGTOW mirrors the "gendered spaces" of radical feminist collectives in its devised non-hierarchal structure, with the same rationale being that their beliefs directly influence the organizational structure of the community. Like radical feminists who furthered a social movement culture in the 1980s and 1990s, MGTOW attempts to create a "men's culture" through MGTOW approved books and songs. Hierarchy emerges in the distinctions of MGTOW media and platforms. *Reddit* MGTOW, who write long posts on message boards, do not seek donations in the way *YouTube* content creators do. Ironically, Sandman has, contrary to "going ghost," enjoyed the elevated status of internet star. He cemented his position by an economy of donations for creating videos on request. Another sign of hierarchization is the control and censorship of ideas, since technically the MGTOW community is about whatever men individually want to discuss. This again, occurs along the division of *YouTube* content versus written posts. On the MRM site, *rockingphilosophy.com*, a message by Tilted in the comments section to the 2013 article: "Face it, MGTOW is a Cult," indicates that Barbarrossaaa repeatedly censored the posts of Tilted that contended Barbarrossaaa's ideas. While *Reddit* message boards provide MGTOW non-hierarchal modes to negotiate male identity formation and is thus truer to the cause of MGTOW, radicalized versions of MGTOW on *YouTube* also stick closer to men's liberationists' packaging of sex role theory symmetry.

While the popular press is quick to find answers in generalized notions of "misogyny" with regard to tragedies and controversies, such as Isla Vista and *#gamergate*, male identity formations on the internet warrant a closer inspection. With MGTOW, MRM and PUA, the numbers are indeed evident of latent and unresolved male identity issues, which the internet has enabled into a "ghost" consciousness of anonymous men in the digital milieu. But which points are salient for "antifeminists" to expand on contemporary gender discourse, if any? The answer may be different with every type of antifeminist. Given the strong undercurrent of antifeminist presence online, the notion of "men as victims" and other types of sex role theory language may begin to play an increased role in gender debates. This is illustrated in the 2013 Columbia University sexual assault controversy between Emma Sulkowicz and Paul Nungesser. Sulkowicz alleged that Nungesser raped her, although they had—previous to the incident—been consensual sex partners. Columbia University reviewed the case and found Nungesser not guilty. Sulkowicz, an art student, responded with an act of protest by creating "Mattress Performance: Carry That Weight," as part of her thesis project. Maintaining that Nungesser had raped her, Sulkowicz carried a mattress with her wherever she went. This garnered so much attention in the popular press and in the art world, that she effectively ruined Nungesser's reputation. At their graduation ceremony, Sulkowicz and her friends also carried the mattress onto the stage. Nungesser sued Columbia University for allowing a "gender based anti-male discriminatory harassment campaign" to take place on the campus,[23] a case which the judge ultimately dismissed. The case put into question the role of educational institutions in presiding over campus violence and rape cases. By accusing Sulkowicz of an "anti-male campaign," the council for Nungesser was using an antifeminist line of argument. A particular antifeminist language, emerging from an earlier men's liberation rhetoric, has entered into the courtrooms. Although sex role theory is not new, its language may still be recurrent in gender politics and discourse.

---

**23** | cf. http://www.nytimes.com/2015/05/29/magazine/have-we-learned-anything-from-the-columbia-rape-case.html?_r=0 cf. http://nytlive.nytimes.com/womenintheworld/2015/06/26/emma-sulkowicz-accused-of-anti-male-campaign/

## REFERENCES

Farrell, Warren (1974): The Liberated Man, New York: Random House.
Farrell, Warren (1993): The Myth of Male Power: Why Men are the Disposable Sex, New York: Simon & Schuster
Fasteau, Marc Feigen (1974): The Male Machine, New York: McGraw-Hill.
Hartley, R. E. ([1959] 1974). "Sex-Role Pressures in the Socialization of the Male Child." In: Psychological Reports 5, pp. 457-468.
Kant, Immanuel (1997 [1920]): Lectures on Ethics, Cambridge: Cambridge University Press.
Kimmel, Michael S. (1987): "Men's Responses to Feminism at the Turn of the Century." In: Gender & Society 1/3, pp. 261-283.
MacKinnon, Catherine (1987): Feminism Unmodified: Discourses on Life and Law, Cambridge: Harvard University Press: pp. 1-19.
Messner, Michael A. (1998): "The Limits of 'The Male Sex Role': An Analysis of the Men's Liberation and Men's Rights Movements Discourse." In: Gender & Society 12/3: pp. 255-276.
Nichols, Jack (1975): Men's Liberation: A New Definition of Masculinity, New York: Penguin.
Pelak, Cynthia Fabrizio, and Taylor, Verta and Whittier Nancy, (1999): "Gender Movements." In: Janet Saltzman Chafetz (ed.), Handbook of the Sociology of Gender, New York: Plenum Publishers, pp. 147-175.
Pleck, Joseph. H. (1974): "Men's power with women, other men, and in society: A men's movement analysis." In: Dana V. Hiller/ Robin Sheets (eds.), Women and men: The consequences of power, Cincinnati, OH: University of Cincinnati, Office of Women's Studies
Pleck, Joseph. H. (1976): "The Male Sex Role: Definitions, Problems and Sources of Change." In: Journal of Social Issues 32, pp. 155-64.
Pleck. Joseph. H. (1982): The Myth of Masculinity, Cambridge, MA: MIT Press.
Pleck, Joseph.H. /Brannon, R. (1978): "Male Roles and the Male Experience: Introduction." In: Journal of Social Issues 34, pp.1-4.
Pleck, Joseph H. /Sawyer, Jack (1974): Men and Masculinity, Englewood Cliffs, NJ: Prentice Hall
Postill, John and Pink, Sarah, (2012): "Social Media Ethnography: the Digital Researcher in a Messy Web." In: Media International Australia 145, pp. 123-134.
Postill, John, (in press): "Doing Remote Ethnography." In: Larissa Hjorth/ Heather Horst/Anne Galloway/ Genevieve Bell (eds.), The Routledge Companion to Digital Ethnography, London: Routledge.

## Websites

"Fap," Accessed: March 28, 2016. http://www.urbandictionary.com/define.php?term=fap

"What is #GamerGate and Why are Women Being Threatened About Video Games?", October 16, 2014. http://time.com/3510381/gamergate-faq/

"MGTOW Philosophy," Accessed: April 15, 2015. http://www.mgtow.com

"Face it, MGTOW is a Cult," Accessed: May 2015. http://www.rockingphilosophy.com/2013/06/face-it-mgtow-is-cult.html

"FAQs," Accessed: March 15, 2016. http://www.slutwalktoronto.com/

"Supreme Court's Evolving Rulings on Abortion," November 30, 2005. http://npr.org/templates/story/story.php?storyId=5029934

"Timeline to 'Retribution': Isla Vista attacks planned over years." May 26, 2014. http://edition.cnn.com/2014/05/26/justice/california-elliot-rodger-timeline/

"Double Standards—MGTOW," Accessed: May, 2015. https://www.youtube.com/watch?v=rfUJX12BaNo

"Introduction to MGTOW," Accessed: May, 2015. https://www.youtube.com/watch?v=odEzVqgyAKE

"The "Ideal" Woman—MGTOW," Accessed: May, 2015. https://www.youtube.com/watch?v=_IBdR3YKL84

"Teenage Girls—MGTOW," Accessed: May, 2015. https://www.youtube.com/watch?v=sbdDyrnv2gs

"Emma Watson UN Speech - MGTOW (HeforShe)," Accessed: May, 2015. https://www.youtube.com/watch?v=EKMWtLUsqsM

"College Girl Debt Bubble—MGTOW," Accessed: May, 2015. https://www.youtube.com/watch?v=UzqqIIk3wLk

"Slutwalk Toronto 2014," Accessed: May, 2015. https://www.youtube.com/watch?v=RQirMw5H5SI

# Exploring the Potentials and Challenges of Virtual Distribution of Contemporary Art

*Jonas Blume*

*Art made by using and reflecting upon new media and new technologies helps us understand how our lives are being transformed by these very media and technologies*
-Charlie Gere, "New Media Art and the Gallery in the Digital Age."

This paper explores the potentials and perils of the distribution of visual art in the virtual realm. Beginning with a mapping of the interplay between artistic practice and computer technology, I attempt to trace the levels upon which art and the Web have been integrated. After examining early instances of virtual exhibitions of physical art and the potentials that the internet bears as a medium of art experience, I will cover digitally nascent art's structural address of the internet and its medium-specificity. In the light of the recent ubiquity of the participatory internet, there is a move toward developing an understanding of the integrative post-medium practices of post-internet art. Exploring the new role that the artist, artistic practice, and the artwork occupy in relation to the internet serves to trace how the Web affects the distribution of contemporary visual art on an individual and commercial level. Also revealed is the degree to which post-internet and new media practices are not autonomous from conventional art institutions, but actively strive to integrate themselves into the existing economic structures of the art market.

## ART AND COMPUTER TECHNOLOGY

With the recent developments of the participatory internet, the so-called Web 2.0, much effort has been made to grasp the effects it has on the production and distribution of visual art. Much of this discussion treats digital art as a new phenomenon. On the contrary, artistic practices using the computer as a production method precede the existence of the internet, dating back to the 1970s. This being said, the osmosis between artwork and computer technology is hardly a recent phenomenon, but it was not until the advent of computer networks that this connection became interesting as a site for widespread artistic engagement with the medium. In 1993, the browser *Mosaic* popularized the World Wide Web due to its capability of efficiently displaying images (Dziekan 1993: 19).

Artistic Web practices of the 1990s became known as "Net art" (alternatively written: net.art). It capitalized foremost on exploring, manipulating, and subverting the internet's technological infrastructure. Net art was made on the Web, existed on the Web, and was experienced on the Web. The non-atomic nature of the work lacked a physical manifestation in "real life." This seems to be acknowledged as less of a problem just recently, in that collectors are starting to purchase digital art. While Net art is a historically demarcated term, Web art and internet art have successively been used. Technologies such as *Flash* further allowed integration of time-based media into websites, resulting in the synaesthetic cacophony of text, image, video, and audio (Carreras/Mancini 2014: 89). Art, whose site of production and primary experience is cyberspace, is today broadly referred to as digital art.

Generally, we would describe Web 2.0 as the current state of evolution of the internet, its main characteristics being participation and user-generated content. In the arts sphere, the term "post-internet" has been suggested. The term does not claim that the internet is over, but rather that it has attained ubiquity and permeated every aspect of our lives. To put it bluntly, it refers to everything that happened after the internet had "happened." "Digital art" and "post-internet art" are terms used to distinguish two separate streams of current artistic practice that are rooted in online culture. I will discuss their defining and distinguishing features further below.

## Virtual Exhibitions

Similarly to artistic engagement with computer technology, virtual exhibitions predated the Web as well. The earliest instances were attempts by museum institutions to make their collections accessible to a wider audience by distributing them via CD-ROM (Silver 1997: 825).

David Silver (1997) gives a very concise definition of early virtual exhibitions in his essay "Interfacing American Cultures: The Perils and Potentials of Virtual Exhibitions," involving four essential characteristics:

First, virtual exhibitions are online and exist as part of and within the global computer network called the internet. Second, they are Web-based, which means that they are designed, mounted, presented, and viewed on the World Wide Web, a networked system whose graphical interface makes possible the inclusion of various forms of media. Third, virtual exhibitions are hyper-textual, an aspect which collects and connects various, hyperlinked texts and can produce elements of non-linearity, de-centeredness, and intertextuality. Finally, they are dynamic, a feature which renders them more perpetual works-in-progress than static collections. ( Silver 1997: 829)

Silver makes references to the 1995 exhibition *Remembering Nagasaki*, which serves as an illustration of the respective dimensions of his definition. The virtual exhibition—*Nagasaki Journey. The Photographs of Yosuke Yamahata*— followed three shows in physical locations running simultaneously: the Ansel Adams Center for Photography, San Francisco[1]; the International Center of Photography, New York; and Chitose Pia Hall, Nagasaki. The exhibitions consisted of photographs as well as text panels detailing excerpts of diary entries by the photographer who had been assigned to document the aftermath of the nuclear bombing. Upon the closing of the exhibitions, the Exploratorium in San Francisco created the online exhibition to make the content accessible beyond the duration of the physical display in the galleries.[2] However, it was also enhanced by participatory elements, such as message-board style forum, where visitors could share their memories, emotions, and opinions on the Nagasaki bombing (Silver 1997:836; Carerras/Mancini 2014:90). This aspect relates to the hypertextuality that Silver ascribes to virtual exhibitions—a non-linear narrative in the sense that navigating the exhibition follows no linear structure in which the pieces are experienced. Furthermore, the forum added an element of dynamism and flux through the accumulation of global voices on the matter.

*Image 1*

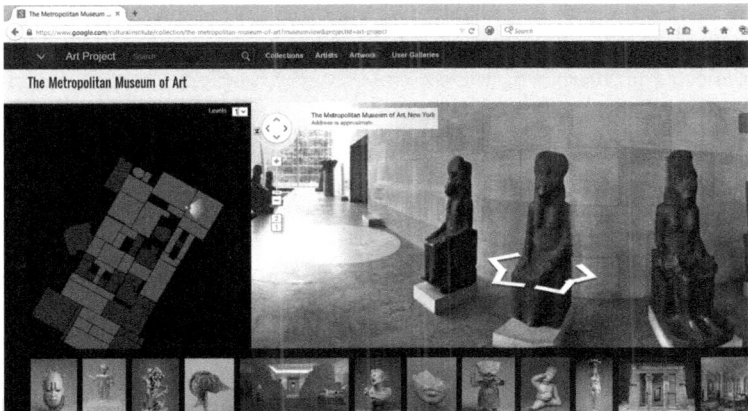

Google Art Project. Metropolitan Museum, New York. Museum view. https://www.google.com/culturalinstitute/project/art-project

---

**1** | Closed in 2001.
**2** | http://www.exploratorium.edu/nagasaki/

With this example in mind, Silver differentiates between three types of virtual exhibitions, which will prove useful in order to follow the delineation of their shape and effect on art distribution. The "virtual version" is the first of such. It means a virtual exhibition that is an online replica of a show in a physical location. During the apex of *Second Life*, art and educational institutions rushed to create digital counterparts of their sites in virtual reality. Museums spent money to have their architectural spaces reproduced very precisely, thus allowing users to get a good idea of movement through the museum space. However, the image quality of the artworks within the galleries was generally too low for facilitating an art experience that could outperform printed, or even digital reproductions. In addition, the focus was so much on the spatial experience that little effort went into providing contextualizing materials and information about the exhibits. A contemporary example of the virtual version would be the *Google Art Project*,[3] a database that collaborates with (mostly high profile) art institutions to make their shows experienceable online. The graphic interface has dramatically evolved from the click-and-slide HTML gallery. Unlike *Second Life*, *Google* abandoned the need for specialized software (that is, the *Second Life Viewer*) and instead utilizes *Flash* in combination with its 360-degree photo capturing technology, which is mostly known through its application in *Google Street View*, to present the exhibitions within the browser window. In fact, navigating the virtual exhibition space is very intuitive for users familiar with *Google Street View*. The experience is enhanced through the interactivity of artworks. Upon clicking on a piece, the user is directed to a zoomable high-resolution reproduction floating on a white background. There is also the digital equivalent of a wall text, providing an art historical and biographical context for the work. As Silver points out, the virtual version is predicated on increasing the accessibility of exhibitions. In most instances, these shows are compiled of objects from public art collections and presented online for educational purposes, rather than commercial ones.

Silver calls the second type of virtual exhibitions "the missing wing". In contrast to *Second Life* museum sites, the *Art Project* contains some elements associated with this type. The "missing wing" is more than a replica of a physical exhibition. It is an extended version, providing additional material and exhibits that enhance the scope of the real-life exhibition, but could not be featured due to financial, logistical or spatial constraints.

The third type is the "hyper-real site", which has no physical original but exists only online (Silver 1997: 829f). This type of exhibition is most relevant to current modes of art production and distribution that are impacted by the Web 2.0 and social media, and will be the main focus of this paper.

---

3 | https://www.google.com/culturalinstitute/project/art-project

## ARTISTIC PRACTICE IN THE POST-INTERNET ERA

Above, I suggested a distinction between Digital art and Post internet art. Practices that are today subsumed under the term Digital art, have a shared heritage with Net art. Even though the terms have evolved from the 1990s Net art or Internet art, to Web art and presently Digital art, the defining feature that bonds these terms is their exclusive existence in a hyper-real site. Early Net art was primarily experimenting with the internet's structural underpinnings, such as coding protocols and the rhizomatic network structure (Gens 2014; Cornell 2011). Through the focus of Net art on its constituting technology, a strong sense of medium-specificity has been attributed to it in the McLuhanesque sense of the medium always being an integral part of the message (Silver 1997: 830).

The kind of work, which exists and is being experienced exclusively on the Web, bears also medium-specific advantages. Jon Ippolito sees its greatest potential in the non-linear viewing experience. He uses the 1963 installation *Random Access* by Nam June Paik to illustrate how the artist attempts to circumvent the restraints of temporal media's linearity before the advent of the Web (Ippolito 2000: 25). Paik constructed a web of audiotape on a wall that could be played by moving a handheld playback head over the tape, without any constraints as to directionality, speed and entry/exit points. Ippolito sees the Web as the technological solution for breaking down the linear experience of audio and video, which he makes clear by using a quote from Paik:

The only reason why videotape is so boring and television is so bad is that they are time-based information. Human beings have not really learned how to structure time-based information in recording and retrieval very well, because it is new. No one says the Encyclopedia Britannica is boring although it has lots of information, because you can go to any page of the encyclopedia, to A or B or C or M or X, whereas when you watch videotapes or television, you have to go A, 3, C, D, E, F, G. (ibid.)

Because of this medium-specific trait along with its aforementioned hyper-textual and participatory dimensions, the site of experience for Net art and its descendants is the Web itself. Contemporary Digital art practices are inevitably indebted to these medium-specific traits, yet the liberation brought about by the new medium was—and still is—juxtaposed to the struggle for integration into the existing structures of how art is institutionally presented (Cornell/Varnelis 2011). Before I assess the implications for distribution of Digital art, I would like to bring to the fore the other contemporary internet-informed practice of post-internet art in order to make clear the distinctions in how the works are produced, distributed, experienced and sold.

Post-internet art is a rather recent term that has been much debated because it is being used very broadly to describe both, an aesthetic derived from online culture (e.g. stock photos, watermarked images, green screens), as well as practices that are a result of online activity. In a wider sense, the term Post internet describes a cultural shift at large, delineating itself from postmodernism, yet without the closure that the prefix *post* implies. Unlike the idea of Digital art, Post internet acknowledges the profound socio-cultural effects that resulted from the conflation of everyday life and the internet. In the post-internet era the distinctions between online and offline have disappeared. Even artists working in "traditional" fine arts media are in no way working outside the force field of the internet. Artist Marisa Olson is widely credited with the invention of the term, which she explains in an interview with curator Lauren Cornell:

What I make is less art "on" the internet than it is art "after" the internet. It's the yield of my compulsive surfing and downloading. I create performances, songs, photos, texts, or installations directly derived from materials on the internet or my activity there. (Cornell 2006)

In the light of this statement, Post internet has been approximated as a term describing a state of mind characterized by the ubiquity of internet culture (Storfner 2014). Artworks produced in this category are "created with a consciousness of the networks within which it exists." (Archey 2014). This awareness has altered the ontological stance on what constitutes art. Nicholas Bourriaud gives two definitions: one pertaining to the postmodern conception; the second taking into account what is now called the post-internet condition.

Art. 1) General term describing a set of objects presented as part of a narrative known as art history. This narrative draws up the critical genealogy and discusses the issues raised by these objects by way of three sub-sets: painting, sculpture, architecture. 2) [...] Art is an activity consisting in producing relationships with the world with the help of signs, forms, actions, and objects. (Bourriaud 2002 cited in: Dziekan 2012: 21)

While the understanding of art has seen a break from postmodernism, the activities that constitute Post internet artistic practice are essentially descended from postmodern techniques. In the 1980s artists of the "Pictures Generation," such as Sherrie Levine and Richard Prince, built their careers on appropriation of culturally circulated images. With infinite amounts of images circulated through the Web together with the ease of such appropriation by digital means, this practice has become ubiquitous. Among the generation dubbed "digital natives"—referring to artists born into the internet era—intellectual property circulated on the Web often lacks attribution and is thus regarded as commons

(Vickers 2013b; Storfner 2014: 15). This stance towards appropriation has to be distinguished from the context of its postmodern predecessors, in which appropriation was a radical gesture in itself. These days, many artists have internalized appropriation as an integral part of artistic practice; be it through reframing and de-contextualization, documenting and archiving, reiterating and altering, or documenting content through research (Joselit 2013: 35-37).

Appropriation as such often operates within the postmodern framework of situationist subversion. Guy Debord, masthead of the Situationist International group, formulated the concepts the concepts of *dérivé* and *détournement* as methods of resisting the forces of spectacle brought about by mass media's invasion of public and social life. The former is based on Walter Benjamin's notion of the *flâneur*, who drifts through the city according to his own impulses and is thus able to circumnavigate the prescribed channels of movement that control urban behavior. The latter describes a subversive action that uses elements of mass culture to turn them around and use them contrary to their intended purpose (Debord 1967). *Détournement* persists in the practice of decontextualizing and reframing appropriated content. The contemporary equivalent of *dérivé* is not to be found in the urban setting, but can instead be seen in browsing cyberspace.

With the postmodern turn, artworks became dismantled as objects of aesthetic unity. Rosalind Krauss described this change in the context of site specificity. With pluralistic sculptural practices in the 1960s, site became recognized as material support and thus amounted to an integral part of the artwork's meaning. This also meant that the reading of an artwork was no longer contingent on its medium only (Dziekan 2012: 191). In contemporary practice, medium-specificity has largely been abandoned altogether.

Art practice is now largely characterized by a collapse of distinction between online and offline identity, author and viewer, art and everyday activity. As these lines are blurred, the artist increasingly functions as an arranger who curates, comments, researches and archives pop-visual culture circulated on the Web (Storfner 2014: 4). This practice regards all output to be part of a larger artwork (Vickers 2013b; Troemel 201c), amounting to a *Gesamtkunstwerk* that relies on an epistemology of rhizomatic referentiality, in which artworks are not considered a discrete aesthetic unity, but an activity that produces relationships in an infinite network of referents with full awareness of its own existence within it (Archey 2014).

## Contemporary Modes of Virtual Distribution

The post-internet practice I have outlined above relies heavily on the participatory Web and social media. Karen Archey (2013) holds the artist as arranger, to be acting as a "consciousness-raising conduit between art and society". Since many artists do not differentiate between online and offline worlds, nor between art and everyday practice, social media holds great potential for leveraging one's audience reach through mediating online activity.

According to most artists I have interviewed, this sort of self-branding is an empowering tendency. In the conventional modes of art distribution, access to a wider audience was limited through authority figures, such as curators and critics, who acted as gatekeepers. Now, access to an audience has thus been largely democratized. Artists are able to bypass curators and reach their audience directly through various means. The cost-effectiveness of creating a blog or website, in contrast to organizing a physical exhibition, allows for diverse ways of increasing visibility. It is common among undergraduate students to create blogs on which they curate shows from their peers' work or from solicited submissions.

Similarly, many young artists founded collectives—not necessarily bound by medium, style, or geographical proximity—that are increasingly utilized as multipliers of networking clout. Networking has always been a determining factor in artists' careers. Commercial success seldom depends on the quality of the work alone, but rather on a set of fortunate circumstances in which acquaintance with the so-called gatekeepers is a decisive factor.

Social media now serves to build an extensively networked audience base that functions in two ways. First, artist websites—but even more so, recent networked applications like *Instagram*—have allowed some artists to bypass the gallery system. It appears to be an increasingly common experience for artists to be contacted directly by buyers who noticed their work on *Instagram*, so that they are able to sell directly from their studio without expending a gallerist's commission. Some artists have acquired such a large following that they are able to sell exclusively through *Instagram*, making a living in doing so. Second, for many artists, *Instagram* leads to access to the gallery system. Many of them report that curators and writers became aware of their work, not by seeing it on the artist's website, but by seeing it on *Instagram* (Fleming 2013).

The effectiveness of such online promotion lies in its multiplying factors. For many contemporary artists having only a website is not enough. Even though it remains the central outlet for professionally presenting one's work, it is often complemented with an active *Facebook* presence, quirky *Twitter* feeds, *Instagram* profiles and *Tumblr* blogs. Promoting one's work on these multiple tracks leads to an audience crossover from one platform to the other.

While *Instagram* reach depends on an individual initiative, the contemporary equivalent of virtual exhibitions may be seen in curated blogs such as *DIS Magazine*[4] and *Contemporary Art Daily*.[5] Such blogs feature coverage of physical exhibitions, as well as artist profiles. Due to the immense number of subscribers, blogs can reach many more readers than any critical review in a printed arts magazine.

On the other hand, the Web also bears potential to realize exhibitions that would be considered unfit or too radical to be presented in an institutional context. Inequality in gallery representation and museum shows persists until today (Wexler 2007). Women artists and artists of color are still underrepresented in the institutional circuit. Virtual exhibitions—such as the recent show *Body Anxiety*[6] that featured female artists with a Web-based practice, organized by artists Jennifer Chan and Leah Schrager—capitalize on the democracy of the Web, which enables marginalized groups of artists to realize shows that are not subjected to the internal power dynamics and restraints of institutional programming and curation, which made shows like this very hard to realize in an institutional space (Fateman 2015).

Websites such as *DeviantArt*[7] have been around for quite some time. The initial appeal lay in the possibility to present one's work online—before personal websites could be programmed with little knowledge of coding—on sites such as *Cargo Collective* or *Square Space*. On the other hand, *DeviantArt* also served as a sort of database that invites users to browse art across mediums, styles, and subject matter. While the promotional function of this website has largely been replaced by the integration of social media into personal websites, it still serves as a platform for amateurs, students, and hobby artists to "get their work out there."

However, the idea of having a website that combines such a diverse array of art in one place has been utilized commercially. Ventures like *Artsicle,*[8] *Art.sy,*[9] *U Gallery,*[10] *Art Space,*[11] or *Saatchi Art,*[12] are proliferating. They rely on a wider or narrower margin of selectivity in their curation that is often synonymous with their credibility. Contrary to *DeviantArt*, their focus is primarily on selling work. Portfolios exclusively consist of object-based art, ranging in prices from

---

4 | http://dismagazine.com/blog/
5 | http://www.contemporaryartdaily.com/
6 | http://bodyanxiety.com/
7 | http://www.deviantart.com/
8 | http://www.artsicle.com/
9 | http://www.artsy.net/
10 | http://www.ugallery.com/
11 | http://www.artspace.com/
12 | http://www.saatchiart.com/

a couple of hundred dollars to tens and hundreds of thousands, depending on the individual online gallery. This business model bears its own advantages and problems. Few artists exclusively sell their work here, but rather do so sporadically to make money. In a similar way to how, for example, in the past, print-makers used to make an edition of small prints that would sell easily in order to raise funds to cover the material costs for the creation of a larger work. This wariness of fully committing to online trade is most likely rooted in the fact that online galleries attract a different audience than "real-life" galleries. Many of the online galleries see it as their mission to make art more accessible and affordable to a wider audience. Granted that the price range is vast, it allows people with a limited budget to start collecting art (Hurst 2012). Also, the horizontal hierarchy of the Web—as opposed to the vertical one in the art world—together with the evident financial transparency, make them a much less intimidating place to be purchasing art (Fleming 2013; Rao et al. 2014). People for whom those are deciding factors in buying work are probably less acquainted with the art world, and likely have different motives for acquisition. On these sites, the art presented seems to be selected according to visual appeal, since the image (as represented on-screen via the Web) is all the prospective buyer has to base his opinion on. If visual appeal is the primary criterion for online buyers, this differs from conventional art collectors. High-profile collectors usually operate within their own programmatic framework that restricts them to a time period, style, medium, or school. Purchases thus are considered in the context of an existing collection—in terms of their demonstrativeness of a practice or time period, in relation to what other collectors of the same standing are purchasing, and also in their potential to yield financial gains through resale at a later point. In the light of the intricate network of factors that influence a high-profile collector's decision for a purchase, it is still rather uncommon for them to be hunting art on these platforms. However, these sites are building a much wider base for the distribution of affordable pieces by little known artists, attracting first-time buyers to the market. This strategy is embraced by the majority of newly established online galleries. Notably, established brick-and-mortar galleries are increasingly taking advantage of virtual distribution methods for their artists through some online outlets. Online galleries operating with a rigorous selection of artists, such as *Art.sy*, enjoy more credibility than their more "democratized" competitors and offer works for sale on behalf of the artists' galleries. In effect, they are able to attract collectors that are already established within the art scene.

Image 2

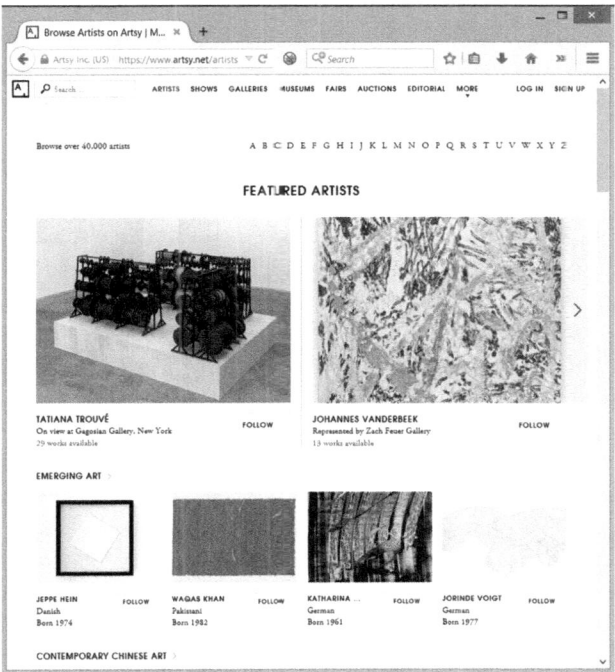

*Artsy.* Featured artist page. http://www.artsy.net

Other commercial players like Christie's are also pushing into the virtual realm. In addition to their postwar and contemporary art auction in May 2014 the auction house's expert for contemporary art, Louic Gouzer, initiated a separate auction: *If I Live I'll See You Tuesday* intending to draw a younger audience. The auction included 30 works of "young" contemporary art by established and emerging artists, which in auction house jargon broadly refers to work created since the 1980s. Gouzer sought to underline the contemporary nature of the pieces, in order to attract younger buyers, by posting them on his personal *Instagram* before they could be seen in a printed catalog (Vogel 2014). The auction results totaled $134.6 million.[13] What impact this promotion via social media really had on the sales results, however, remains obscure.

This rudimentary use of social media, for what is essentially advertisement, is somewhat symptomatic of the slow-turning wheels of auction houses that generally cater to a less internet-savvy audience. Phillips de Pury took a leap of faith by putting on their first auction of digitally produced art in October

---

**13** | Christie's website.

2013, in partnership with the blogging platform *Tumblr* (Fei 2013). The lots included GIF animations, videos, websites, and inkjet prints. As the auction house declared on their website, the auction was intended to "bring together artists who are using digital technology to establish the next generation of contemporary art." (Phillips de Pury). The 20 pieces included in the auction sold for prices between $800 and $16,000, totaling $90,600. The auction may be considered groundbreaking for the fact that digital art has been notoriously hard to sell, even in the primary market. Introducing virtual works to a secondary market audience thus marks an important step towards dissolving the prevailing emphasis on object-hood and scarcity as factors in determining an artwork's value.

*Tumblr* seems intent on forging a permanent connection with the art world, manifest in its partnership with established performance artist, Marina Abramović. Her 2014 installation, *Generator,* at Sean Kelly Gallery turned the exhibition space into an empty arena through which viewers would move while being deprived of hearing and vision by way of blindfolds and noise-canceling headphones. The installation was documented on a dedicated *Tumblr* post that displayed snapshots of the space and its occupants in regular intervals.[14] However, the virtual documentation and the ensuing circulation of the images by the visitors, is not regarded as integral to the piece. Rather, it seems, lifting the work into virtual space is a promotional move aiming to increase audience reach. There have been rumors that Abramović had permanently partnered with *Tumblr*, which would actually constitute a new way in which artists team up with tech companies and so gain more autonomy from the institutional communication outlets that currently document exhibitions. How exactly the suggested exchange of content and compensation works in this particular partnership has not been publicly disclosed. However, a noticeable result was that most major galleries can now be found, liked, and followed on *Tumblr*.

---

**14** | http://generatorskny.tumblr.com/

*Image 3*

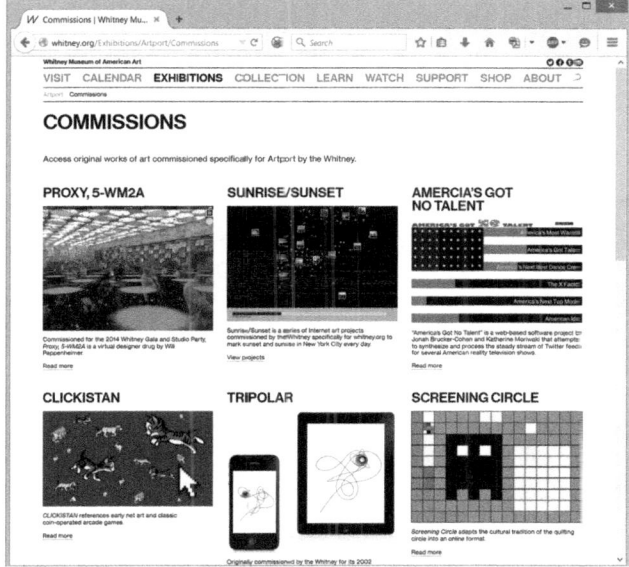

Overview of works commissioned by the Whitney Museum of American Art for Artport. http://whitney.org/Exhibitions/Artport

Beyond the individual and commercial engagements with virtual distribution, art institutions have been very reluctant to integrate new media and digital art into their exhibitions and collections. The tradition of the museum as the site of art experience has led to much discourse of how to integrate the virtual experience into the physical exhibition site. Some efforts are being made to integrate digital interfaces such as PC-stations and video goggles into exhibition spaces to enable browsing of virtual art. More salient approaches have been made by a handful of institutions that acknowledge that the primary site for virtual experience does not have to be located in the physical museum, but may very well be made accessible online. The Whitney Museum of American Art has been commissioning digital art for more than ten years, most of which is viewable on their dedicated internet art portal, *Artport*.[15] Similar long-standing efforts to systematically showcase virtual works online have been made by the Walker Art Center in Minneapolis with projects like *Gallery 9*[16] and *Adaweb*;[17]

---

**15** | http://whitney.org/Exhibitions/Artport/
**16** | http://gallery9.walkerart.org/
**17** | http://adaweb.walkerart.org/home.shtml

as well as the digital art archive created by the New Museum in New York, *Rhizome Artbase*.[18]

## CHALLENGES OF THE VIRTUAL

During interviews I conducted with artists and curators as part of my research on virtual exhibitions, I encountered a much-echoed critical observation: the tendency in post-internet art production to create work for the camera. Brian Droitcour, the associate editor of *Art in America*, discusses this phenomenon at the example of Kari Altmann's installation *Hhellblauu*[19] (2008-2012) in an article, stating that the artists' websites may actually be the most suited space for encountering the work:

In the gallery, it looked like nothing—a dingy wading pool filled with water, where some prints of the Paramount logo and other found images on chunky foamcore floated about and piled up at the periphery. [...] But when I saw the documentation I did a double take. The colors in the image—especially the sky blue named in the title—were intensely vibrant in comparison to the dull ones I remembered. [...] In short, this bad installation had suddenly looked like a good one, thanks to the way the lens of the camera and the lights worked on the materials when Altmann took the photo. (Droitcour 2013)

In a similar vein, New York based artist and curator Dakota Sica told me about the practice of documenting physical exhibitions for virtual circulation, and how documentation complicates the process of reviewing artists' work:

We've gotten so used to documenting shows for the internet. We're using the wide-angle lens in the gallery, we're perfectly tuning the photo to white balance. So—and this is kind of creepy—a lot of artists are actually making art shows for Instagram, or for being photographed. That does it amazing justice online, but when you come to see the actual work, it has nothing to do with what is being presented [online]. [...] I find when I look at the documentation of work, and when I see the works in person, the works are less impressive most of the time, than they are online.

This tendency of creating work for sharing through images is understandable considering the potentials of online self-promotion. However, most artists treat the virtual presentation of their work as the preliminary way of finding an audience. In this sense, individual and commercial virtual exhibitions and online galleries are regarded as mere stepping-stones to gain access to

---

**18** | http://rhizome.org/artbase/
**19** | http://karialtmann.com/work/2008/hellblau/

the "real" art world. Ben Vickers, Curator of Digital at the Serpentine Gallery, voiced his concern about this during his talk at the 2013 SWIM Conference in Copenhagen:

[...] Many artists don't opt for building their own foundations. Instead, it's been rather seen as a stepping-stone or a short-cut into existing institutions. One of the reasons why existing institutions, collections, and museums maintain power in the face of these new abilities is fundamentally because they still have the money that pays for the art and the property that displays it. And I think nothing can be said to have radically changed in the age of the network society until we see a radical shift in this dynamic. (Vickers 2013b)

However, existing institutions—and their limited capability for facilitating digital art—are a rather bleak prospect for digital artists. Most of today's museums are still rooted in their 19$^{th}$ century heritage, having been founded to provide for the conditions of art production and reception at that time, and are presently not equipped to appropriately present new media work (Gere 2008b: 24). In addition, institutions tend to marginalize non-object-based practices because their funding is tied to conventional exhibitions (Cornell/Varnelis 2011).

For this reason, many artists take to materializing their essentially digital work specifically to make it accessible and possible to be experienced in a conventional white cube gallery setting. Critic Droitcour (2013) sees this paradox as the epitome of post-internet art. "Here is a self-styled avant-garde that's all about putting art back in the rarefied space of the gallery, even as it purports to offer profound insights about how a vast, non-hierarchical communications network is altering our lives." Although Droitcour is correct in identifying this dynamic, he criticizes it as an opportunist compromise to cater to the existing market. While post-internet art does often have a peculiar appearance, likening it to sloppily executed sculpture, this might be less a result of laziness, and rather one of being forced to chose among inadequate ways of translating a virtual piece into a physical one. Lauren Cornell, currently curator at the *New Museum*, New York describes the notion in her experience with new media art:

I find it constantly disheartening to speak with young artists who feel compelled to translate performance, video, Web-based projects or sound works into something gallery-ready, because physical exhibitions still remain the dominant way that art is named, seen, reviewed and converted into a saleable asset. (Cornell/Varnelis 2011)

Digital art is inherently medium-specific, yet the market has not been able to accommodate this change, and continues to depend on object-hood, scarcity and conferring value by authority figures. As long as these values remain untouched, there will be little appeal to commercial galleries and institutions in fully integrating Digital art into existing structures of physical art exhibition.

## REFERENCES

Archey, Karen/Peckham, Robin (2014): "Art Post-Internet", Beijing: Ullens Center for Contemporary Art. May 11, 2014. http://www.karenarchey.com/artpostinternet/

Barthes, Roland (1978 [1967]): "Death of the Author." In: Roland Barthes/Stephen Heath (eds.) Image, Music, Text: Essays, New York: Hill and Wang, pp.142-148.

Burgin, Victor (1969): "Situational Aesthetics." In: Claire Doherty (ed.), Situation. (Documents of Contemporary Art), London and Cambridge: Whitechapel Gallery, and The MIT Press, p. 41.

Boyers, Robert/Danto, Arthur/Fisher, Philip/Sontag, Susan/Fried, Michael/ Dietz, Steve/Gurstein, Rochelle/Tucker, Paul/ Diggory, Terence (2003): "Session V: Panel Discussion." In: Salmagundi 139/140/1, pp. 201-208.

Carreras, Cesar/Mancini, Federica (2014): "A Story of Great Expectations: Past and Present of Virtual/Online Exhibitions." In: DESICOC Journal of Library & Information Technology 34/2, pp. 87-96.

Colman, Alison (2005): "Constructing an Aesthetic of Web Art from a Review of Artists' Use of the World Wide Web." In: Visual Arts Research 31/1, pp. 13-25.

Cook, Sarah/Graham, Beryl (2010): Rethinking Curating: Art After New Media, Cambridge: MIT Press.

Cornell, Lauren/Varnelis, Kazys (2011): "Down the Line." In: Frieze 141, September 2011. http://www.frieze.com/issue/article/down-the-line/

Cornell, Lauren (2006): "Net Results: Closing the Gap Between Art and Life Online." Time Out New York Magazine. February 9, 2006. http://www.timeout.com/newyork/art/net-results/

Debatty, Régine (2008): "Interview with Marisa Olson." We Make Money Not Art. http://we-make-money-not-art.com/archives/2008/03/how-doesone-become-marisa.php

Debord, Guy (1986 [1967]): The Society of the Spectacle, Detroit: Black and Red.

Dietz, Steve (2002): "Ten Dreams of Technology." In: Leonardo 35/5, pp. 509-522.

Droitcour, Brian (2014): "The Perils of Post-Internet Art." Art in America, November 2014. http://www.artinamericamagazine.com/news-features/magazine/the-perils-of-post-internet-art/

Dziekan, Vince (2012): Virtuality and the Art of Exhibition: Curatorial Design for Multimedia Museum, Bristol & Chicago: Intellect.

Fateman, Johanna (2015) "Women on the Verge." Artforum. April 2015. https://artforum.com/inprint/issue=201504&id=50736

Fei, JiaJia (2013) "Contemporary Art is Digital Art." The Exhibitionist. October 31, 2013. http://the-exhibitionist.com/contemporary-art-isdigital-art/

Fleming, Olivia (2014): "Social Media and the Art World: Buying and Selling Art on Instagram." Vogue Online, May 13, 2014. (Accessed: March 4, 2015) http://www.vogue.com/872448/buying-and-selling-art-on-instagram

Gens, Mark (2014): "A Critical Analysis of Art in the Post-Internet Era." http://www.markgens.com/text?

Gere, Charlie (2008a): Digital Culture. Expanded Second Edition, London: Reaktion Books.

Gere, Charlie (2008b): "New Media Art and the Gallery in the Digital Age." In: Christine Paul (ed.), New Media in the White Cube and Beyond: Curatorial Models for Digital Art, Berkeley and Los Angeles: University of California Press, pp.13-25.

Hopkins, David (2000): After Modern Art. 1945-2000. (Oxford History of Art), Oxford and New York: Oxford University Press.

Hurst, Nathan (2012): "Curatorial Competence: How the Internet is Changing the Way Fine Art is Bought and Sold." WIRED. September 2012. http://www.wired.com/2012/09/five-years-in-20x200-and-the-growth-of-online-artgalleries/

Ippolito, Jon (2000): "Does the Art World Really 'Get' the Internet?" Artbyte 2/6, pp. 24-25.

Ippolito, Jon (2002): "Ten Myths of Internet Art." Leonardo 35/5, pp. 485-493.

Ippolito, Jon/Blais, Joline/Smith, Owen F./Evans, Steve/Stormer, Nathan (2009): "New Criteria for New Media." Leonardo 42/1, pp. 71-75.

Joselit, David (2013): After Art, Princeton: Princeton University Press.

Jungman, Andrea/Cwilich, Sebastian/Grosz, David/Konvitz, Ezra/Mehta, Nahema/Norton, Robert/ Pevzner, Boris/Teran, Dan (2012): "New E-Models in the Art Business." International Art Industry Forum 2012, Vienna. https://www.youtube.com/watch?v=lk1hf6zNFN4

Kimbell, Lucy (ed.) (2004): New Media Art. Practice and Context in the UK 1994-2000, Manchester: Cornerhouse Publications.

Lin, Po-Hsien (2005): "A Dream of Digital Art: Beyond the Myth of Contemporary Computer Technology in Visual Arts." In: Visual Arts Research 31/1, pp. 4-12.

McHugh, Gene (2011): Post Internet: Notes on the Internet and Art, December 29, 2009-September 5, 2010, Brescia: LINK Editions.

Miranda, Carolina A. (2014): "The New World of Net Art." Art News, December 6, 2013. http://www.artnews.com/2013/06/12/the-new-worldof-net-art/

Paul, Christiane (2003): Digital Art. (World of Art), London: Thames & Hudson.

Rao, Mallika/Tanenbaum, Stephen/Vroom, Christopher/Wilson, Rebecca / Tyron, Alexis/Cwilich, Sebastian (2014): "The Online Art Industry—What's Next?" NYCxDesign, May 15, 2014. https://www.youtube.com/watch?v=V_Jo4W7pMH8

Silver, David (1997): "Interfacing American Culture: The Perils and Potentials of Virtual Exhibitions." In: American Quarterly 49/4, pp. 825-850.

Sontag, Susan (1966): "Notes on Camp." In: Susan Sontag (ed.), Against Interpretation, and other Essays, New York: Farrar, Straus & Giroux.

Stallabrass, Julian (2003): "The Aesthetics of Net.art." In: Qui Parle 14/1, pp. 49-72.

Stallabrass, Julian (2003): Internet Art. The Online Clash of Culture and Commerce, London: Tate Publishing.

Storfner, Laura Isabel (2014): "Post-Internet-Art: Moderne Archaeologie? Eine Bestandsaufnahme zum Einfluss der Digitalisierung auf die Gegenwartskunst." BA Thesis, Universitaet der Kuenste Berlin.

Troemel, Brad (2010): "What Relational Aesthetics Can Learn From 4Chan." Art F City. September 9, 2010. http://artfcity.com/2010/09/09/img-mgmt-what-relational-aesthetics-can-learn-from-4chan/

Troemel, Brad/Vierkant, Artie/Vickers, Ben (2012): "Club Kids: The Social Lives of Artists on Facebook." DIS Magazine. http://dismagazine.com/discussion/29786/club-kids-the-social-life-of-artists-on-facebook/

Vickers, Ben (2013a): "Learning from the Limits of Digital Space." Post-Digital Cultures Symposium, Lausanne, December 6-7, 2013. https://www.youtube.com/watch?v=U43O27ho4ys

Vickers, Ben (2013b): "The Art of Curation in a Digital Society." SWIM Conference, Copenhagen, November 14-15, 2013. https://www.youtube.com/watch?v=vqu7Dn3DRI

Vierkant, Artie (2010): "The Image Object Post-Internet." http://jstchillin.org/artie/pdf/The_Image_Object_Post-Internet_a4.pdf

Vogel, Carol (2014): "For Those Who Can Afford It, Christie's Is Selling Anxiety." New York Times, March 26, 2014. http://www.nytimes.com/2014/03/27/arts/design/a-christies-contemporary-art-auction-with-an-edge.html

Weibel, Peter (1994): "Context Art: Towards a Social Construction of Art." In: Claire Doherty (ed.), Situation. (Documents of Contemporary Art), London and Cambridge: Whitechapel Gallery, and The MIT Press, 2009, pp. 46-52.

Wexler, Alice (2007): "Museum Culture and the Inequities of Display and Representation." In: Visual Arts Research 33/1, pp. 25-33.

Christie's: "If I Live I'll See You Tuesday: Contemporary Art Auction." http://www.christies.com/sales/if-i-live-ill-see-you-tuesday-new-yorkmay-2014/

Phillips de Pury: "Paddles On! Auction & Exhibition New York 5-12 October 2013." http://www.phillips.com/auctions/auction/PD010213

## Virtual Sites

Body Anxiety http://www.bodyanxiety.com/
Google Art Project https://www.google.com/culturalinstitute/project/art-project/
MIST Gallery http://www.mistgallery.com/
Remembering Nagasaki http://www.exploratorium.edu/nagasaki/
Artsicle http://www.artsicle.com/
Artspace http://www.artspace.com/
Artsy http://www.artsy.net/
Deviantart http://www.deviantart.com/
Saatchi Art http://www.saatchiart.com/
UGallery http://www.ugallery.com/
Contemporary Art Daily http://www.contemporaryartdaily.com/
DIS Magazine http://dismagazine.com/blog/
Generator by Marina Abramovic http //generatorskny.tumblr.com/
Adaweb, Walker Art Center http://adaweb.walkerart.org/home.shtml
Artport, Whitney Museum http://whitney.org/Exhibitions/Artport/
Eyebeam Art+Technology Center https://eyebeam.org/
Gallery9, Walker Art Center http://gallery9.walkerart.org/
Rhizome Artbase http://rhizome.org/artbase/
Super Art Modern Museum http://spamm.fr/

# Blind and Online
An Ethnographic Perspective on Everyday Participation Within Blind and Visually Impaired Online Communities

*Olivier Llouquet*

...disabled people are continually being written out of the future, rendered as the sign of the future no one wants...It is my loss, our loss, not to take care of, embrace, and des re all of us. We must begin to anticipate presents and to imagine futures that include all of us.
Alison Kafer, "Feminist, Queer, Crip."

## Introduction

The rise of the internet as a global network for human exchange is deeply transforming our lives. As more people around the world connect to the network and make it part of their everyday life, the potential of technology to enable knowledge sharing and facilitate inclusive forms of interactions and social participation has never been greater. However, the so-called "informationalization" of society is "intertwined with rising inequality and social exclusion throughout the world" (Castells 1996; in: Goggin/Newell 2003: 68). In particular, Chaudhry (2005) suggests "visually disabled people are arguably the marginalized group most drastically affected by the information technology industry because of the visual bias of so many ICT products."

This paper adopts an ethnographic approach to examine the everyday participation of members of blind and visually impaired online communities.

---

1 | I use community here to refer to a group whose members interact with each other primarily via the internet. It should be noted that visually impaired people are as different from one another as sighted people are, and that I adopt the view of Barbara Pierce, President of the National Federation of the Blind of Ohio, in her article posted November 2008: "There is No such Thing as Blind Culture." cf. https://nfb.org/images/nfb/publications/bm/bm08/bm0810/bm081007.htm

Through online encounters, I attempt to look—with my informants—at how they appropriate the possibilities technology offers and the challenges they face in their everyday life. While these narratives are partial and incomplete, they are personal accounts of lives lived with a visual impairment. I discuss the methodological and ethical aspects of the research and reflect on how this experience has led me to expand conventional ethnographic methods beyond the visual.

## Methodology

Ethnography involves the practice of spending time observing and participating in a particular environment—the fieldwork—and using a range of data collection techniques to describe human practices in that environment (Leander, 2012). With the rise of the internet, ethnographers (e.g. Boellstorff 2008; Miller 2011; Pink/Postill 2012) have extended the notion of fieldwork to encompass the 'online' realm of the internet, and social networks such as *Facebook* or *Twitter*.

Over a period of two months, I joined several *Facebook* groups run by and for visually impaired people ("VI")[2]. Groups vary in size, from a few members to more than 4000. Members are widely dispersed over broad distances, but most are based in European countries or the United States of America. The study is limited to groups using English as a language of communication.

I started the research focusing on assistive technology and joined the group: "iPhone and iPad Apps for the Blind and Visually Impaired.[3]" In my required introductory post, I explicitly stated my role as an anthropologist and the objectives of the research. Within a few minutes I received a phone call through *Facebook*; I felt unprepared but decided to answer. The call was from John, from California. He is an accessibility consultant and ICT trainer for VI but he had just lost his position due to job cuts in his company. He tells me about his experience working as a technology trainer and confirms the popularity of Apple devices amongst VI. John was born blind, and he says maybe that is why he does not care much about photographs and does not use a profile picture. He says his friends know who he is, so a picture is not required. For him, the group is a great place for hanging out, and hearing about other VI daily experience.

After two weeks spent gathering technical information on assistive technologies, I joined groups where people engage in more personal inter-

---

**2 |** I make use of this term as members commonly employ it.
**3 |** https://www.facebook.com/groups/iPhoneiPadAppsfortheBlindVisuallyImpaired/ Accessed: March 2016.

actions. The group[4] in which I participated most regularly was created in July 2015 and has since gathered a steadily growing membership (nearly 3,000 members at the time of the research). Publicity for the group is gained mostly through word of mouth and the promotional efforts of its administrators, who are all visually impaired. The group is not reserved exclusively for people with visual impairment, but the majority of users are VI. However, it is a private group and one has to ask to join. Once accepted by an administrator, new members are invited to read the group rules, posted permanently at the top of the group Wall. In particular, members have to use their real names and should not send friends requests to persons they have not previously interacted with. Administrators have the possibility to exclude sighted "spammers" who "add friends to only send scams," or anyone who does not comply with the rules. Observations were based on every day interaction through *Facebook* and also private interviews. I usually spent a couple hours per day engaging with members on the group Wall or messaging privately through *Facebook Messenger*. Over the course of the study, no surveys were conducted; seven semi-structured interviews were held over the phone through *Skype* or *WhatsApp*, ranging in length from thirty minutes to two hours. By way of response to the issue of the "researcher gaze"—discussed below—I decided to only interview participants who reacted to my posts or comments or befriended me, therefore signaling their willingness to interact.

The study is independent of parameters such as gender, age or country; it represents a sample of online encounters that reflect the availability of participants and their willingness to engage with me. For each interview, I sought authorization to record the conversation and the informed consent of the participant toward the publishing of the edited recording; I also asked for permission to use audio extracts and quotes—transcribed in written form and made anonymous.

## A Brief Overview of Assistive Technology

In 1998, Section 508 of the Rehabilitation Act of 1973 required Federal Agencies of the United States of America to make their electronic and information technology (EIT) accessible to people with disabilities. According to this section, "an accessible information technology system is one that can be operated in a variety of ways and does not rely on a single sense or ability of the user" (United States Department of Justice, Civil Rights Division, 2009).

---

4 | For data protection, this group will remain unnamed (otherwise administrators could be easily identified).

This amendment was a high commercial incentive for multinational companies to include accessibility features in their operating systems if they intended to sell products to the US Government (cf. Brown/Collier 2015). This sparked the development of commercially affordable, voice-aided Assistive Information Technology (AIT), also referred to as "screen readers." By reading on-screen text through a voice synthesizer, screen readers greatly facilitate electronic communication and basic browsing. However, since they are limited to text, many graphic interfaces remain unreadable and make the navigation an arduous task, especially since online content is moving toward more visual media—like GIFs and videos—that cannot be interpreted by screen readers.

Many times people make an image with a message on it, when really it could just be words and this is very annoying. —Abbie

Since 2005, all Apple computers have come with a built-in screen reader called *VoiceOver*. From 2009, *VoiceOver* has been available on all IOS mobile devices along a screen magnifier. This has been a milestone for VI users as they were able for the first time to use the iPhone, a mainstream device, without the need to purchase additional assistive third-party technology. Many users expressed their appreciation towards the brand.

I am a big Apple fanatic. I live and breathe Apple. I have an Apple watch on my left wrist, an Apple wristband on my right. I have Apple socks, even Apple sneakers. I have an Apple Shirt and never take it off. I have Apple glasses, and I also have an apple tattooed on my left arm. – Miko

The progressive shift to mobile devices, in combination with GPS and geo-located services such as *Uber* or *Google Maps*, brought another positive evolution in terms of mobility. Latest innovations include apps like *TapTapSee* or *CamFind*, which utilize the recent advances in artificial intelligence together with use of the camera, identifying anything taken with the phone or—in the case of the more recent *AiPoly Vision*—through real time video. They replace the first generation of apps, such as *BeMyEyes* or *VizWiz*, which relied on sighted volunteers to help identify things via video calls. These particular advances allow a more independent social life.

I sometimes use *CamFind* when I am at a party, to take a photo of the drinks in front of me and to know what's available, so that I don't have to ask someone else. – Abbie

While technological innovation has improved conditions of life for many blind or visually impaired people, there is also growing concern over dependence on technology. Members often discuss the impact of technology on their life and reinforce the importance of Braille literacy.

The majority of people now are so reliant on their technology. I consider myself as a bit old-fashioned but if someone told me to get rid of my laptop or phone for, lets say, seven days, I would find it very difficult. – Fabian

An informant also pointed that while technology has solved many problems for VI, a tendency to technological determinism often masks the social reality of living with disability.

People would say, "isn't it amazing what technology can do?" Or, "isn't it amazing what medical science can do?" But they don't really know what is there. They just know there is stuff out there. They don't really connect with it. There is a presumption that technology solves everything. The problem is that people assume that because the technology is there you can do anything. – Daniel

The problem is not necessarily simply what is accessible to VI, but the ignorance of the existing support structures.

The main problem is that my blindness is a problem for others. It prevents me to get into jobs because what tends to happen is that people would think hiring a visually impaired person would cost too much, but it is not necessarily true. For example a lot of employers in the UK don't know about the access to work scheme, which provides financial support to buy assistive technology[5]. – Fabian

Most of members use a profile picture and therefore ascribe to the form of visuality inherent to social networking sites. Being social through this visual medium requires members to engage in specific strategies to portray themselves accurately. A common way is to ask a sighted friend to take a photo with one's phone. Fabian, a freelance radio host, uses a staged photograph to represent himself; he portrays himself wearing a pair of headphones whilst talking through a microphone and using a laptop and audio mixer.

If you want to change your portrait or the way you present yourself, how do you make sure that you do that accurately? For example I started growing a beard. Now I know that it needs to be tidy, it needs to be "presentable". So particularly as a visually impaired person, on a visual basis, if you want to consciously change your portrait how do you do it in a suitable way? – Daniel

---

**5** | In the UK, an Access to Work grant can pay for practical support for workers with disabilities. cf. https://www.gov.uk/access-to-work/overview

## Support Groups

Isolation is a common issue with people living with disabilities. Group members reach out to other members. They can either write to the entire group, or message each other privately.

I think isolation happens everywhere actually, but US is a very big country. Many blind people live in places that are very rural because it is cheaper there and they don't work. As a result, they don't really have anyone to talk to, or sometimes they also have other conditions beside blindness, and that makes them very isolated. – Ava

Most people are cautious and will generally interact first through the public Wall to get a sense of who the person is before accepting a friend invitation.

If I think they're a bit dodgy, I don't talk to them. For instance, if I get a friend request on Facebook and I don't know the person, I would always message the person and ask why are you messaging me. – Isa

Support groups on *Facebook* allow members to engage in social interactions more frequently and develop an informal virtual support network.

What I love about this group is that when I have a problem/question regarding the computer or devices that I use, as soon as I post the questions...bam! People help right away. Great technical support! – Ava

Sometimes members may feel like starting their own group based on shared interests, goals or age; some groups gather a following, other stagnate or are abandoned, forming a complex ever-changing network where the private and public are interwoven. Most members interact privately within their personal network of friends. As the study progressed, I joined other groups created transversally on other platforms such as *Skype* and *WhatsApp*. These groups were effectively smaller and more private, because members need to provide their *Skype* ID or phone number in order to join. Also, these channels imply a more intimate exchange, since members engage with each other through voice. Participants post voice messages regularly as they are engaged in their daily routines. It is an effective way to fight boredom and be involved with things, as well as maintaining a regular contact.

Other important sites of the blind digital "ecosystem" are the many online community-based radio stations such as *Dodge Radio, Mushroom FM* or the *VIP Lounge*. These stations are significant as they offer "a place to make friends, find out about current trends in the VI community and help people who want to become broadcasters" (*VIP Lounge* website)[6].

The *VIP Lounge*, a global community-based radio station for the visually impaired, has fostered an innovative network linked with chat rooms on *WhatsApp* and *TeamTalk* platforms. According to one informant, it could have close to 10,000 members worldwide.

## Emerging Sites of Possibility

In their on-going decade long anthropological research on disabilities, Ginsburg and Rapp (2015) argue that "making disability count requires attention to sites of cultural production that reflect a growing desire to communicate about the reality of living with disability in arenas of representation." They continue by noting that "'the disability publics' [they] are studying are building new social imaginaries in which people with disabilities have horizons of possibility." The sites they engage with in their fieldwork are cultural entities—such as museums, educational structures, dance and theater projects or film festivals—but I believe their approach could be extended to online communities of people living with disabilities. For example, some members are experimenting with the live feature of *Facebook*, broadcasting themselves and performing in front of the camera. A group member proposed to organize a multi-located real time concert on *Skype*. Musicians and singers upload videos, poets share rhymes, writers post extracts of their stories; transforming the Wall into a stage for creative experimentation. Besides an arena for creativity and entertainment, *Facebook* groups also are public forums where "members can voice their concerns, release the pressures they face in their daily life and engage in a collective rewriting of what could be a life lived against the grain of 'normalcy.'" (Ginsburg/Rapp 2015).

Here's a question for you all. Do you get bothered by your family, friends, and/or strangers making jokes about your blindness? It can be small or something big but how do you feel and deal with it? My dad for years called me blind bitch. He apologized after I told him that had always bothered me. I don't know if it was a sincere thing or not, but that got to me a lot since he picked on me about other things about myself. My siblings did things as well at times [...] sometimes I remind them and sometimes I don't bother giving into they just don't realize how much it hurts me. My mom the other day commented on my outfit cause some colors were a bit off and she was like "oh just tell people your color blind." I laughed it off and she was like "see, you find our jokes funny,

---

6 | http://theviploungeradio.com/ Accessed: March, 2016.

it isn't that big of a deal to you." I didn't feel like arguing over the matter and let it go. - Post on the group Wall.

## Sensory Ethnography

In a reflexive review of her ethnographic research on blindness, Gili Hammer (2014) reflects on the ocular-centrism characteristic of most qualitative methods, and questions terms such as "participant observation" or "the researcher gaze." She asks: "What are the sensory dimensions of the ethnographic project? What does participation-observation entail? And can participant observation be ethical when my informants do not have the possibility to know where is the 'researcher's gaze'?" (Hammer 2014).

Although Hammer's research took place "offline," I felt the same ethical and methodological questions surface during my online study, conducted remotely. As a sighted user of an interface designed for optimal visual control, I am—*de facto*—in a situation where I posses more information than my informants.

The visual interface has been optimized for the visual scanning of information. Space on the screen is a fixed, detailed and stable entity divided in areas associated with specific functions. The center of the screen is reserved to browse through the archive: Time is contained into space, and scrolling down effectively makes one move back in time, revealing archived public interactions that have taken place till the very first post. What is written here stays forever. While sighted users can quickly browse through the timeline, accessing the information through screen readers would take a considerable amount of time. - Extract from research diary

Boellstorff (2008) advises that ethnographers adopt the principle of care as a response to "the asymmetrical power relations and imbalance of benefit between investigator and investigated" (ibid: 129). With this in mind, I progressively became more aware of the challenges faced by visually impaired people. I also reflected on my own bodily engagement with the machine and noticed my attention shifting from the visual to the auditory in order to make sense of the information:

It feels more natural to close my eyes. It helps me to focus on the conversation, to feel the richness of the voice of my interlocutor. I notice the changes in intonations, the pauses and silences, the rhythm, the accent. Acoustic intimacy. I can hear voices in Chinese coming from a show on TV playing in the background. The static noise reveals the derelict state of the Eastern European network; calls from Africa are incessantly dropped. A layering of synthesized voices and digital sounds, fragile and precious traces of ephemeral encounters on the network. These groups are like sound oases in the vast ocean of images that is the internet. Here, it is the sounds themselves that create time and space. If there is no sound, nothing happens... – Extract from research diary

## CONCLUSION

Lack of awareness, poor public policies and the visual bias of ICT products make content difficult to access for visually impaired users. However, blind and visually impaired online communities are support groups through which members enrich their technical and social capital. They are emerging sites of possibilities where members collectively engage in the rewriting of disability and regain a sense of agency against the privilege of able bodies. To be able-bodied is—over the course of a lifetime—a shifting, transitory and uncertain state. The social model of disability has sought to redefine disability as a social problem, one that can be overcome through social change. As trans human communication technologies become more prevalent, it is critical that they remain accessible to all. In his book *Orality and Literacy*, Walter Ong (1982) suggests, "with telephone, radio, television and various kinds of sound tape, electronic technology has brought us into the age of 'secondary orality'. This new orality has striking resemblances to the old in its participatory mystique, its fostering of communal sense, its concentration on the present moment..." (ibid: 133). The visually impaired groups offer opportunity to redefine how we imagine and use technology to interact with each other since the sensory and auditory sense are brought to the foreground. Sensory ethnography in particular, and the "sensuous scholarship" (Stoller 1997) it entails, can contribute to the exploration of alternative forms of sensory engagement with technology; thereby promoting inclusive, rather than assistive, technologies.

## REFERENCES

Boellstorff, Tom (2008): Coming of Age in Second Life: An Anthropologist Explores the Virtually Human, Princeton: Princeton University Press.
Brown, Justin/Hollier, Scott (2015): "The Challenges of Web Accessibility: The Technical and Social Aspects of a Truly Universal Web." In: First Monday 20/9, September 7, 2015. http://firstmonday.org/ojs/index.php/fm/article/view/6165 Accessed: March 23, 2016
Castells, Manuel (1996): The Rise of the Network Society, The Information Age: Economy, Society and Culture, Vol. 1, Malden, MA: Blackwell.
Chaudhry, Vandana/Shipp, Tom (2005): "Rethinking the Digital Divide in Relation to Visual Disability in India and the United States: Towards a

Paradigm of 'Information Inequity'." In: Disability Studies Quarterly 25/02, http://dsq-sds.org/article/view/553/730 Accessed: March 23, 2016.

Ginsburg, Faye/Rapp, Rayna (2015): "Making Disability Count: Demography, Futurity, and the Making of Disability Publics," http://somatosphere.net/2015/05/making-disability-count-demography-futurity-and-the-making-of-disability-publics.html Accessed: March 23, 2016.

Goggin, Gerard/Newell, Cristopher (2003): Digital Disability: The Social Construction of Disability in New Media, Lanham, MD: Roman & Littlefield.

Hammer, Gili (2014): "Ethnographies of Blindness: The Method of Sensory Knowledge," In: Ronald J. Berger/Laura S. Lorenz (eds.), Disability and Qualitative Inquiry: Methods for Rethinking an Ableist World, London: Routledge.

Kafer, Alison (2013): Feminist, Queer, Crip, Bloomington: Indiana University Press.

Leander, Kevin (2008): Toward a Connective Ethnography of Online/Offline Literacy Networks. In: Julie Coiro/Michelle Knobel/Colin Lankshear/ Donald J. Leu (eds.), Handbook of Research on New Literacies, Mahwah, NJ: Lawrence Erlbaum, pp. 33-66.

Miller, Daniel (2011): Tales from Facebook, Cambridge: Polity Press.

Ong, Walter J. (1982): Orality and Literacy: The Technologizing of the Word, London: Taylor and Francis.

Pink, Sarah (2009): Doing Sensory Ethnography, London and Thousand Oaks: Sage Publications.

Pierce, Barbara (2008): "No Such Thing as Blind Culture," https://nfb.org/images/nfb/publications/bm/bm08/bm0810/bm081007.htm Accessed: March 10, 2016.

Postill, John/Pink, Sarah (2012): Social Media Ethnography: The Digital Researcher in a Messy Web, Queensland: Media International Australia.

Stoller, Paul (1997): Sensuous Scholarship, Philadelphia: University of Pennsylvania Press.

U.S Department of Justice, Civil Rights Division, Disability Rights Section (2009): "A Guide to Disability Rights Laws," http://www.ada.gov/cguide.htm Accessed: March 23, 2016.

# How Has Social Media Changed the Way We Grieve?

*Ellen Lapper*

It was 1:30 a.m. My family had been trying for hours to contact me and a point had been reached where our social media ties prevented them from informing others. "I don't want her to find out over *Facebook*," said my Mum The dilemma being, the more people were told of the news—close family even—the greater the risk would be of one of them posting online. Today, those privileged with online access rarely log out. As our offline selves become increasingly dictated by our online presence and our lifestyles rely on mobile devices and social media, it becomes all the more pressing to investigate the impact of this phenomena on the inevitable accompaniment to our existence: death. Our social media platforms alert us of a death before traditional forms of media such as newspapers, radio or television have the chance (Carroll & Landry 2010). This phenomenon was clearly demonstrated by frenetic activity on UK social media sites following the passing of David Bowie and Alan Rickman at the beginning of 2016. The news of both deaths became '*Trending Topics*' on *Facebook*. Media coverage was dominated by now familiar announcements stating that thousands of tributes were pouring in via *Twitter*. One user posts a photo, another shares a video and the *hashtag* '#RIP[insert celebrity's name]' goes viral.

*Image 1*

An English *Facebook* user's post on a friend's Timeline the day after David Bowie died. January 2016.

Due to the scope and sensitivity of this topic, it would require extensive analysis to address all the surrounding issues fully, something I quickly appreciated from the outset. I began looking into the role of memory in the digital age with the rather broad question: how do technological advancements affect, aid or hinder the way we remember someone who has passed away? However, as my research progressed, the nature of my question changed slightly. Despite the original enquiry still playing a prominent role, my specific focus became: To what extent has social media changed the way we grieve?

## DIGITAL TRACES

My father, who was not an active social media user (*WhatsApp* only), passed away recently. Despite his physical absence, I continue to notice ways in which his digital presence seeps through. I constantly scroll through his iPhone photos and re-read his *WhatsApp* chat; essentially I'm becoming dependent on digital means to remember him. Hannah Arendt (1970) expressed her fear of technology in doing the thinking for us, predicting the takeover of machines long before the invention of the smart phone. Our answers are now at the push of a button and our dependency on such tools has increased. It is becoming rare to hand-draw a route in advance of a journey—*Google Maps* will simply show us the way on our portable device. If it is becoming optional to remember, does this imply we are becoming better at forgetting?

For Adi Ophir (2005), traces are things that something, or someone, has left behind once they have disappeared or become lost. These traces relate to reminders for the memory. In terms of death, we are (to an extent) prepared for physical traces to remain present as relics, acting as a trigger to activate and unlock a deeper thought—for example, I knew my Dad's shoes would still lie by our front door and his guitars would sit gathering dust. Despite operating in the same way, what I was not prepared for, and what I believe has changed with technology's dominance, are these same triggers lingering within our digital environments.

For the past few years, I have accidentally left myself logged into my *Gmail* account, which is synced to *YouTube* on my father's iPad and laptop. Whenever he watched a video, my account took note. As a result, my recommendations were always an odd mix of bike videos, live performances of the band 'Big Country', bass guitar tutorials (Dad's videos) and things that I had watched, such as bunny show jumping, food challenges and 90's R&B. This underlines technology's omnipresent ability to curate a digital persona for us. This online curatorship of the self may not be as obvious as a *Facebook* profile, where the user actively mediates the information they reveal, however, it is nonetheless an online reflection of an offline personality.

Four months after my father's passing, my *YouTube* recommendations were devoid of any of his videos (except perhaps one of the 'Buzzcocks')—everything else I could vouch for. In the absence of my father's viewing, my *YouTube* profile acquainted itself once more to my taste. "Disappearance to the second degree; the gradually diminishing presence of the traces, the gradual depleting identity of what disappeared, to the point where all that can be said is: 'There was something there'" (Ophir 2005: 52).

Dad's swift exile from *YouTube* struck me. Perhaps he just did not watch enough videos, but what would it be like to lose someone more active? One moment: notifications, event invitations, comments, Tweets on *Twitter*, *Facebook* timeline domination, and then … silence; a digital presence lost. Or is it really gone—in a physical sense? When thinking of others in recent mourning, I realized that I had invariably discovered the news of their losses on *Facebook*. How then are social media platforms such as *WhatsApp*, *Facebook* and *YouTube* affecting grief?

I am an active *Facebook* user and therefore required no real introduction to the site. Once contact was made over *Facebook*, the aim was to explore the grief experiences of others on alternative social media platforms; however, the scope was too large. Primarily this research became about *Facebook*. I initially reached out to five *Facebook* users through the platform itself and later met them in person. Further research would require not only an extension outside of my social network but also an extension outside of England. The majority of my *Facebook* network consists of, though is not limited to, other English-speaking users based in England. Having said that, I have also noticed that people within my *Facebook* network who reside in England are much more active on social media than friends who reside elsewhere, partly explaining my selection. The idea that social media has decreased our privacy in England (Miller 2016) cannot be a worldwide generalization, so the geographical focus must be taken into consideration. My questions extended to:

How is a person remembered on a social media site such as *Facebook*?

What are the motives for users, close family even, for carrying out this form of remembrance?

How has social media changed the boundaries between public and private?

What are the implications of such posts?

## METHODOLOGY

Social media allows us to easily participate in an otherwise passive world; it's not like television (Agger 2012). Agger is critical of the overly sharing nature of *Facebook*, stressing the need for a return to the division between public and private. I must admit, I too held a skeptical stance over publicizing a death or sharing a memory of someone who has passed away on *Facebook*. One *Facebook* user, Patti, whom I knew personally and had recently suffered a loss, told me that she would never consider announcing that news on *Facebook*. "I will tell the people I want to know. I don't want my whole *Facebook* network knowing that information; it's very private. It's just selfish and attention seeking." No doubt, Agger too would call for a retreat back into the private sphere. However, announcing a death was seldom a private affair; in England obituaries are not new and traditional gravestones in cemeteries are accessible to the public. Still, social media has created a bridge between public broadcasting and private communications (Miller 2016). Unlike a printed obituary, which goes out once to a mass audience, close to the time of death and with no real invitation for response, such notifications of grief on social media are immediate and interactive. They come directly from a user, with a curated profile, friend list, previous posts and the ability to mediate an audience.

*Image 2*

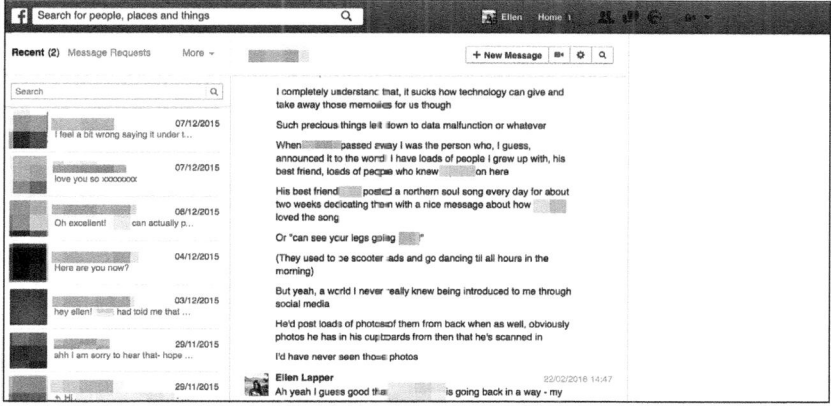

Facebook Messenger chat with Dominic. February 2016.

The instantaneous nature of publicly expressing grief on social media paradoxically presents us as vulnerable to a wider audience, yet the technological distance somehow protectively shields us. Agger's (2012) criticism is based on the belief that people overshare online in ways they wouldn't face to face. For Stella, a *Facebook* user who lost both her father and brother (the former before the prevalence of social media, the latter in the midst of it), it was exactly this factor of distance that helped her share the news of her loss; she didn't know where to begin in person.

It took me forever, to put it up on *Facebook* and what to write, blah blah but then, it was kind of like a sense of relief. But then you know when you're a bit like, oh my God, now what?! It was just really hard [...] but I was so glad that I could put it up on *Facebook* cos people know and people were like, "When can I come to the funeral? When is it?"

Stella's last sentence shows exactly how such posts invite immediate interaction and the support that people need at times of instability. The appeal of technology becomes clear when we are most vulnerable, as Sherry Turkle stated in her TED talk[1]. She elaborated that—in using this medium, as opposed to physical interactions—we have the ability to edit our content and present the self as we prefer to be seen. This could partly explain why, when announcing sensitive news concerning death, users find comfort and ease in communicating over sites such as *Facebook*, as the written form allows for better formulation.

---

**1** | Turkle, Sherry: "Connected, but alone?" Filmed February 2012. TED video, 19:41. https://www.ted.com/talks/sherry_turkle_alone_together?language=en

When initiating contact with *Facebook* users in my network, I began by using the *Messenger* tool. The messages (Image 2) I exchanged with one user, Dominic, are grouped together as they were sent seconds after each other. The narrowing of the audience and the chat set-up allows us to create a more rapid, intimate dialogue; however, a slight delay in the construction of the text gives us the ability to recompose. Dominic's messages revealed positive repercussions of posting his loss online. It triggered "a world I never really knew being introduced to me through social media." Stella also noted this "nice" revelation of another side to the deceased's life through pictures shared on *Facebook*. Arguably, these shared photos uploaded by friends could have been brought physically to the bereaved person. However, the potential immediacy of a response from an extensive audience elicits a different kind of interaction. Distance aside, users can choose to what extent they engage with the variety of media-sharing *Facebook* offers. *Facebook*'s language of 'sharing' and 'friending' entice us to feel comfortable in using social media.

The sharing of a memory on social media accelerates Maurice Halbwachs' (2011) otherwise natural theory that all our individual memories are formed within a societal structure, and can then only be understood in a group context. Does online sharing then add another layer to its collectiveness? By allowing others access to this perhaps once-private memory, we force it out of our personal sphere and into the minds of others. When exposed to shared trauma or traumatic knowledge, past events can seem to constitute the memories of the generation that follows; their memories become our memories (Hirsch 2011). What effect does social media have on this form of collective memory? Do the memories of people on our *Facebook* timeline become our memories? When we see something within our social network, are we lured into thinking it is ours? I discussed this with Faye, who recently lost a friend and put out a tribute to her on *Facebook*. Faye agreed that *Facebook* often has the ability to make you believe you knew something about someone, or were present at the time an event took place, only later to discover that you learnt it via passive observation online. In this sense, others' posts are subconsciously becoming our memories or our collective memories.

Faye elaborated, "I wouldn't normally post something like that but it was the way she lived her life—she was very open on *Facebook* about everything and I wanted to honor that. It invited such a response; I got so many, so many messages, all such lovely words, was so comforting." We concluded that perhaps it helps to share the pain. The conversation in which we shared our experiences might not have taken place had I not seen her *Facebook* post. The interactivity of such shared information on *Facebook* is exactly what makes it different from printed obituaries—it invites an immediate response. Similarly, Stella enjoys sharing memories concerning her lost loved ones for their interactive connectivity—on an anniversary or birthday, for example. This is what I understood from everyone to be most comforting. As these memories are shared within their networks, others can comment, 'Like' and attempt to share the experience.

*Image 3*

Facebook post from Natasha, one user in my network, on the day of her brother's funeral. December 2015.

For Arendt, whatever is experienced internally is valueless unless shared with another. "Pain [...] is so subjective and removed from the world of things and men that it cannot assume an appearance at all" (1970: 51). She expands her view on physical pain within our body as being the only thing that you cannot share, however, I would argue that grieving is physical pain. The bereavement posts on *Facebook* could be a result of our struggle to share this physical, internal pain by using the alternative forms that social media offers to us. Texts and words aside, users can share videos, post photos or use emoticons; all these options endeavor to express something where vocalization fails. The process of *posting* offers users opportunities to connect with others who may share similar experiences or offers messages of support, as illustrated in Image 3. The emoticons replace text. Some 87 people 'Liked' the post and 97 comments were made—many of which stated: "so sorry to hear that", indicating it was the first time they learned of this news. Somewhat ironically within this context, though

I do not doubt the sincerity, the comment shown at the bottom—"Memories we hold in our hearts forever" almost pulls us back to humanity for a second and out of this virtual sphere. I would argue that online sharing and the use of technology to express grief and memorialize has the ability to become the new form of collective memory, although perhaps we are not fully conscious of it yet.

## WAILING OVER *WHATSAPP*

Halfway into this research, I became a victim of my own stupidity, curiosity and digital culture. Upon seeing an image online, supposedly from Apple, claiming to show you what your iPhone would have been like in 1970, I followed the instructions and set the date to January 1$^{st}$ 1970. In an instant, I had 'bricked' my phone and it refused to turn on. I cried. I wasn't crying over the device itself, rather the loss of the *WhatsApp* chat and *iMessage* history held in my 'phone—essentially the last conversations with my now deceased father. I was wailing over meaningless chat, usually in the form of attempts to organize something banal like who was going to pick the milk up, which, if written down on paper, would most definitely be in the bin right now. I truly believed I needed to resurrect this "biological development of mankind" (Heisenberg 1955: 14-15). Thankfully after a stint in the Apple store, the iPhone was restored but my chats were wiped. I could still log on to my father's phone and read it there, but it wouldn't be the same. I couldn't bring myself to activate Dad's digital presence by changing: 'last seen 20 November 2015'—the day he died (Image 4).

Stella and I exchanged our devastating *WhatsApp* experiences. She had lost her conversation with her brother Trev, which along with a written letter, he had used to say goodbye.

Luckily I went into a phone shop and they connected [his phone] back up for me. So I got [the *WhatsApp* conversations] back, but they're not on my phone and it's not the same. I don't want them on his phone. I thought 'I'll send them to me'. And then I thought 'I don't wanna do that', but obviously the date changed.

Stella referred to the same issue I had with the "last seen online..." which is displayed on most users' *WhatsApp*:

And then people were like, "what the hell, his phone's on?" Texting me and Mum and I was like, "No it's me! It's me." I thought do I put the *WhatsApp* status up saying, "it's his sister"? But he'd put his status as "I love you Stella and Mum, I'm sorry". And that was like his last status, and I thought I don't wanna delete that but these people were like "fuck all my messages are sending".

Bernadette, an active *Facebook* and *WhatsApp* user, spoke of her loss:

He's still in our uni WhatsApp group. I found it odd at first when I saw his name at the top but we've just had it since uni so we're just gonna keep using it. Obviously when we make new groups to arrange stuff we don't add him in like we used to but yeah, he's still there in the main one.

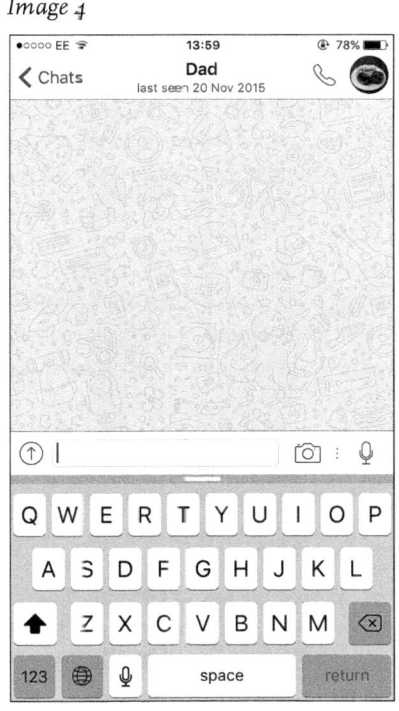

*Image 4*

A screenshot of my WhatsApp chat with my father after my phone had been wiped. February 2016.

The digital presence for *WhatsApp* requires a separate analysis in comparison to *Facebook*. Generally, it is for private, instant messaging—usually just one-on-one—but also useful for groups to communicate, normally with people they know personally. Messages often contain a mix of banal and significant exchanges, the latter demonstrated in Trev's goodbye. Stella's resurrection of Trev's *WhatsApp* sparked a disturbed response; I am also reluctant to bring my father online again. We are ill-equipped in dealing with the remains of a digital presence and we can't bear to lose them. Aside from *YouTube* perhaps, this illustration reinforces the impact of social media presences on our society; they cannot be easily removed. Our initial exposure leads us to believe that we need these presences to remain in order to remember. As Stella said, "If I didn't have it at all then I wouldn't feel that much pain over something." I am also now struggling to recall what I wrote about with Dad, what pictures we exchanged and who picked the milk up. It is tough; I want that little device to help me. However, perhaps we need to forget in order to remember (Augé 2014).

## DIGITAL GHOSTS

The preservation of a digital presence became more apparent as my research continued. Bernadette told me that the *Facebook* profile of her late friend remains unchanged and has not been memorialized.[2]

Bernadette went on to express her annoyance when people write on her friend's *Facebook* Wall:

He's not there anymore, he's not going to read it. But maybe that's just because I always think scientifically. I don't know why it annoys me. His best friend got so irritated 'cos it sparked loads of other people to write on his wall. People that didn't even know him. Even this girl he dated for just a few months. I don't know who has access to his *Facebook*.

Ari Stillman (2014) discusses the possibility of a collaborative identity construction based around the deceased's *Facebook* Wall. His idea, that the "identity of the deceased belongs to those who construct it" (ibid: 59) in turn helps shape a collective memory of the individual. Could it be that the *Facebook* profile becomes a memorial, even if it has not been officially memorialized through *Facebook*'s given terms? I would argue, yes. There are some individuals, like Bernadette, who do not like the idea of the profile being active as it invites others to craft an identity of the deceased. She elaborated on the posts of the "girl he dated for a few months"—in that they didn't correspond to anything she or the close friends knew—yet appeared publicly on his profile, asserting her apparent relation to him. Despite this, she said she wouldn't want it otherwise—she couldn't imagine the deletion of his profile. It is simply easier to do nothing, which in turn risks misinterpretation as disbelief of the death.

Faye explained her interaction with her late friend's *Facebook* profile:

---

2 | *Facebook* offers a "memorialized account" as a way of remembering the deceased. Essentially, the profile remains and current friends can interact with it, however no new friendship requests can be sent and the user does not appear in searches or birthday reminders. Memorializing a profile was a function introduced by Facebook in 2009. https://www.facebook.com/help/103897939701143 Accessed April 29 2016.

I just can't stop going on it. But it's weird, I can't search for her and click on her profile. I have to do it through someone else who is a mutual friend, and then I see her photo there and I just click on her via this other friend. I just want to look at her profile. But I don't want her to appear in my recent searches. I don't know why.

When asking if it was because people had posted things on her *Facebook* timeline, she said, "No. She has like a Timeline Review, so what you can see on her wall is very limited." *Facebook* profiles are ultimately private, individual constructs of a user yet, at the same time, they are not the only ones crafting their online identity (Davis, Sieder & Gardner 2008). Social media is social. When a user passes away, despite Timeline privacy restrictions, the interaction with what remains can still maintain this collaborative process and develop into a form of collective memory.

Ophir (2005) talks about the inseparable interchangeability between disappearance and appearance much in a similar sense to Marc Augé's (2004) discussion of memory's relationship to oblivion. For Augé, we must forget in order to remain present. To an extent I agree, however, I would rather argue for us to push these memories aside to make way for new ones. The reduction of these memories into traces allow for their dormant storage. Then, as Ophir explains, "Some thing has to remain present 'to this day,' and first and foremost here and now, in order to testify to what has disappeared" (Ophir 2005: 52). The digital reminders I have discussed are testament to that loss. Stella explained how she never had the option with her first bereavement. Only now the feeling of deprivation arise:

They're like old pictures, they're like really crap pictures, whereas Trevor's are like amazing, it's almost...made it harder or my Dad, cos I think, God it was so long ago. I don't feel like it's a long time ago, but I don't have any of the things, like I can't remember my Dad's voice. And it kills me. I can't remember it at all, like what his tone of voice was or anything. And I hate that and I feel like I've forgotten it. With Trev, I'm like always gonna be able to hear that. I'm always gonna hear his laugh. And that is only through having a video on my phone. But other times people hate having all that, cos you know, you've gotta be in the right mood, and ready for it, and if you're not, then it like takes you like ten steps back.

There is actually no difference between the effect of the physical and digital reminders left behind when someone passes away; when unprepared, both can set you back. The differences lie in the possibilities that digital technologies offer us now, as Stella describes:

With Trev, I can put so many pictures up [on *Facebook*] and I love it. And I can just change pictures all the time and then I feel like, oh my God am I letting my Dad down? I need a picture of my Dad but there's like only the set 7 or 8 I've got of him.

Loss in the digital age simply provides us with more. Despite our integration into digital technologies, it is this bombardment that we are still coming to terms with and are currently unable to process. Initially, one thinks of the bombardment as constant reminders, however when relating this back to Augé (2004), the increase provided by the digital age could potentially make it harder for us to forget.

## Conclusion

This preliminary research into grief and social media has primarily revealed its extensive complexities, in which humanity is constantly catching up with technology. As worlds between offline and online blur, we must become better acquainted in how to deal with the loss of an online presence. Particularly within *Facebook*, there remain many unexplored topics, including the memorialization of a *Facebook* profile (which none of my sources were aware of) and—through *Facebook*'s introduction of a legacy contact—the problems in acquiring access to digital assets in the case of the bereaved (see Image 5.).

Other considerations also arose, such as the possibility to continue crafting your online identity after death (using apps such as *If I Die*), the nature in which we remember on *Facebook* (changing profile pictures) through to the manner in which people interact after death ('Like', comment, share, private message, etc.). My study touched upon three social media platforms used by England-based users, however worldwide there are plenty more with varying purposes and modes of interaction which would produce a different cohort of results.

*Image 5*

Screenshot of automated private Facebook message after one user was selected as a legacy contact by her mother. February 2016.

Of the users I spoke with, the ones who announced their loss or posted tributes regularly share information, so perhaps, despite the difficulty in phrasing, grieving on social media is a normal and comfortable outlet for those who are already integrated and accustomed to posting. The breakdown between private and public provided by social media creates a protective, technological shield. Most people simply announced their loss via a status update, however in the case of Stella, she regularly uses *Facebook* to share a memory (normally photos) of her lost ones. The benefits of such actions are highlighted through the speed and immediacy of the scope in which we can interact, connect and share. It is consoling to receive messages, share photos and form a collective memory of a late individual. If anything, this study has opened my opinion on the 'oversharing' nature of grief on social media. Whilst I am still hesitant to perform it myself, it is essentially just like in real life. Grieving is a natural process that requires the comfort and support of others to heal. Social media platforms, as extensions of our brains, are aiding us. *WhatsApp* interaction requires additional research but currently serves to highlight our unpreparedness in dealing with a loss online. As our digital presence bleeds into our lived reality, everything—including death—must take its course. Similar to the physical reminders left behind by the deceased, as our lives become digitalized, these naturally take form online; only we are still acclimatizing.

## REFERENCES

Agger, Ben (2012): Oversharing: Presentations of Self in the Internet Age, New York: Routledge.

Arendt, Hannah (1970): The Human Condition (Sixth Impression), Chicago; London: The University of Chicago Press.

Augé, Marc (2004): Oblivion, translated by Marjolin de Jager, foreword by James E. Young, Minneapolis: University of Minnesota Press.

Boellstorff, Tom/Nardi, Bonnie/Pearce, Celia/Taylor, T. L. (eds.) (2012): Ethnography and Virtual Worlds: A Handbook of Method, Princeton: Princeton University Press.

Caroll, Brian/Landry, Katie (2010): "Logging On and Letting Out: Using Online Social Networks to Grieve and to Mourn." In: Bulletin of Science, Technology & Society 30/5, pp.341-349.

Davis, Katie/Seider, Scott/Gardner, Howard (2008): "When False Representations Ring True (and when they don't). In: Social Research 75/4, pp.1085-1108.

Halbwachs, Maurice (2011): from "The Collective Memory" In: Jeffrey K. Olick/Vered Vinitzky-Seroussi/Daniel Levy (Eds.), The Collective Memory Reader, New York: Oxford University Press, pp. 139-149.

Hirsch, Marianne (2011): from "The Generation of Postmemory" In: Jeffrey K. Olick/Vered Vinitzky-Seroussi/Daniel Levy (eds.), The Collective Memory Reader, New York: Oxford University Press, pp. 349-347.

Lewis, A. David/Moreman, Christopher M. (eds.) (2014): Digital Death: Mortality and Beyond in the Online Age, Santa Barbara CA: Praeger.

Miller, Daniel (2016): Social Media in an English Village, London: UCL Press.

Miller, Daniel/Costa, Elisabetta/Haynes, Nell/McDonald, Tom/Nicolescu, Razvan/Sinanan, Jolynna/Spyer, Juliano/Venkatraman, Shriram/Wang, Xinyuan (2016): How the World Changed Social Media, London: UCL Press.

McEwen, Rhonda/Scheaffer, Kathleen (2013): "Virtual Mourning and Memory Construction on Facebook: Here are the Terms of Use" In: Bulletin of Science, Technology & Society 33/3-4, pp.64–75.

Ophir, Adi (2005): The Order of Evils, New York: Toward an Ontology of Morals, Rela Mazali/Havi Carel (trans.), New York: Zone Books.

Stillman, Ari (2014): "Virtual Graveyard: Facebook, Death, and Existentialist Critique" In: Digital Death: Mortality and Beyond in the Online Age, A. David Lewis/Chistopher M. Moreman (eds.), Santa Barbara CA: Praeger.

Turkle, Sherry: "Connected, but alone?" Filmed February 2012. TED video, 19:41., last accessed April 12 2016. https://www.ted.com/talks/sherry_turkle_alone_together?language=en

"How we grieve on social media", April 25, 2014 http://www.theatlantic.com/health/archive/2014/04/grieving-in-public-tragedy-on-social-media/360788/

"What will happen to my account if I pass away?", last accessed April 12 2016 https://www.facebook.com/help/103897939701143

"Memories in the Digital Age", January 14, 2012 http://www.theguardian.com/lifeandstyle/2012/jan/14/memories-in-the-digital-age

"Tributes to David Bowie pour in internet and on social media", January 11, 2016 http://www.theguardian.com/music/2016/jan/11/tributes-to-david-bowie-internet-social-media

"If I Die", last accessed April 2016. http://ifidie.net

"The Future of Memory", February 4, 2016. http://www.kunsthallewien.at/#/en/exhibitions/future-memory

"June 2006 Update", June 2006. http://public.oed.com/the-oed-today/recent-updates-to-the-oed/previous-updates/june-2006-update/

"If you don't have anything nice to say, SAY IT IN ALL CAPS". Accessed January 23, 2016. http://www.thisamericanlife.org/radio-archives/episode/545/if-you-dont-have-anything-nice-to-say-say-it-in-all-caps

"Digital in 2016", Accessed January 27, 2016. http://wearesocial.com/uk/special-reports/digital-in-2016

# Watch Me, I'm Live
## *Periscope* and the "New-Individualistic" Need for Attention

*Dario Bosio*

## Introduction

I'm on a small boat off the coast of Hawaii, the sky is as blue as the sea, a young girl is playing with a toy whale as she looks at the horizon. Suddenly, in the middle of the blue, a white spurt appears in the middle of the waves some hundreds of meters from us. It's a whale. The girl salutes the animal with an excited shout. I wish I could do the same, but I don't have any other option than typing "WOW" on my smartphone keyboard, even knowing that it will get lost in the flood of comments and hearts that are now streaming across the screen.

> I'm not actually on the boat.
> I don't know the young girl.
> I'm just watching a live video streaming set up by her mother.
> A few minutes later, the screen turns black; she signed off.
> I'm back at my desk in Florence.

*Image 1*

"Have you seen any whales yet?" *Periscope* from Hawaii (Grifagno s my username on *Periscope*)

The experience described above, taken from my field notes, is only one among many I had since I started using *Periscope* some weeks ago. *Periscope* is a live video broadcasting app for smartphones that is owned by *Twitter*. It was launched in April 2015 and immediately gathered millions of users.

*Periscope* and apps alike (i.e. Meerkat) allow users to broadcast live directly from their smartphones. A smartphone and a decent internet connection are all one needs to set up a live video broadcast which could potentially reach the entire world. The live visual aspect and the ephemeral nature of the communication (all broadcasts are permanently deleted 24 hours after they end) has radically redesigned the way that people interact with one another on the internet, especially with strangers.

Over a period of three weeks I studied the way that people made use of *Periscope*, focusing on content produced by ordinary people, avoiding enterprises or companies. The aim of the research was to understand what motivates the users of these live broadcasting tools to disclose their intimacy in front of an audience of strangers and what the implications of such behavior could be.

Drawing from existing literature on the phenomenon of personal *vlogs* on *YouTube* by Michael Wesch and studies exploring the incentives of online relationship building (Valentine 2006; Fernback 2007; Turkle 2015), I will discuss how live broadcasting apps like *Periscope* challenge some of these findings and at the same time reinforce and confirm some of the worrisome predictions found in studies on the implications of digital connectivity on real-life relationships.

## CONSIDERATIONS ON THE THEORETICAL BACKGROUND OF THE PROJECT

Given the object of this study, which is a mobile phone app and the types of questions raised during the research, this paper may be of interest to those studying Media and Digital Anthropology, particularly for those focusing on online relationships. During the course of the research, I also found some theoretical tools from the fields of sociology and psychology that were useful to the study.

### Research Group

The scope of this study lies in comprehending how ordinary people make use of *Periscope*, and what the reasons are that prompt users to connect with strangers through this particular tool. I considered content produced exclusively by people who were not promoting a brand, a company or a religious movement and disregarded broadcasts of major news events, even if they were filmed by ordinary (non-affiliated) people.

The research subjects include people that chose to record and broadcast segments of their everyday lives and intimacy while chatting with strangers. Although the focus was not set on any particular age group, due to the app's demographics, the vast majority of the subjects observed were in their teens or twenties.

On account of language barriers, I could only consider broadcasts in English, Italian, French and Spanish. Nonetheless, while *Periscope* has indeed gathered users from all across the globe, most of them are based in Europe, the United States, Russia and Turkey. The *digital divide;* referring to access to fast internet connection or smartphones in Africa or Asia, as well as internet access restrictions and censorship, are among the reasons for the geographical concentration. Maps depicting the phenomenon of the digital divide support this thesis. The correlation between *Periscope* users and geographical areas where broadband internet is widely available is evident.

*Image 2*

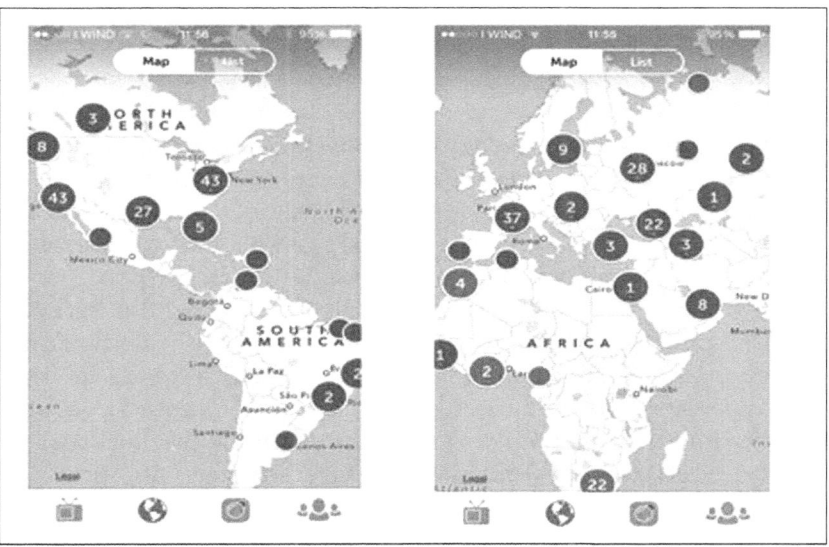

"The Digital Divide". Two screenshots taken from Periscope showing the number of active users. The discrepancy in access between the Northern and Southern hemisphere is evident.

## Methodology

The research was conducted through participant observation and short single interviews carried out via *Periscope Chat* whenever possible. I downloaded and signed into *Periscope* through my personal *Twitter* account and made sure to write the reason why I was on *Periscope* on my public profile ("a visual anthropological research"). I logged into *Periscope* on a daily basis over a period of three weeks, sometimes for hours, and observed and interacted with dozens of *scopers* (namely, people broadcasting live video).

In order to fully understand the research methodology and the difficulties I encountered during fieldwork, it is necessary to understand how the app works.

After logging in, the user is presented with a world map filled with red and blue dots. Red dots represent the live *scopers* and blue dots the broadcasts that just ended. Broadcasts, or *scopes*, are stored on the system for twenty-four hours and then deleted permanently. Even if some apps like katch.me allow users to save the *scopes* that they watched on their hard drive, my research suggested that this practice is not very widespread.[1]

By clicking on a red dot on the map, you are presented with a live *scope*. The smartphone replicates what the camera of the *scoper's* smartphone is recording. Other elements on the screen include: a text box at the bottom where the user can type in text to chat with the *scoper*, a series of balloons with text streaming on the left (chat messages) and a stream of hearts floating on the right of the screen from bottom to top. The hearts represent the equivalent of *Facebook likes* in *Periscope*: users give hearts to show their appreciation for the *scoper* or for what they have broadcasted. The entire interaction is live, meaning that once the *scope* ends, the users are no longer able to chat with the *scoper* nor with the other users; the screen turns black and the window closes.

The ephemeral nature of the *scopes*, together with the fact that there is no thematic search engine inside *Periscope* other than the aforementioned world map made it difficult to narrow down the focus of the research. I followed some *scopers* whose broadcast I knew fit the research topic, however I generally found myself jumping from *scope* to *scope* hoping to find something valuable, guided only by the user's short title descriptions (which, in many cases, were misleading).

---

**1** | This ephemeral nature of the content shared replicates a trend that has emerged over the past years since the launch of ephemeral messaging apps like *Snapchat*. Uploading something on the internet no longer means that it will stay there forever. The possibility of replay, which characterized the internet so far, is gradually being abandoned by most recent apps. The implications of this change include the loss of "the possibility of recognition" as theorized by McLuhan:. "the amazing thing about replay is that it offers the means of recognition—the first time is cognition the second time is recognition, and the recognition is even deeper." (Dr Fallon: 2008).

The chat system itself proved to be far from ideal to conduct research given that the questions of the researcher were unnoticed in *scopes* in which more than five or six people were attending; but also because chat messages disappear from the screen after seconds. To cope with this problem, I sometimes joined conversations and used the app like everyone else, trying to find the answers to my questions through participant observation. In a few cases, when the broadcast was attended by less than five people, *scopers* became interested in my research and collaborated in answering questions I had for them. As long as no other *scopers* changed the topic, we conversed about my research.

I observed a few *scopers* reacting negatively when asked about the reasons why they scope, perceiving my question as an attack on their practice. In more than one case in which the *scoper* was asked, "Why do you scope?" They would attack back with answers like "Nobody is forcing you to watch this if you do not want to." or "Do you think that I do not have any friends in real life?" The presence of several *trolls* in the chat also made the research difficult in more than one case.

I would also like to raise some ethical considerations regarding the content of the *scopes* since many of them were broadcasted by teens, sometimes as young as fourteen years old. Regarding this matter, I would like to share the following passage from my field notes:

Every time I started watching the *scope* of a teenager I felt like I should not do it It feels like I am intruding, invading the kid s privacy and wrong on many different levels. Yet, it is completely legal to do so—it is completely legal that I, as an adult, can watch a teen talking about private matters with his/her peers and showing his/her own room and intimacy, while remaining completely anonymous and silent. This is very dangerous.

In more than one case I stopped the vision of a certain *scope* because I felt uncomfortable with what I was watching, deeming it too "personal" for the public. The manner in which teenagers are using Periscope and the way they perform for the camera—through extensive use of make-up, posing and "cool" clothes—proves that they are very aware of the way they should behave in front of a camera, and that they are expected to play "a heightened version of themselves" (Grindstaff 2012: 27).

Image 3    Image 4

"Open Boobs." A 16 year-old girl is seen performing a dance for the camera, while the anonymous audience asks for her to undress.

Alone together. A group of young women on *Periscope*. Each of them is focused on their smartphone rather than interacting with one another. One of them was watching the same *Periscope* in which she was featured.

In several situations, *scopers* were prompted to undress, especially when the *scoper* was female. In fact, many young people promised nudity in the title of their *scope* in hopes of gathering more users. Given the anonymous nature of the service and the possibility of lying about your age and gender, there are various reasons for concern for underage *scopers* to be regarding what and how much they reveal; the images could easily be captured and used for pornographic purposes. *Periscope*'s terms of use ban nudity and illegal activities like the consumption of drugs. However, due to the sheer volume of *simultaneous scopes*, policing the platform is impossible. Being that most abuse reports come from the users themselves, this remains an open issue.

## CONTENT

*Periscope* co-founder, Kayvon Beykpour, came up with the idea for the app during a trip to Turkey in 2013 when protests were raging in Taksim Square. While he could *read* about what was happening through his *Twitter* feed, he regretted that he could not *see* it. His initial intention for *Periscope* was to be "akin to teleportation, a technology and user experience that lets you be anywhere and witness anything" (Shontell 2015: par. 7).

Despite this intention, however, the vast majority of content being shared on the platform is not about exceptional events. While indeed there are *scopes* that let users see "news as it happens, see sporting events from the sidelines, see behind the scenes of anything official" (ibid: par. 29), these constitute a very small minority among the thousands of simultaneous broadcasts available at any given moment. Interestingly, most of the broadcasts feature one *scoper* pointing a camera at him/herself in what I would call a *selfie-fashion* while talking to their audience, performing for the camera, answering questions or simply reading aloud what people are writing in the text chat. In most cases, there is no exceptional landscape or relevant events to be shared. My research concluded that most common people are using *Periscope* just to be on camera and talk to strangers, even more so if the situation they find themselves in is too "boring"[2].

I found a strong similarity between the use of *Periscope* and Turkle's description of how people are making use of text messages. In describing how people use mobile phones, she writes:

These days so many people—adults and children—become anxious without a constant feed of online stimulation. In a quiet moment, they take out their phones, check their messages, send a text. They cannot tolerate time that some people I interviewed termed "boring" or "dull." (Turkle 2015: 23)

Most of the *scopes* I watched took place in situations where the broadcaster was bored or had to spend time alone. Sometimes the *scope* would feature groups of friends. In such cases, the people being featured were mostly observed in quiet situations or "killing time" together, and used the app as a way of breaking their boredom. Interestingly, as soon as the camera was rolling, most of them dedicated their entire attention to it - in a way that reminded me of the way we treat newborns, a sort of reverent and absolute attention - with a preference for an abstract and ephemeral relationship as opposed to real life conversations.

*Periscope* offers its users the possibility of breaking this boredom by providing them with "so many automatic listeners" (ibid.). As soon as you log in and start broadcasting, an audience is available and you no longer have to spend time on your own.

In contrast to text messages that imply a sort of real-life relationship between sender and receiver, the audience on *Periscope* is largely made up of anonymous viewers. Apart from private *scopes*, which can be directed to specific users, public broadcasts can be attended by anyone. The kind of bond between broadcaster and viewer in this sense is a very loose one and practically non-existent. Most of the conversations hardly go beyond simple questions and answers regarding the geographic location of the broadcaster or viewers, comments on one's appearance or sexually charged requests, particularly if the broadcaster is female.

---

**2** | As evidenced by the numerous scopes with titles like "bored", "keep me company", "come in and talk" or similar.

The kind of relationships that are established through *Periscope* confirm previous studies of online communities regarding the type of bond that is created through online social tools, namely the creation of a *connection-without-constraint* (Fernback 2007). The results of my research also concluded that the kind of relationship that users are building is in most cases aimed at filling dull-time and not to create a long-lasting bond.

Similarly, by studying the phenomenon of personal *vlogs* on *YouTube*, a practice that in many cases is similar to these numerous *selfie-scopes*, Wesch defined the kind of bond between viewer and viewed as a "deep and profound but not strong" one, characterized by its being "in most cases completely anonymous, fleeting and ephemeral. It is a diffuse experience of connection; an anonymous hand with the message: You are not alone." (Wesch 2009: 28). It looks like this fight against loneliness is in many cases what drives people to broadcast their own lives on *Periscope* as well.

In contrast to *Periscope, vlogs* on *YouTube* can become very personal and in some cases self-revealing for the subject, given the inherently reflexive nature resulting from the possibility of replay and the non-simultaneous nature of the communicative act (Wesch 2009). *Periscope* lacks the structural tools needed for an introspective conversation with oneself. The fact that there's an audience watching at the time of the broadcasts puts the *scoper* under a performative pressure that is inherently different from the one experienced by the *vlogger* who can record the same monologue over and over again, watch it, edit it and change it. *Periscope* is live; a fact that puts the *scoper* under the impression of having a certain kind of obligation towards his/her viewers. This becomes evident in the performative nature of many broadcasts. I would like to give a few examples from my field notes:

I am watching an American girl singing in front of the camera - probably before going to bed, it must be 2.30am where she is. She is smoking weed from a glass pipe and singing songs following the requests of the audience. You can hear her friend spitting and vomiting in the other room, calling her. She doesn't reply, but stays and performs for the camera.

Watched a video by a teenager in France. The title is "prof=pute" (teacher=bitch). They are in class and are filming a helpless young teacher while shouting swear words at her from their desk. Roughly eight hundred people are watching the *scope*. They are suggesting what swear words to shout at the teacher. He follows their suggestions.

Both examples show how users are able to transform a "dull" moment (like the one before going to bed or a high school class) into something possibly more exciting. These also exemplify how important the anonymous audience is in addition to the act of being watched.

Many broadcasters complain about a lack of viewers during their *scopes*, stressing how important it is that somebody is watching; as though one could get some sort of validation through the very existence of an audience and not through his/her actions. The fact of being watched is satisfactory enough, regardless of the exceptionality of the content. Concerning this point, the triviality of the activities that people chose to broadcast does remind, in some ways, of reality-TV, where ordinary life turns into something exceptional for the mere fact of being broadcasted—and the character's social validation arises from being watched during their daily routine.

If we start conceiving the communicative act happening through *Periscope* as a form of reality-TV, then it becomes easier to understand the shallow nature of the communication and equally as important - the bonds created. As Grindstaff evidenced in her studies of reality-TV, the content of such programs hardly rely on the quality of the communicative act, rather the potential of the transmission function of the media to convey strong messages is hardly taken into consideration. What's at play, instead, is a different set of goals, namely: validation, to be part of the discourse and part of the scene [...] If there [is] a communicative dimension at work here, the communication is 'I exist' rather than 'here's what I think'—the talking body rather than the talking head" (Grindstaff 2012: 31).

This focus on the bodily appearance of the *scopers* might also be one of the reasons why many *scopers*, especially young ones, promise to "flash" (slang for "showing briefly") their intimate parts on camera if they reach a certain number of viewers, a trend that proved to be successful, at least in the words of some of the users I encountered during my research. As a young boy from Italy told me:

Periscope used to be cool, but now it only works if you put in a title like "le esco" ["I show my tits"], or if you do something pornographic, like [name of another *scoper*] who showered during his *scope*.

*Image 5*

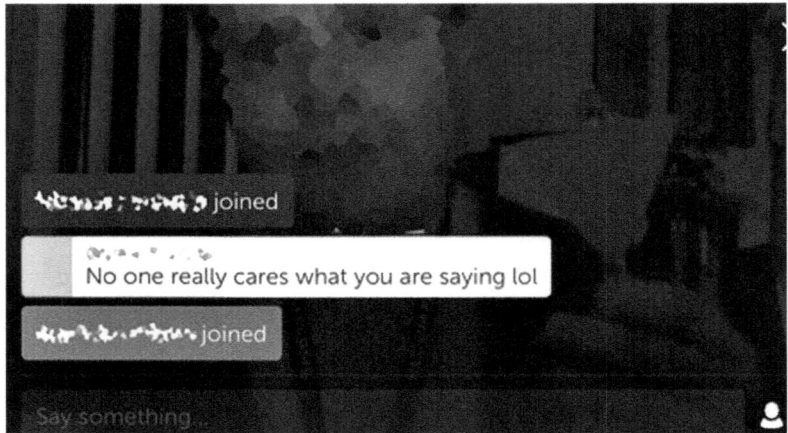

"No one really cares what you are saying lol"—"If there [is] a communicative dimension at work here, the communication is "I exist" rather than "here's what I think"—the talking body rather than the talking head" (Grindstaff 2012: 31).

The research suggests that there's little interest by the *scopers* to create a relationship or bond with the audience through this kind of communication and that what one aims at is *being watched* and *appreciated* by his/her audience. This also explains the obsession of counting hearts (the tool provided by *Periscope* to show appreciation) that some broadcasters have during their *scopes*. These hearts represent a lasting mark of validation for oneself and can be consulted at any time by checking the *scoper*'s personal profile.

## Conclusion

The scope of my research concluded that *Periscope*, despite the intentions of its founders, has been re-appropriated by a large number of its users to pursue personal intimate goals, compared to the concept that it was originally intended to be. Through usage of the app, users are able to fill dull moments and experience a form of relationship with an audience, even though it is generally an ephemeral one.

Not surprisingly, the observed behavior is strongly related to existing theories on "New Individualism" as an age where traditional roles (family, relationships) and social orders (state) collapse and the "ethics of individual self-fulfillment and achievement is the most powerful current" (Beck-Gernsheim 2002: 22). *Periscope* destroys every spatial and hierarchical context and puts individuals on the main stage; a stage whose audience can potentially reach millions.

*Periscope*, in this sense, is a product of a cultural trend that is specific to our time and its success is tightly linked to the fact that the cultural context for its emergence was ideal at this historical moment. After all, *Life-casting*, or the act of broadcasting one's own intimacy, is not a new phenomenon on the internet and a great deal has been written about the very first attempts at this practice since Jennifer Ringley set up a webcam that broadcasted her dorm room in 1994 on the website *jennicam.com*. When interviewed about the motivations that inspired her to expose her life, Ringley didn't deny that "there were certain elements of insecurity that go along with being, you know, 19 years old" and claimed that she was doing it to seek approval (Reply All: 2015). At the same time, she admitted that the presence of the camera also made her feel less lonely (Burgin 2000: 80). Ringley is a programmer and scripted the software that broadcasted her life herself. What *Periscope* offers its users is nothing but an easy and accessible way to satisfy those very same needs that pushed Ringley into her *cam-girl* experience, reinforced by the cultural background of a generation that grew up watching reality-TV in which the division of *private* or *public* became unclear.

The use of *Periscope* by ordinary people therefore reinforces the theories that perceive the longing for online relationships as a symptom of a diffuse incapacity of being alone. Nonetheless, they offer a surrogate for the lack of real-life relationships (Valentine 2006; Turkle 2015) and satisfy the need for sharing one's own life as a form of social validation exemplified by the formula: I share, therefore I exist (Turkle 2015).

Given that online bonds need constant connection in order to be lived fully by the user (Franklin 2009), there's a risk that users give priority to "connections" over "relationships", pushing away the possibility of a fulfilling bond in real life.

This analysis of *Periscope*, which is a relatively new phenomenon (launched in March 2015), reinforces some of the most worrisome predictions for the impact of mobile devices on individual, *real-life* relationship skills. Given that there's no sign that the trend is going to stop or revert in the short future, as new apps and tools for ephemeral, anonymous and instant connectivity emerge at a faster pace, it would be of great interest to carry out in-depth studies on how connected individuals, particularly younger generations build and live their relationships through this new set of tools. It would also be significant to examine how the spread of these forms of *connected loneliness* are developed at the expense of *real life relationships*. Given that online relationships are often characterized by "narcissism, disinhibition and the failure to care about the feelings of others", the risk of finding ourselves living in 'a world devoid of empathy" (Weisberg 2015) should be something we should be concerned with when studying the way users satisfy their relational needs through online interactions.

## References

Beck, Ulrich/Beck-Gernsheim, Elizabeth (2002) Individualization: Institutionalized Individualism and its Social and Political Consequences, London, New Delhi and Thousand Oaks: SAGE Publications Ltd.

Brooke, Knight A. (2000): "Watch Me! Webcams and the Public Exposure of Private Lives". In: Art Journal, 59/4, pp. 21-25.

Burgin, Victor (2000). "Jenni's Room: Exhibitionism and Solitude". In: Critical Inquiry 27,1, pp. 77-89.

Carpenter, Edmund (1975): The Tribal Terror of Self—Awareness, in: Paul Hockings (ed.), Principles of Visual Anthropology, Chicago: Mouton, ,pp. 451-461.

Fallon, Patrick (2008). Fr. Patrick Peyton Interviews Marshall McLuhan (Part 1). Last accessed March 2016. Video posted to http://youtube.com/watch?v=1uZYR3jmMng

Fernback, Jan (2007): "Beyond the diluted community concept: a symbolic interactionist perspective on online social relations". In: New Media & Society 9/1, pp. 49–69.

Firth, Simon (1998): "21st: Live! From my bedroom". Last accessed March 2016. http://www.salon.com/1998/01/08/feature_354/

Franklin, Adrian S. (2009): "On Loneliness". In: Geografiska Annaler. Series B, Human Geography 91/4, pp. 343-354.

Gradim, Anabela (2009): "Digital Natives and Virtual Communities: Towards a New Paradigm of Mediated Communication". In: Estudos em Comunicação 5, pp. 53-73.

Grindstaff, Laura (2012): "Reality TV and the Production of 'Ordinary Celebrity': Notes from the Field". In: Berkeley Journal of Sociology 56, pp. 22-40.

Miller, Daniel (2008): "What is a mobile phone relationship?" In: Erwin Alampay (ed.) Living the Information Society in Asia, Singapore: Institute of Southeast Asian Studies, pp. 24-35.

Rosen, Christine (2012): "Electronic Intimacy" In: The Wilson Quarterly 36/2 pp. 48-51.

Shontell, Alyson (2015): "What it's like to sell your startup for ~$120million before it's even launched: Meet Twitter's new prized possession, Periscope". Last accessed March 2016. Online article on Business Insider: http://www.businessinsider.com/what-is-periscope-and-why-twitter-bought-it-2015-3?IR=T

Turkle, Sherry (2012): "Connected but Alone" TED Talk. Last accessed March 2016. Video on https://www.ted.com/talks/sherry_turkle_alone_together

Turkle, Sherry (2015): Reclaiming Conversation: The Power of Talk in the Digital Age, London: Penguin Pr.

Valentine, Gill (2006): "Globalizing Intimacy: The Role of Information and Communication.
Technologies in Maintaining and Creating Relationships". In: Women's Studies Quarterly 34/1/2, pp. 365-393.
Weisberg, Jacob (2015): "We are hopelessly hooked". New York Review of Books, February 25.
Wesch, Michael (2009): "YouTube and You: Experiences of Self-Awareness in the Context Collapse of the Recording Webcam". In: Explorations in Media Ecology, pp.19-34.

# Part 2

# Political Digital Environments and Activism Online

# Hair, Blood and the Nipple

*Instagram* Censorship and the Female Body

Gretchen Faust

## INTRODUCTION

Every*body* has the possibility of becoming a content creator within the realm of social media, allowing for limitless cultural creation. Social media is an open forum permitting anyone to be heard. Content creation provides networked individuals opportunities to reach wider audiences, creating an online community and capacity to broaden discussion. Shared media contributes to expanding knowledge and generates infinite ways of being.

However, these ideals are not echoed by the application of content control in social media venues. *Facebook*, *Instagram* and *Twitter* are well-known social media outlets that focus on networking, sharing images, and brief words of thought. Despite the magnitude of variety in the realm of the internet, social media exercises different degrees of censorship to control the portrayal of male and female identified bodies. This paper is going to explore the censorship of female identified artist's bodies on the social media platform *Instagram*[1].

## METHODOLOGY

This study is navigated with feminist qualitative methods that focus on the subject's experience within their self-imaging practice. The exploration is reflective in a sense, as I identify myself as a feminist artist who deals with the issue of the body. However, I do not share my work on the social media

---

[1] | The illustrated images were hand drawn by the author to provide an idea of the sources referenced in the essay while respecting the ownership of those who are featured in regards to copyright despite the well circulated nature of the Instagram photos.

platform. Identifying myself as female may have given me more access to sharing similar experiences as my subjects.

My research was based on "following" two female artists (Petra Collins and Rupi Kaur) on their *Instagram* accounts as well as the *#FreetheNipple* movement. Additionally, I interviewed a female artist, Scar, on the topic of her experience as a female identifying artist who posts work on *Instagram,* and its issues of censorship. Scar runs an *Instagram* account[2] that is solely dedicated to posting on "menstrual experience"; posting submissions of art, photographs, comics, poems, etc. to the feed since March 2015. Unlike Petra Collins or Rupi Kaur, none of Scar's postings have been removed or banned despite similarities in content. This may be because of the difference in the amount of followers—possibly the lower volume of traffic onto their feed may protect their visibility from the *Instagram* moderation team.

What is particular to the art that has been shared on *Instagram* is that it is a "self-imaging practice," where the artist is both object and the subject at the same time. This is a challenge towards the conceived social order of image production and consumption in our general visual culture. A "self imaging practice" of a female identified artist questions the stereotypical role of image production that is controlled through a patriarchal lens. This study is important in today's image-centered society because, while the feminist movement has improved the progression towards social equality, there is still a particular ideal and image exerted over a woman's body.

## INSTA-*WHAT*?

In simple terms, *Instagram* is an online, mobile, photo-sharing, video-sharing and social networking service. It enables its users to take pictures and videos and simultaneously share them on a variety of social networking platforms such as *Facebook, Twitter, Tumblr* and *Flickr. Instagram* is an interactive way to share your life with friends through a series of pictures. *Instagram* allows one to experience moments in your friends' lives through pictures as they happen, proclaiming the hope of "a world more connected through photos.[3]"

The declared goal of *Instagram*'s service presents the possibility of sharing diverse ways of being and experiences, however their terms of service present boundaries that readily contest their mission. *Instagram*'s main concern is to have users post photos and videos that are *appropriate* for a diverse audience. The detailed explanation given in their "terms of use" states, "for a variety of

---

2 | Scar, *Instagram* user: xxgirlflu, has over 797 followers.
3 | *Instagram*'s "Community Guidelines," April 2015. Accessed: May 24, 2016. https://help.instagram.com/477434105621119/

Hair, Blood and the Nipple   161

reasons, we don't allow nudity on *Instagram*. This includes photos, videos, and some digitally-created content that show sexual intercourse, genitals, and close-ups of fully-nude buttocks." This censorship also extends to some photos of female-identified nipples, but photos of post-mastectomy scarring and women actively breastfeeding are allowed. Nudity in photos of paintings and sculptures is acceptable.

*Image 1*

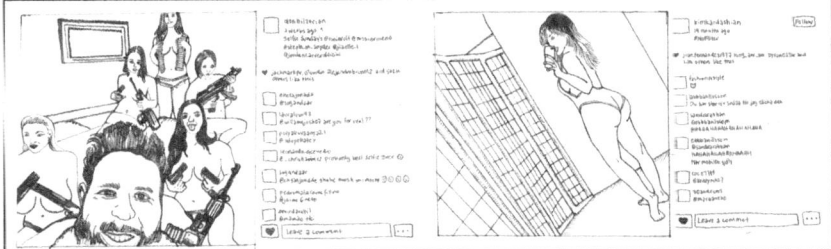

(Left) Illustration of Dan Bilzerian's *Instagram*, Bilzerian is known as the "King of Instagram." (Right) Illustration of a well known "selfie" from Kim Kardashian's *Instagram* feed. Kardashian is within the top ten *Instagram* most followed users— only second to *Instagram* itself. Illustration by author.

Social media's definition of what constitutes "nudity" and what is permissible regarding the female nipple is constantly contested. There is the common idea that if you wouldn't show the photo or video you are thinking about uploading to a child, or your boss, or your parents, you probably shouldn't share it on *Instagram* (Raiss 2015). As with the rest of *Instagram*'s "Community Guidelines," the familiar tone of this cautionary statement contradicts the manner of enforcement. A photo that violates the ban on "nudity or mature content" will be taken down, the user will be served with either a perfunctory warning or a suspension of their account and content; in some cases the person's account will be terminated.

Similar to *Facebook*, *Instagram* doesn't get into the messy business of distinguishing between pornography and art. Their blanket ban on so-called "mature content" and the inconsistency of enforcement has users struggling to wade their way through ill-defined concepts relating to the morality around photo sharing. Male nipples and the thong-clad asses that populate the famed "Instagram King" Dan Bilzerian's feed[4], together with posts of Kim Kardashian

---

**4** | Dan Bilzerian is an American professional poker player, actor and internet social media celebrity with over 16.4 million followers. Bilzerian commonly posts photos of women, guns and trips to Vegas.

West's[5] bottom are allowed to stay. While female nipples and bare buttocks that don't belong to Kim Kardashian are asked to leave the platform (Raiss 2015). Representations made by *Instagram* often state that they try to find a balance between allowing people to express themselves creatively whilst retaining policies that maintain a "comfortable experience for our global and culturally diverse community". However, this line of what is acceptable is always in flux, with constant revisions and what *Instagram* often refers to as mistakes. The platform is well aware of this inconsistency in their policies, and honestly states "we recognize that we don't always get it right" (Vagianos 2015).

## WHAT STARTED THIS RUMBLE? PETRA COLLINS AND THE VISIBLE, IMPERMISSIBLE HAIR

On the outskirts of the celebrity-driven *Instagram* feeds, there have been a few social personalities that have brought attention to what is permissible and what is inacceptable on the social media feed. What makes the cut and what does not in the social feed, is a mirror of what our plugged-in culture promotes within its values.

Petra Collins is a portraiture photographer, fashion photographer and fashion designer from Toronto, Canada[6]. Her work addresses "what is hidden from our culture". Common themes in her work surround what is natural to a post-pubescent body, the menstrual cycle of young women and masturbation. She sparked an internet discussion after designing a t-shirt for *American Apparel* that featured a line drawing of a vagina bleeding.

Her rise as a social media sensation began in March 2013, when Collins' *Instagram* account was deleted for a photograph of herself that showed her own pubic hair emerging from bikini bottoms. Collins claims the account deletion was unfounded because it did not break any of *Instagram*'s terms and conditions. When asked about her intention with her work, "I guess I was trying to combat feelings of the male gaze through my images. I wanted to create images that represented *my own* sexuality, not a sexuality that was dictated by someone else–like, 'How do I make this *mine?*'" (Collins, 2013). Collins openly wrote about her experience of *Instagram* taking down her photo stating: "What I did have was an image of MY body that didn't meet society's standard of 'femininity'" (ibid.).

---

**5** | Kim Kardashian West is an American television and social media personality, socialite, and model. She has over 65.4 million followers on *Instagram*. Kardashian released a book called *Selfies* in May 2015 that contained over 445 photos of her chronological "selfie" photographs.

**6** | Petra Collins has 300,000 followers on her *Instagram* account.

Hair, Blood and the Nipple    163

*Image 2*

Illustration of the image Petra Collins had posted on her *Instagram* in March 2013 and was subsequently removed and later allowed on the social platform. Illustration by author.

It is perplexing that such an image, apparently so harmless and familiar, could be banned alongside accepted imagery posted by celebrities that promote an aggressive sexuality and gender. This situation is salient in illustrating the capacity for society to be shocked and appalled by what is otherwise "natural" amidst a proliferation of sexually violent or disgustingly derogatory images that regularly populate our media as a whole. It highlights the hypocrisy at play; *Instagram*'s community standards deem someone's body in a more "natural" state to be unacceptable.

Responding to the inescapable reach of social media, Collins offers images of unflinching honesty, exploring the aspects of privacy and publicity of growing up as a woman at a moment when female bodies are ubiquitously hyper-mediated by *Photoshop* and social media. Collins writes, "I'm used to being told by society that I must regulate my body to fit the norm." The point that makes Collin's essay on censorship and social media significant is the idea that the internet is an outlet from real life and if an image or concept is banned in this apparently limitless realm, then how can other ways of being manifest in our real time experience? If particular imagery of bodies are silenced or censored in a place of boundless possibility, then is there any place to be free?

## Rupi Kaur and 'Leaking Patriarchy'–What Type of Blood is Tolerated?

When Rupi Kaur[7] decided to make the taboo around menstruation the theme of her university photography project, she wasn't expecting to become the focus within *Instagram*'s continuous censorship war. The Canadian poet and artist uploaded an image from her photographic series onto *Instagram* in March 2015, depicting her fully clothed but with a spot of blood between her legs and on the sheets. *Instagram* removed it—twice—claiming that her photo violated their terms of service.

Kaur decided to convey menstruation to demystify the cultural stigmas that surround it. She developed the series of work with her sister Prabh over a weekend. After the photo series was created Kaur decided to share it online; this action formed a component of the project, tracking how different medias embraced or rejected the material (Tsjeng 2015). Before the image was taken down by the *Instagram* team, her page was swarmed by internet trolls[8], leaving comments like "come over here and let me make your vagina bleed" and "fuck your feminism". *Instagram* deleted the picture less than 24 hours after it was posted. Kaur stated that *Instagram* did not give her any reason, nor did they contact her before the removal of her image.

The response to, and subsequent censorship of, the photo series amplified Kaur's motive behind her work. Kaur discussed that "it wasn't just a project for my school course anymore, it felt like a personal attack on my humanity" (Tsjeng 2015). Kaur did not complain directly to *Instagram*, but instead posted the photo again with the hope of informing her audience of the nature of the censorship happening on *Instagram*. Kaur repeated the post of the image that same night it had been removed; again it was removed the following morning (Tsjeng 2015).

Interestingly enough, *Instagram* only claims to prohibit images that are "violent, nude, partially nude, discriminatory, unlawful, infringing, hateful, pornographic or sexually suggestive". Within this list there is no mention of menstrual blood. Nonetheless, Kaur's image of a blood spot was removed twice. Kaur moved her image to *Facebook* to discuss the censorship on *Instagram*. In her *Facebook* post, Kaur discussed that she is aware that some communities and cultures go out of their way to shun and oppress a woman for the duration of her period. In a *Facebook* post, she wrote, "*Instagram* is another one of them. Their patriarchy is leaking. Their misogyny is leaking. We will not be censored."

---

7 | Rupi Kaur has 387,000 Instagram followers.

8 | An internet troll is someone online who posts comments with the deliberate intent of provoking readers into an emotional response. Comments may be inflammatory, off topic, or harassing.

The post immediately went viral—it was shared 6,339 times and liked by more than 36,000 people. Kaur's photo had suddenly reappeared on her *Instagram* page within the next morning.

*Image 3*

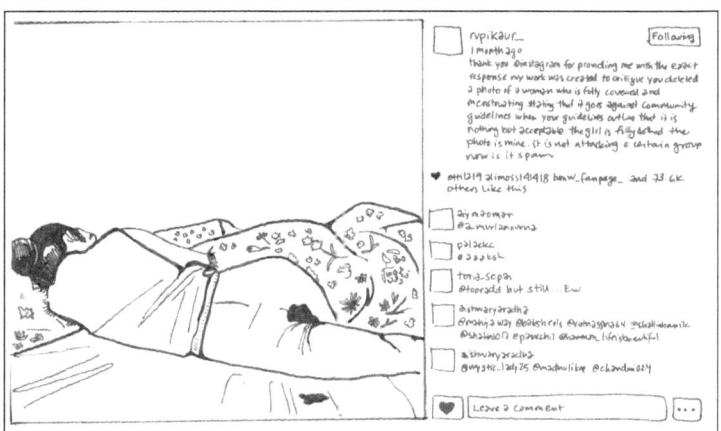

Rupi Kaur's image that was removed twice from her *Instagram* feed, first posted in March 2015. Illustration by author.

It is important to keep in mind that Kaur's image was censored on a platform where revealing imagery is persistent. The natural cycle and monthly experience of the women is not tolerable to be seen; as Kaur puts it "It is okay to sell what's between a woman's legs, more than it is okay to mention its inner workings." Kaur is still surprised the image was as controversial as it ended up being, stating, "I never thought it was such a big deal, it's just a red spot."

## But Whose Nipple Makes the Cut? #FreeTheNipple

Image 4

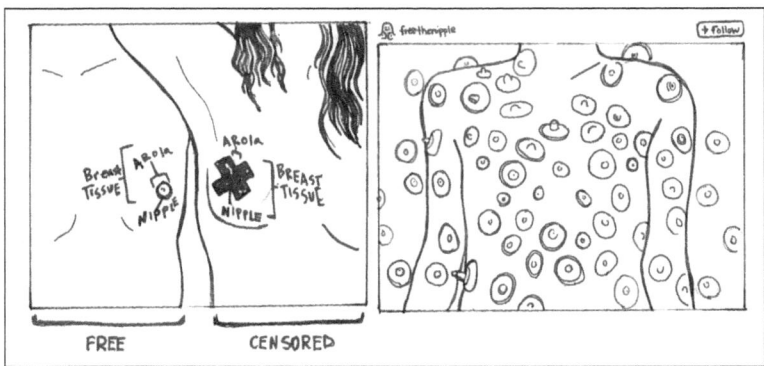

Images taken from Freethenipple's *Instagram* feed https://www.instagram.com/freethenipple/. Illustration by author.

Standards of acceptance of nudity between genders are far from equal in most cultures. This can be seen in the casual example of a bathing suit: how many women are obliged to cover their chest area, while it is cultural accepted for a male identifying person to be bare-chested. Female bodies are still subject to intense scrutiny and censorship when it comes to nipples—a form of disapproval to which, unfairly, men are not subject. Women are regularly expelled from *Instagram* for posting photos with any portion of the areola exposed, while photos *sans* nipple—degrading as they might be—remain unchallenged.

The *#FreetheNipple* movement was sparked by various *Instagram* users, however celebrity Scout Willis was able to use her public leverage to bring more light to the matter. Willis used her body to campaign against gender inequality and the double standard of censoring women more than men. During summer 2014, Willis walked around the streets of New York City topless to protest against *Instagram*'s rules on nudity. She did this to point out "that what is legal by New York state law is not allowed on *Instagram*." (Willis, 2014)

Willis has been criticized for relating the visibility of nipples with equality, however to her, "nipples seem to be at the very heart of the issue." Willis highlighted the historic point in 1930s American society when men's nipples were just as provocative and shameful as the nipples of women are now. Willis recounts the public action taken in 1935 where a flash mob of topless men descended upon Atlantic City in New York City, 42 of whom were arrested. Men fought and they were heard, so changing not only the law but also social consciousness. By 1936, male bare chests were accepted as the norm in New

York City. Unfortunately, the divide still stands and it wasn't until 1992 that women were *allowed* to be topless in public in New York City (Ridge 2013).

However, one thing to keep in mind while scrolling through *#freethenipple* is that many of the postings share some common features: a lot of the people posting are white, thin and able-bodied. Many are conventionally attractive and most of those posting are young. For a campaign that is asking for equality and visibility, it brings to question the nature of exactly *what* is allowed to be celebrated. The movement claims to work against sexual objectification and censorship—something that arguably affects all women at some point in their lives—however the lack of diversity within its *hashtag* community only perpetuates what the movement is working against.

*Image 5*

Scout Willis' action in New York City, posted on *Twitter* during Summer 2014 that sparked publicity on *Instagram*'s nipple ban. Illustration by author

## CONCLUDING THOUGHTS

As Jessica Valenti (2015) from *The Guardian* points out, "the very nature of social media has made it easier for women to present a more diverse set of images on what the female form can look like." However, the continuous act of concealing something by removing the image from public view makes it seem that the posted matter is illicit.

Upon following the issues of hair, blood and nipple in different social situations, it becomes apparent that aspects of internet culture bear an unhealthy disconnect between bodies and personal identities. It is interesting that an image of a nipple is more offensive than the violent imagery that is posted throughout the internet. I am still left questioning why features of basic physiology are more threatening than firearms. Kaur's photographs and her act of sharing them on social media makes the blatant point that society is uncomfortable with women menstruating but is comfortable with women being objectified.

While imagery that does not fit the mold has been flagged on social media, it is the use of social media that has made it possible to bring attention to such censorship. Digital connectivity provides women with a very public way to assert their identities, build a supportive private or public community, and in some ways liberate their bodies from injustice or oppressive societal norms (Ruiz 2015). The censorship of the hair, blood and nipple shed light on a still murky facet of the vast social media universe. Imagery is censored by a geographically dispersed group of photo moderators who work 24/7 on the moderation of *Instagram*'s social platform. The moderators are not robots; they are human beings. Their cultural differences may mean that a certain photo is either banned, accepted, flagged for moderation, or approved in different global contexts. A set of corporate guidelines can prove insufficient for a network of photo moderators with their own preferences and biases (Shapiro 2012).

This type of gendered moderation or harassment has severe implications for women's status on the internet, as it is a reflection of the inequality that exists in our physical world. I recognize that I may have bias in my methods with this paper, but I believe that the photographs speak for themselves in actualizing the content that is allowed or not allowed on *Instagram*.

## REFERENCES

Bernard, Katherine (2013): "The Power of Instagram: Petra Collins and Kim Kardashian in the Age of the Selfie". In: Vogue. http://www.vogue.com/872835/the-power-of-instagram-petra-collins-and-kim-kardashian-in-the-age-of-the-selfie/

Bourdet, Kelly (2015): "Women With Body Hair: 16 NSFW Photos Of The Real Deal". In: Refinery 29. http://www.refinery29.com/body-hair-pictures#slide

Cliff, Aimee (2015): "Why Is Pop Still So Scared Of The Vagina?" In: The Fader. http://www.thefader.com/2015/03/30/why-is-pop-still-so-scared-of-the-vagina

Collins, Petra (2013): "Why Instagram Censored my Body". In: Huffington Post. http://www.huffingtonpost.com/petra-collins/why-instagram-censored-my-body_b_4118416.html

De Cicco, Gabriela (2013) "Women In Arts: Activism And Censorship". In: Association for Women's Rights in Development. http://www.awid.org/News-Analysis/Friday-Files/Women-in-Arts-Activism-and-Censorship

Greenhouse, Emily (2015): "Facebook Can't Tell the Difference Between Art and Porn". In: Bloomberg Politics. http://www.bloomberg.com/politics/articles/2015-03-12/facebook-can-t-tell-the-difference-between-art-and-porn

Harrity, Christopher (2015) "Why Does Facebook Censor Gay Images?". http://www.advocate.com/politics/media/2015/01/30/why-does-facebook-censor-gay-images

Hass, Amanda (2014): "Why Women Aren't Welcome on the Internet". In: Pacific Standard. http://www.psmag.com/health-and-behavior/women-arent-welcome-internet-72170

Heins, Marjorie (2014): "The Brave New World of Social Media Censorship". In: Harvard Law Review. http://harvardlawreview.org/2014/06/the-brave-new-world-of-social-media-censorship/

Hill, Milli (2014): "By removing photos of childbirth, Facebook is censoring powerful female images" In: The Guardian. http://www.theguardian.com/commentisfree/2014/oct/22/facebook-removing-childbirth-female-images

Kinsella, Felicity ( 2015): "Why We Need to Stand Up to Social Medias Outdated Rules on Censorship". In: i-d magazine. https://i-d.vice.com/en_gb/article/why-we-need-to-stand-up-to-social-medias-outdated-rules-on-censorship

Mayfield, Kerrita (2015): "Challenging the Ideal Female Form". In: *Pacific Standard*. http://www.psmag.com/books-and-culture/challenging-the-ideal-female-form

O'Neil, Lauren (2014): "#FreeTheNipple: Scout Willis goes topless in NYC to protest Instagram's nudity policy". CBCNews. http://www.cbc.ca/newsblogs/yourcommunity/2014/05/freethenipple-scout-willis-goes-topless-in-nyc-to-protest-instagrams-nudity-policy.html

Olszanowski, Magdalena (2014): "Feminist Self-Imaging and Instagram: Tactics of Circumventing Sensorship". In: Visual Communications Quarterly 21/2, pp. 83-95.

Raiss, Liz (2014): "How Social Media Censorship Impacts Self-Expression". In: The Fader. http://www.thefader.com/2014/12/23/6-creatives-on-the-consequences-of-social-media-censorship

Ridge, Hannah (2013): "Topless Women in Public Not Breaking the Law, Says NYPD". In: Mic. http://mic.com/articles/42359/topless-women-in-public-not-breaking-the-law-says-nypd

Ruiz, Rebecca (2015): "These women used social media to reclaim their bodies" In: Mashable. http://mashable.com/2015/03/23/women-empowerment-social-media/

Shapiro, Ezira (2012): "Network of 'Moderators' Decide What Photos Can Be Posted on Facebook, Google, Other Social Media". The Daily Beast. http://

www.thedailybeast.com/articles/2012/09/12/network-of-moderators-decide-what-photos-can-be-posted-on-facebook-google-other-social-media.html

Sigrun (2015): "Natural female bush gets shamed" Instagram censorship—A talk with Ainsley from Sticks and Stones Agency". In: C- heads Magazine. http://www.c-heads.com/2015/01/12/natural-female-bush-gets-shamed-instagram-cencorship-a-talk-with-ainsley-from-sticks-and-stones-agency/

Stoeffel, Kat (2013): "Instagram Censors Artistic Bush". In: The Cut. New York Magazine. http://nymag.com/thecut/2013/10/instagram-censors-artistic-bush.html

Taylor, Aleix (2014): "Your Concise Guide to Social Media's Female Nipple Policies". In: Hyperallergic. http://hyperallergic.com/131620/your-concise-guide-to-social-medias-female-nipple-policies/

Tsjeng, Zing (2015): "Why Instagram censored this image of an artist on her period". In: Dazed Digital. http://www.dazeddigital.com/artsandculture/article/24258/1/why-instagram-censored-this-image-of-an-artist-on-her-period

Vagianos, Alanna (2015): "Instagram Admits They 'Don't Always Get It Right' When It Comes To Nudity" In: Huffington Post. http://www.huffingtonpost.com/2015/01/21/instagram-pubic-hair-censorship-sticks-and-stones_n_6515654.html

Valenti, Jessica (2015): "Social media is protecting men from periods, breast milk and body hair". In. The Guardian. https://www.theguardian.com/commentisfree/2015/mar/30/social-media-protecting-men-periods-breast-milk-body-hair

Villenave, Samantha (2013): "The New Digital Puritans: Social Network Censorship #NSFW". In: Hyperallergic. http://hyperallergic.com/64648/the-new-digital-puritans-social-network-censorship-nsfw/

Weinstockh, Tish (2015): "Are #breastfeeding selfies the new #freethenipple?" In: ID-Magazine. https://i-d.vice.com/en_gb/article/are-breastfeeding-selfies-the-new-freethenipple

Willis, Scout (2014): "I Am Scout Willis And This Is The Only Thing I Have To Say About Walking Topless Down The Streets Of New York Last Week". In: XO Jane. http://www.xojane.com/issues/scout-willis-topless-instagram-protest

# Berlin. Wie bitte?[1]
## An Exploration of the Construction of Online Platforms for the Mutual Support of Young Spanish Immigrants in Berlin

*Teresa Tiburcio Jiménez*

The economic crisis that erupted in 2008 and spread throughout much of the global economy severely affected many countries in Europe, notably Spain. Unemployment rates soared and youth unemployment rates peaked at over 50 percent. These figures, together with the austerity measures agreed on by the Spanish Government, influenced the adjustment of employment regulations and prompted a mass exodus. Thousands of young people began their march to other countries, especially in Northern Europe and Latin America, to seek employment and better working conditions. Germany became one of the desirable destinations and, within Germany, Berlin was established as a favorable place. Given the high growth in the numbers of Spanish immigrants moving to Berlin, many of them highly influenced and inspired by the demonstrations against austerity measures that had spread through Europe in 2011 the Spanish community decided to organize and create networks of solidarity and mutual support. They shared common principles: self-management and assembly-based decision-making. Groups that were organizing themselves outside of public institutions made the internet their field of operation; this allowed them to experiment and create innovative civic alternatives.

With this research, I tried to understand the origin and evolution of these groups: What are their roots? What motivated members to participate? How do they work and operate, and how to they embody social innovation? I also sought to understand the extent to which the use of digital tools affects their daily practices and sociability. How do these groups create bridges between the "digital culture" and the daily interactions that constitute the group work in the city of Berlin? In order to answer these queries, I found a central question that constituted a starting point, an issue that underpins all the enquiries listed

---

**1** | My translation from German: 'Berlin, sorry, what did you say?".

above: What are the needs and everyday experiences of Spanish immigrants living in Berlin? Then subsequently, what alternatives or possible solutions have been created with the use of the internet?

My main objective in this research therefore was to locate the needs of Spanish immigrants living in Berlin and to understand how the collective groups created strategies and mechanisms to find and confront those needs. Additionally, there were two further issues that I considered in order to explore the phenomenon of Spanish migration to Berlin in depth. Firstly, I intended to describe how these groups make use of new information technologies and how their members integrate them into their daily activities. Secondly, I tried to understand the philosophy underlying the practice and to comprehend to what extent the ideological position of social actors influences the search for solutions to these needs.

## An Outline of the Field of Study

I will briefly outline the research context in order to answer some initial questions:

- What are the current studies around contemporary Spanish emigrants?
- What is the relationship between the country of departure and the economic crisis?
- What have been the main responses of the current Spanish Government, the political parties, the civic collectives and the media to Spanish migration?

In short, it is my aim to address the current phenomenon of Spanish migration, a topic that currently lacks institutional and academic study.

## How Many Leave? Are the Numbers Important?

In politics, the manipulation of figures is a commonly used weapon. A political entity can map out a certain political, economic and social landscape to suit particular interests, as in the case of migration, illustrated by the numbers below. As an example, in May 2015, the Spanish Prime Minister Mariano Rajoy from the People´s Party[2] (PP) stated that his opponent in parliament, Pedro

---

2 | The People´s Party(PP) has governed in Spain since 2011. In the political spectrum they are defined as center-right.

Sanchez of the Socialist Workers Party[3] (PSOE), had lied when he stated that 500,000 young Spanish people left the country during Rajoy's term in office (2011-2015). Rajoy quoted the National Statistics Institute's figure of "exactly 24,658" (Castro 2015). The PP parliamentarians applauded, but the war of numbers did not remain inside parliament; the People's Party launched a *Tweet*[4] within a week of the elections, comparing the data on migration provided by both main parties, and accusing the Socialist Party of lying.

*Image 1*

Really, have 523,358 young people emigrated? Who lies? Estimates of the Socialist Party: They have included immigrants between 18 and 35 years of age, regardless of nationality or country of birth [including German and Dutch students ...who came back to their respective countries]. (My translation)

---

**3** | The Spanish Socialist Workers Party (PSOE) is the main opposition to the PP, and is center-left.

**4** | https://twitter.com/PPopular

The journalist, Irene Castro, pointed out in a later analysis that from the beginning of the crisis, 1,200,000 people aged 18 to 35 left the country, and 550,000 of these did so during the mandate of Rajoy. Castro stated that her sources also belonged to the National Institute of Statistics and that the discrepancy in numbers stemmed from the way in which people were counted. Simultaneously, several newspapers debated the figures (Grasso 2013; García de Blas 2015), bloggers made their own estimations[5], and Spanish migrants discussed the shame of the Government statement on their *Facebook* and *Twitter* walls because they did not publicly accept that so many people were leaving the country.

Two months later, on June 25, 2015, *Marea Granate*[6] ("Garnet Tide")—a non-partisan public platform aiming to make visible the situation of Spanish migrants abroad—distributed a press release which included graphs and data published by other foreign statistical agencies. This information was widely disseminated across *Facebook*, *Twitter* and other social media. During the campaign they used the following hashtags: #cifrasINExactas ("inaccurate figures"), #Somosmas ("we are more"), and #nonosvamosnosechan ("we do not leave, they kick us out"). This press release accused the government of deliberately distorting the figures, using the National Institute of Statistics for their benefit and, in particular, "being proud of data that was completely falsified so as not to recognize the failure of their social and labor policies." (*Marea Granate* 2015. My translation)

---

**5** | Blog created by a civic group for the visibility of the new Spanish migration called: Así nos Vamos ("So We Go"). http://asinosvamos.es/
**6** | http://mareagranate.org/

*Image 2*

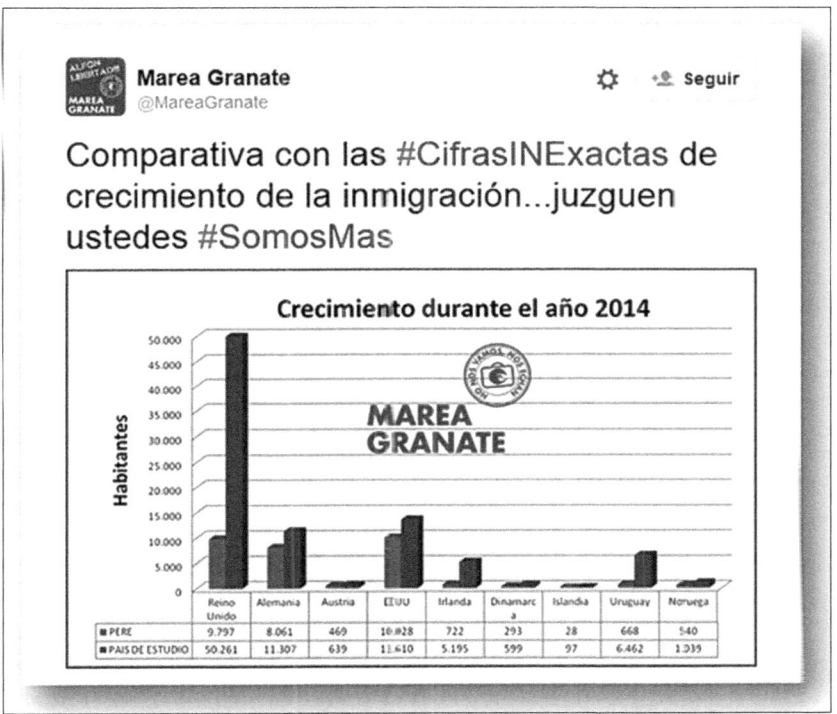

A comparison[7] of #*cifrasINExactas* figures for emigration growth. …judge for yourselves #*Somosmas*

Why did the President of the Spanish government use the data provided by the National Institute of Statistics, when even the institution itself recognized its limitations? What relationship, if any, could be identified between the statistics and the social aspects of the migration phenomenon? According to some authors (Alba et al. 2013; Ortega Rivera et al. 2014), the relationship lies in the use of terms such as *brain drain, migration, economic exile* and so on. These expressions are directly related to the economic crisis and the unemployment rate (23.8 percent overall, 51.4 percent under 25 years of age)[8] that, despite the famous austerity measures, has not improved.

---

7 | Vertical axis: The Register of Spaniards Resident Abroad (PERE: *Padrón de Españoles Residentes en el Extranjero*) data denoting total figures for emigration, set alongside the figures issued from statistical agencies for total number of Spanish immigrants in each country of destination. 2014.

8 | Data from the first quarter of 2015. http://www.datosmacro.com/paro-epa/espara

The official discourse is abstracted from the economic context in which the departures happen [...] Some commentators have noted how the governmental language that presents the new emigration as a positive phenomenon is an exercise of concealment, in a broader context of a kind of "newspeak" which confronts the brutal reality of the economic crisis and its effects.[9] (Alba et al. 2013: 33)

At this period in time, the Spanish media started to confirm that indeed: "We are leaving Spain." In turn, the magnification of the migration phenomenon in the mass media could well have encouraged the increase in departures, thus causing what Ortega et. al. (2014: 42) calls, the "self-fulfilling prophecy," something which many of those I interviewed perceived years ago.

María, a 30-year-old social scientist from Alicante—says: "Well, I noticed right away, because there comes a time when most of your friends have gone. And you realize that you too are not the exception to the rule. Almost all who were in Madrid have left. All. Berlin was not the only destination, we scattered throughout Europe."

## WHERE DO THEY GO? DESTINATION GERMANY. NO, SORRY, RATHER BERLIN

Why Germany? No, why Berlin? Our work is a project about a group of young people and their interaction with a particular city. Therefore, I think it important to consider briefly why they decided to migrate to Berlin. There are various attractions that this city offers, not only to young people from other countries, but also to young Germans. The relatively affordable rent, cultural attractions, and vibrant nightlife make Berlin a city that serves many purposes beyond the purely professional.

There are no specific studies on the current Spanish migration situation in Berlin today. There are, however some studies on the *Gastarbeiter*[10] that arrived during the 60s and 70s. In fact, one study conducted by Garcia Fernández (1965), anticipates Germany to be a country that young Spaniards will choose to emigrate to, although the language will pose a significant barrier (Ortega et al. 2014: 58). Fernández speaks of a "migratory psychosis," a kind of myth promoted by word of mouth through the media and the German authorities that actually helps to perpetuate this trend in migration. Navarrete (2014: 174) restates this theory and Alba Monteserín et al. (2013) agree.

---

**9** | My translation.
**10** | Immigrant workers invited to Germany in the 60s and 70s.

## WHO ARE WE? THE PRECARIOUS YOUTH

Unemployment rates do not seem to fully explain the rate of migration. Whilst the rate of unemployment in Spain is significant, there are deeper social-economical and structural reasons that also might explain why a person decides to leave a country. Santos Ortega (2006, 2013) and Antonio Muñoz (2014, 2015) are two Spanish scholars who have most recently written on the subject. Their stance is critical. They believe that, on the one hand, mass media plays a huge role in generating a certain level of social alarm, as already noted above. On the other hand, it promotes the idea of better working conditions for Spanish emigrants abroad, which also plays an important part in the decision making process. What is important and remarkable about their analysis is their finding that large labor companies—in collusion with universities and governments—educate, create and plan a hyper-flexible, highly qualified and mobile workforce, which is perfectly conditioned for job insecurity.

The clearest effects of this narrative of labor activation is the attempt to legitimize the forced departure of the country (the so-called brain drain), making it appear as part of a cosmopolitanism that increases employability, a kind of investment in themselves the young people who leave in search of a job.[11] (Santos Ortega/Muñoz Rodríguez 2015: 659)

These authors argued that the narrative used to boost departures and thus reduce youth unemployment levels is camouflaged, so that it does not appear as an economic and social necessity but rather an "opportunity" that should not be missed, even something for which to be grateful. These authors emphasize the need to rethink the dynamics of today's labor market system because:

These "young," that seemingly had everything, turned their pockets out on the table and showed they were not only empty, but also had structural holes: a labor market that penalizes them, a property market that ignores them and, ultimately, a social and political construction that naturalizes the link between youth and vital precariousness.[12] (Santos Ortega/Muñoz Rodríguez 2015: 653)

To conclude this chapter, I would like to state that, beyond the age considerations and the current configuration of statistics, seeking profiles to accurately outline the actual migration process could be illusory and outdated because the phenomenon develops and transmutes over time. The assumed and obsolete categories of age, and issues around job insecurity, mean that we are not

---

**11** | My translation.
**12** | My translation.

alert to a significant number of the migration population. In this essay I have considered those subjects that I think are useful, not necessarily with regard to understanding the migration phenomenon in its entirety, but those that I think will contribute to outlining a small but key area of immigration, in line with the objectives set out in the introduction.

## THE ONLINE PLATFORMS

The internet may, at times, seem like an incomprehensible, quasi-infinite universe composed of texts, images, videos, memes, likes, hashtags, etc.; it is like a hyperactive factory producing an ever-expanding culture, as well as complex behavioral dynamics. In view of this, it is necessary to draw on important anthropological concepts in an attempt to give some order to this nebulous universe.

Manuel Castells (2007; 2009; 2012), Boellstorff (2008; 2012), Hine (2000) and Daniel Miller (2011; 2012) have all contributed a great deal to this expansive and complex area of investigation. A series of concepts have helped to develop our approach to the internet as a field of study. These were also vital in the development of ethnography more generally. However, in recent years this field has undergone a renewal process (Postill 2008; Ardèvol 2014; Miller 2011), especially in matters such as digital culture and the virtual community. These new theoretical frameworks invite us to seek new strategies and analytical alternatives. In order to find approaches that go beyond the online/offline dichotomous perspective (Estalella 2011), I decided to dedicate this chapter to the specific platforms and theoretical approaches in which my field of exploration takes root. I want to show that this field of research goes beyond the online/offline dichotomy, demonstrating the hybridity of technological culture and space.

Since the internet is immense, we should narrow the arena, not in order to create permanent and immovable boundaries, but to present an overview of the field of exploration and get a sense of where the lines blur. To do this, I rely on a concept developed by Sarah Pink in her book, *Doing Sensory Ethnography* (2009). I also rely on the concept of "ethnographic place" (Postill/Pink 2012), which deals with understanding how the ethnographer uses terms such as "routines," "mobilities" and "socialities," as opposed to the more traditional terms of "virtual community" and/or "network." The main aim of this approach is to understand "how social media ethnography produces 'ethnographic places' that traverse online/offline contexts and are collaborative, participatory, open and public" (Postill/Pink 2012:124). Digital technology is not limited to a computer screen or smartphone and the offline interaction is decisive when it comes to understanding what the screens reflect and mean for each user. It is important for us to understand that "techno-social spaces" are hybrid spaces in which technology is embedded in the everyday life of its users (Dominguez-Figaredo 2012). Therefore, my "ethnographic place" is not only comprised of digital spaces such as websites, social networks—such as *Facebook* and *Twitter*—and mailing lists; it is also those areas where face-to-face interaction occurs, such as in assemblies, cafés and at street meetings. These civic platforms are delimited; that is to say they are not just a physical or digital space, but "a scattered constellation of practices-idea-people-objects sharing common principles"[13] (Corsín, cited by Dominguez-Figaredo 2012: 205).

From here onwards, I will refer to these *techno-social spaces* as "platforms" for two reasons. First, because they are civic platforms in the traditional sense—they are comprised of a group of people who share common social-political principles and goals. Second, because the social actors themselves have so referred to these spaces as platforms.

## A Presentation of the Online Platforms: Our Ethnographic Place

I will now present the civic platforms founded by Spanish immigrants in Berlin, on which I have chosen to base my study. As stated before, there is a certain set of principles and related practices shared by those who interact with these platforms. Also of note is the point in time in which these platforms were created, namely the 2011 Spanish uprising. This is when the social movement, 15 *de Mayo* ("15th of May") aka *Toma la Plaza* ("Take the Square"), or #spanishrevolution, began.

The 15M movement—or *Indignados* ("the Indignant")—that began in the Plaza de Sol[14] in Madrid in 2011, was a spontaneous social movement. It was the catalyst in creating many other citizen initiatives that are active today. This social movement attracted interest on many levels, in part because of the wide use of recent technological developments. It used various social media sites on the internet to organize groups issuing various social demands; this helped to realize the potential of the anti-austerity movement across Europe (Flesher Fominaya/Cox 2013). Another remarkable feature of this movement is that it based itself on the model of the *open assembly*. This means, theoretically, that anyone and everyone who wants can join it and partake in the "consensus" decision-making process (Castells 2012: 133-136; Corsin/Estalella 2013). Here I

---

**13** | My translation.
**14** | Puerta del Sol is one of the central squares of the city of Madrid—epicenter and heart of the city. The square and its name has become a symbol that can be compared to Syntagma Square in Athens or Taksim Square in Istanbul.

highlight three key authors and their work, partly because of the volume they have published in this field of work, but also to reinforce the importance of the internet in the development of this social movement: John Postill (2013; 2014a; 2014b; 2015), who was in Barcelona during the birth of the 15M Movement; Javier Toret (2013), who is a researcher at the internet Interdisciplinary Institute (IN3) and also led a thorough investigation into the 15M; and finally Manuel Castells (2012), who wrote a monograph devoted to the internet and, in particular, the social movements of 2011.

As context for this field of study I will trace a brief outline of events that occurred in Spain, 2011. On May 15, two civic platforms: *Juventud sin futuro* ("Youth Without Future") and *Democracia real ¡Ya!* ("Real Democracy, Now!"), called a protest meeting at the Puerta del Sol in Madrid. The main slogans at the demonstration were: "We are not merchandise in the hands of politicians and bankers"[15] and "Real Democracy, Now!"[16] Following the official end of the demonstration, a small but significant number of people decided to remain and camp in the square, similar to the way they had witnessed the Egyptians do in Tahrir Square. The Police responded by detaining some of the protestors. Following this decision, many took to the various social networking sites to appeal to the Spanish people to occupy squares in their resident cities. More than 50 Spanish cities responded to the call, leading to major unrest throughout Spain. After more than a month of occupation, the various assemblies established official ties with each other. This was achieved with the use of the internet. These assemblies decided to leave the permanent camps in order to continue working on the growth and solidification of the movement throughout the country and by the time the protestors had left the square, the movement had established various stable civic platforms in different parts of the country, with different concerns such as health, education and emigration.[17]

The hashtags: *#spanishrevolution* and *#tomalaplaza* went viral. In Spain, activists spread the call for mobilization to Spanish communities in other countries, encouraging them to demonstrate at the doors of Spanish Embassies. In Berlin, as in other cities, Spanish citizens heeded the call to mobilize and, following the example of what was being done in Madrid, Barcelona, and Seville, called for demonstrations at the Brandenburg Gate. *Twitter*, *Facebook* and *Livestream* were used as a means of showing support for what was taking place on the streets of Spain. This also meant that the actions of the movement were highlighted abroad.

---

**15** | My translation.
**16** | My translation.
**17** | These platforms are known as Mareas ("Tides") and each is represented by a color.

We followed from the beginning what was going on in the Plaza de Sol because we were watching the interviews. People keep a close eye on the media in Spain. People living elsewhere ...looking online at their country of origin. Then following events, as if we too are almost in the same place with them; as if in Alicante, Barcelona or Seville. –María, social scientist, 30 years old, from Alicante. (My translation)

The 15M Movement was instrumental in the development of the current civic platforms at work in the Spanish community in Berlin, and this is evidenced by the fact that the members of the civic platforms recognize the part played by the demonstrations in Spain in forming their own support groups.

At the beginning, the Oficina Precaria (Office Precarious) was named "Berlin, Wie bitte?" (Berlin, sorry, what did you say?). La Oficina Precaria was founded as a product of the concerns and interests of 15M. After a while, we have decided to become Precarious Office using the pull that other "precarious offices" have in Europe. We discussed if we were still part of 15M as collective and in an assembly we decided to continue being part of 15M. – Rosa, historian and web content writer, 32 years old, Valencia. (My translation)

Well, the Grupo de Acción Sindical (Labor Action Group) is a working group of 15M Berlin. I went there because it seemed interesting too. Because I find the workers' struggle interesting, I was keen to gain experience there. I also thought it was a very good extension to 15M Berlin Assembly. – Rafa, Ph.D. candidate, 28 years old, Madrid. (My translation)

## 15M BERLIN

15M Berlin is a non-partisan, horizontal self-managed and feminist political group whose main goal is the political coordination of immigration from Spain in its fight against the effects of capitalism. Likewise, it's involved locally in other issues affecting the whole society such as the fight for housing rights and the reporting of labor exploitation.[18]

On their website, 15M Berlin outlines the main working groups of the organization.[19] They also publicize the topics from both past and forthcoming meetings, as well as the decisions taken at each meeting. They also publish the work that each member has to carry out together with the list of general

---

**18** | https://www.facebook.com/Berlin15M/info?tab=page_info
**19** | http://15mberlin.com/

organizational activities—ranging from demonstrations and lectures, to media campaigns.

This group is actively involved in local Berlin politics, which means they support events organized by other groups in the city alongside their work to generate policy initiatives that deal directly with Spain and the fight against austerity measures and job insecurity.

15M Berlin has a presence on the major social networks like *Facebook* and *Twitter*.[20] Through social networking websites they share events, spread media campaigns, and publish articles, videos, and pictures etc. that may be of interest to those following them. They also work to generate publicity for events and information created by other similar groups.

The 15M Berlin Assembly meets every two weeks in the Sama-Café (a collective based in the neighborhood of Friedrichshain). The meetings are announced via *Facebook*, with the creation of a *Facebook Event*. Here, they specify the main talking points of an imminent meeting and nominate the person who will moderate the discussion. 15M Berlin also uses a mailing list, which consistently sends out several messages daily.[21] Through this mailing list, many other issues are discussed, along with being the means to give notification of general organizational activities.

## OFICINA PRECARIA

The *Oficina Precaria* formerly "Berlin, wie bitte," is a working group of 15M Berlin. It is "a platform of support and information to accompany you in your experience as an immigrant. You can consult us about bureaucratic, legal, labor, Krankenkasse, general information about Berlin...We are here to help.[22]

This division also emerged as a working group of 15M Berlin. It organizes consultations each week in Friedrichshain. They are the members of a collective who work to inform others about issues of particular concern to immigrants. They give advice on various issues; the website has six main sections: *Hartz IV* (social assistance), *Wohngeld* (housing benefit), *Krankenkasse* (social security), *Administration* (registration, debts, bank accounts, recognition of qualifications, etc.), *Personal Advice* and a specific section on *Labor Rights*.

---

20 | https://twitter.com/acampadaberlin
21 | I am subscribed and I usually receive around ten e-mails per day.
22 | https://www.facebook.com/oficinaprecariaberlin?fref=ts

*Image 3*

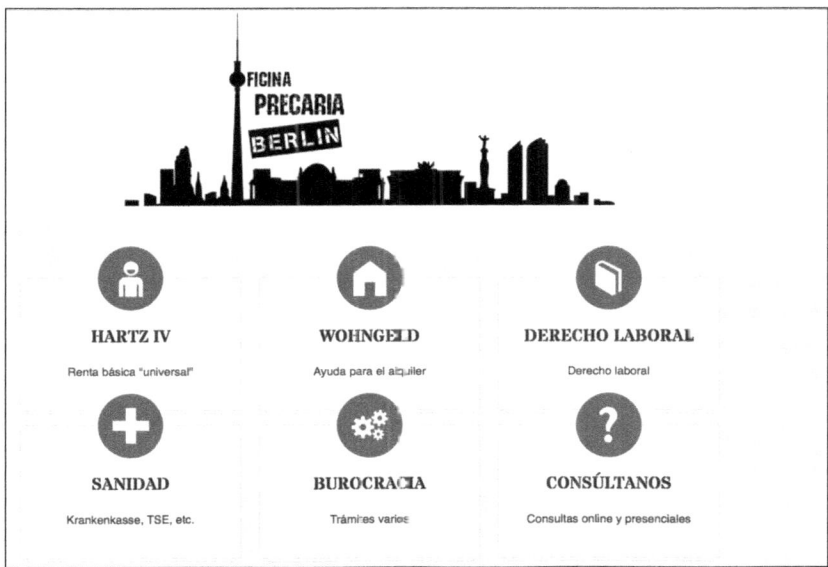

Icons on the main page of the *Oficina Precaria* website. (http://oficinaprecariaberlin.org/)

The *Oficina Precaria* website provides information on all the documents you might need on entry into Germany and all the bureaucratic procedures required in order to become resident. It outlines, for example, the necessary procedure for registration in a city in Germany. It explains exactly what type of documents that are needed, where to apply and what numbers to call when trying to make an appointment. The information is quite meticulous, even describing in detailed steps how to use the local council website for any particular need. Translations of relevant forms are available to download.

This platform exists in a broader network of replicas scattered throughout Europe. The network is called *Precariedad Everywhere* ("Everywhere precariousness"). Clicking on an area reveals a link to the location and opening times of the different offices in Europe.

## Grupo de Acción Sindical (GAS)

The Labor Action Group is an internationalist movement. They help migrant workers of every country to improve their working conditions, along with their German co-workers and with the support of German unions. They fight against wage dumping, exploitation and discrimination. Stand up for your rights and those of the working class as a whole![23]

GAS is a labor union that operates independently of institutions in either Germany or Spain. It arose out of the high demand for labor support. "Oficina Precaria" realized that some of the demands of individual immigrant workers required a "collective solution" (Trabajar en Alemania, 2014). In Spain they were released to appear in a TV program, well-known for its political analysis (Pastor 2015).[24]

Image 4

Screenshot of Spanish television program *El Objetivo*. Members of GAS and "Oficina Precaria" are interviewed by the journalist Ana Pastor.

---

**23** | http://www.accionsindical.org/
**24** | http://www.atresplayer.com/television/programas/el-objetivo/temporada-3/capitulo-24-objetivo-alemania_2015031400185.html

*Image 5*

In Germany, GAS became known for an article published in the *Süddeutsche Zeitung* (Stremmel 2014).[25] Young Spaniards are lured, by the hundreds, into the German Care sector. There they find lousy working conditions and restrictive contracts. In Berlin they are now coming together in resistance.[26]

I posed the question in an interview: What made GAS relatively well known in Germany and Spain?

I do not know, did many interviews. I cannot tell now, but 30 or 40 had or offered. We did not give supply. We called on all sides for us to give interviews. [...] We had to adapt ourselves because we had no time, so there are things that did not go in the end but many other. Süddeutsche Zeitung interview had much effect. From there it was a nonstop. -Mayte, Translator, 30 years old, Murcia. (My translation)

---

**25** | http://jetzt.sueddeutsche.de/texte/anzeigen/589582/zu-Gast-bei-Ausbeutern
**26** | My translation.

GAS meets every two weeks at Café Commune in Kreuzberg. Immigrants who want to present their cases are invited to do so at these gatherings. Once the "conflict" is clear, the group discusses what can be done and how they can organize around a specific case to achieve a particular goal. Their current campaigns range from fighting for a group of nurses—who have an unfair contract and are currently being forced to pay a fine of 12,000 euros—to supporting the claims of truck drivers, and giving advice, in Berlin and Brandenburg.

In a similar way to 15M Berlin, GAS also has a major online presence, utilizing the social network sites such as *Twitter* and *Facebook*, to share all kinds of information on the labor situation in Germany and Spain, as well as other campaigns, with which they identify and support. As an example, they openly supported the "No" campaign in the Greek referendum.

## THE CONSTRUCTION OF THE DIGITAL COMMONS

In this section, I will explain a number of the conceptual tools I applied while analyzing the qualitative data in search of a synthesis. These theoretical approaches have been very useful in that they have fostered a tighter focus on the aspects most interesting to me and most relevant for the research.

First, as noted above, we outlined a *hybrid techno-social space* where online and offline perspectives merge. People involved in these platforms not only interact in the Network, but also regularly participate in face-to-face events. We must therefore understand and address the practices and behavior of this group based on its hybrid characteristic and its ability to move from one space to another. We must also add an extra dimension to this group's hybrid character: its transnational nature (Schiller 2012). This could be understood as what Bernal (2006) has called "transnational third space." Why? Because besides being a hybrid space, the Network is also a "place in which geopolitical boundaries are blurred, which encourages experimentation and the creation of new socio-political practices." These spaces are liminal zones where creativity is significant. I consider this experimental and creative characteristic very interesting as a focus for data analysis. As a main focus, I am able to observe the social realities and perspectives of the social actors and understand how they are able to generate innovative behavioral dynamics. In this case, the social actors map their own needs; they conceptualize the problems they face every day, share and discuss experiments together with the results and new alternatives or possible solutions to their problems. All of these processes are carried out collectively, and they use strategies based on *asamblearismo* (Corsin/ Estalella 2013), a term which is difficult to translate but involves the act of taking decisions by consensus and the means of self-organization in an attempt to stay out of public and private institutions. The fact that the platforms operate outside of institutions is not accidental. Many of the people with whom I spoke feel ignored by public institutions. The sharing of daily experiences and the feelings of empathy that occur in this "third space" is something that neither the market nor the state provides.

What is meant by the alleged ineffectiveness of state institutions in this context? In order to offer a better understanding, I refer to another concept that I considered during my research. The exchange of information and knowledge circulating in this alternative transnational third-space is termed by some authors as *commons* (Ostrom 1990 cited in Lafuente/Corsín Jiménez 2010). This term outlines the ways in which a group of people decide to manage the resources necessary for survival in any given context. These resources are not treated as privately owned and so cannot be capitalized, and cannot "evoke the imagery of exclusion, but of cooperation" (Lafuente/Corsín 2010: 24). In this "alternative market" *commons* circulate in a space that is governed by the logic of collective organization and the principles of self-management. These last two attributes are essential for platform's members as, for them, "what runs is not something [cheap or expensive] or a value [fair or unfair], but the community" (Lafuente/Corsín 2010: 34).

In such a space, the circulation of resources and the various mechanisms for their distribution should be carried out without the limitations of pricing and/or valuing: "the economy that regulates these exchanges bases its success on the ability to meet needs. It is not oriented to individual benefit. Possession of something, whether an object, conjecture or formula implies exchange because he only owns what is shared" (Corsín 2010: 25).[27]

In this situation, the concept of *commons* is all a very useful one, based on the qualitative information gathered on the experiences of the participants of these civic platforms. Online platforms are not only spaces, in which *commons* are put into circulation; they are also where the production mechanisms are created and reinvented. In this *third space* all kinds of valid resources are in circulation: views, opinions, experiences, frustrations, fears, knowledge (Rocha et al. 2013).

The *common* I try to understand also has various particular features. The first is that it caters to the specific needs of a particular people belonging to a moment in history, namely those Spanish immigrants living in Berlin, Germany following the recession of 2008. The second peculiarity, is that it is a *digital common* (Fuster 2011; 2012) because it involves the "sharing and collaborative production of common resources [...] [and] open access in the digital environment" (2012: 229) and therefore its production and distribution in the Network has a determining value.

---

**27** | My translation.

## Conclusion

My primary objective was to understand the needs of Spanish immigrants living in Berlin. When mapping needs I did not do so based solely on personally chosen participants, but rather on solutions and alternatives to these needs these groups suggested and established. I did so because in this way I could establish a situation analysis that was more representative and comprehensive, since the very function of these groups was to conceptualize needs and offer possible solutions. The needs I observed went beyond bureaucratic, linguistic or monetary difficulties. I witnessed and heard of the frustration, guilt, and loneliness that many experienced. We often only see the basic necessities of a people; the psychological and/or emotional components are not always given the importance they deserve. In this regard, we see that needs are interrelated. Not having contacts to help you fill in a document because you do not know the language can result in loneliness. Having a "mini-job"[28] for which you are overqualified can generate frustration. If an employer hires you and pays you less than you deserve, this can give way to indignation. The groups I studied took into account these less visible emotional needs and, through campaign work, they opened up a debate and delved into what they believed to be the core problem.

Regarding the sense of belonging to a community, it is impossible to avoid the idea of community when discussing the online platforms and the people who interact on them. Whether you are a consummate activist or a sometime user, the participants involved are socialized and build on this feeling of belonging to a group. I observed a number of things that can perhaps bring to light the various elements of this particular community.

A shared nationality was not fundamental to this community; it is true that the vast majority of those participating on the platforms were Spanish, but there were many people with whom I spoke who identified as independent militants—mainly from Cataluña and the Basque Country—as well as other independent movements. Some activists and users were of German and/or Latin descent, or other EU countries, that had previously lived in Spain and had also decided to emigrate to Germany because of the crisis. The issue of language was, however, a shared aspect of the community.

I observed a variety of ideological perspectives whilst carrying out my research and, while I would not want to reduce down all the perspectives to one main ideology, it is true that many perspectives were of the political left. There were also, however, people who did not claim to be of any political persuasion

---

28 | Mini-job contracts are jobs with a maximum of 50 days per year and gaining a maximum of 450 euros. This kind of contract has been modified in 2015. Now 8,50 euros per hour must be charged for time worked and social insurance is required.

and who were highly involved. Notably, as stressed before, two basic principles defined the character of the collective: self-management and an assembly-based political system. Both principles belong to, and are influenced by, leftist social movements. These principles materialize in the practices that seem logical and practical at organizational level; they do not seem routed in political or ideological dogma.

I believe that the main bonding element of the group is empathy. It is this element that apparently provides the strength and structure to the community. Nationality, language and ideology shape the profile of the collective but, in my opinion, in these spaces, what unites the participants is the sharing of needs and related difficulties experienced. The desire to find common resolution— with the basis of shared empathy—is really what generates a sense of unity and community.

The use of the internet as a fundamental tool has been critical in my research. In this research I have had to reject the offline/online dichotomy and emphasize the hybrid nature of this community. The question I asked in the introduction was how the various platforms I looked at used the internet to alleviate the needs of immigrants in Berlin; I have since carried out thorough analysis in order to describe this process. The internet is not only a tool through which useful information is circulated, it is a space in itself in which users are constantly interacting with each other, sharing information stories and opinions. As explained above, one of the values of the internet is not only the sharing and managing of information, but also the fact that it provides the tools for knowledge production. The example of how to write press releases collectively is a good example. Use of the internet complements the principles of self-management and an assembly-based political system. It facilitates these principles at an operational level—because it is used to carry out collective work—but also at a political level—because members can "own" means and methods of knowledge production and dissemination. This is what gives autonomy to operate effectively outside public institutions.

Locating and understanding the needs of immigrants, creating a community through empathy, and using and developing digital tools in order to generate and disseminate useful information for immigrants, has ensured the creation of effective mechanisms of support. This creation and reinvention of a "digital commons," had meant that many more immigrants have been able to share common problems and seek collective solutions in a dynamic and creative way. The collaborative production of common resources, accessible to all via digital means, has not only helped immigrants in their practical daily lives but also in their emotional daily lives: feelings of frustration loneliness, guilt and individuality have all been mitigated and channeled through the community. From simple things—like the translation of documents—to the more complex, such as the exchange of emotions, experiences, opinions etc.

the digital commons has helped to alleviate the daily pressures of immigrant life.

In short, the main resource of the community is knowledge. Knowledge is jointly produced and released via the Web, where it is built upon. As knowledge is collectively created, it has no owner; it is not private property, nor does it belong to the state. It is in itself a collective good, circulating and representing the whole community (Lafuente/Corsín 2010: 34).

However, there are a series of questions that I cannot, or have failed to, address in this study. We must ask whether the action taken on these platforms affects those who do not partake in them. That is to say: does this online community have relevance to the whole community of Spanish immigrants in Berlin, including those who do not share identical political perspectives, or who do not use the internet in a similar way?

Regarding the resolution of needs, it is clear, at a practical level, they are covered. For example, if advice is needed regarding an employment contract then there is immediately access to relevant information to be found through "Oficina Precaria." However, it reveals the question whether the discourse and narrative generated by these groups is having broader impact beyond the computer screen. That is to say, how does what happens in this community impact on wider political discourse? For example, how does it have an impact on the job market and education system of today? Does it merely empower members or is it a reflection of what we might become? The essential question is: can these platforms change daily life in a lasting way? I wonder if participation within this community makes members feel that they can take control of their future can create real social change.

The above-mentioned point has not only to do with the individual practice of social actors but also in relation to the effect that their own practices can have on the decision-making process in public and/or private institutions. Can the work of these groups influence the policies of government agencies at different levels, whether in the political or economic sphere? I believe my research will be helpful for future questions in this area of study for two main reasons:

First, the qualitative analysis of the digital space, from the perspective of its hybrid character, represents a new trend in digital ethnography. My work involved a consistent attempt at maintaining a balance between exploring the offline and online world, making sense of the hybridity of these two worlds and exploring new methodologies and theories in participant-observation in a digital space.

Second, this research is highly socially relevant. Not only does it explore the digital space, it explores self-organized initiatives within this space. It could prove useful for further studies that, as a consequence, have impact on decision-making, especially when considering integration policies and new waves of immigration. This could contribute not only to decision-making at an institutional level, but also to new immigrant groups that might base their organization on new media technologies.

Finally, and most importantly, I think it helps to steer the gaze and consider a generation in which new technologies, combined with new social proposals forged in times of crisis, form a new political and social landscape. Likely it is not a complete picture, but simply an attempt to understand the current situation of thousands of young migrants—not only Spanish, and not only in Berlin—from a global perspective that transcends, and provokes us to rethink, the current situation of labor markets and citizen's alternatives to our current political-economic system.

## REFERENCES

Alba Monteserín, Susana/Fernández, Ana/Martínez Vega, Ubaldo (2013): "Crisis Migratoria y Nuevo Panorama Migratorio en España." In: Fundación 1 de Mayo. Centro de documentación de las migraciones.

Ardèvol, Elisenda (2014): "Visualidades y Materialidades de lo Digital: Caminos Desde la Antropología." In: Anthropologica 33, pp.11-38.

Behar, Ruth (2002):"Ethnography and the Book That Was Lost." In: Ethnography, 4/1, pp. 15-39.

Bernal, Victoria (2006): "Diaspora, Cyberspace and Political Imagination: the Eritrean Diaspora Online." In: Global Networks, 6/2, pp.161–79.

Castells, Manuel (2007): "Communication, Power and Counter-Power in the Network Society." In: International Journal of Communication 1, pp. 238-266.

Castells, Manuel (2009): Comunicación y Poder, Madrid: Alianza Editorial.

Castells, Manuel (2012): Networks of Outrage and Hope. Social Movements in the Internet Age, Cambridge: Polity Press.

Corsin, Alberto/Estalella, Adolfo (2013): "Asambleas al aire: la arquitectura ambulatoria de una política en suspensión." In: Revista de Antropología Experimental, pp. 3-88.

Domínguez-Figaredo, Daniel (2012): "Hybrid Scenarios, Transmedia Storytelling. Expanded Ethnography." In: Revista de Antropología Social 21, pp. 197-215.

ElConfidencial.com. "Casi dos millones de personas han dejado España en cuatro años por la crisis" August 14, 2013 http://www.elconfidencial.com/espana/2013-08-14/casi-dos-millones-de-personas-han-dejado-espana-en-cuatro-anos-por-la-crisis_17666/

ElDiario.es "Rajoy olvida a 500.720 jóvenes que han emigrado durante su mandato", May 13, 2015 http://www.eldiario.es/politica/Rajcy-olvida-jovenes-emigrado-mandato_0_387411724.html

ElPais.com "¿Cuántos jóvenes han emigrado? ¿24.000 o 500.000?" May 13, 2015 http://politica.elpais.com/politica/2015/05/13/actualidad/1431517709_288571.html

Estalella, Adolfo (2011): Ensamblajes de Esperanza. Un Estudio Antropológico del Bloggear Apasionado. Barcelona: Universitat Oberta de Catalunya.

Flesher Fominaya, C. /Cox, L. (2013): Understanding European Movements. New Social Movements, Global Justice Struggles, Anti-Austerity Protest, London: Routledge.

Fuster, Mayo (2011): "Acción Colectiva a Través de Redes Online: Comunidades de Creación Online para la Construcción de Bienes Públicos Digitales." In: Redes, 6, pp. 229-247.

Fuster, Mayo (2012): "The Free Culture and 15M Movements in Spain: Composition, Social Networks and Synergies." In: Social Movement Studies, 11/3-4.

Hine, Christine (2000): Virtual Ethnography. London: Sage Publications.

Lafuente, Antonio/Corsín, Alberto (2010): "Comunidades de Afectados, Procomún y don Expandido." In: Fractal 57, pp. 17-42.

Marea Granate: "No nos Vamos nos Echan." June 25, 2015 http://mareagranate.org/2015/06/el-gobierno-minimiza-deliberadamente-los-datos-de-la-emigracion-espanola/

Miller, Daniel (2011): Tales from Facebook, Cambridge: Polity Press.

Miller, Daniel (2012): "Social Networking Sites." In: Heather. A. Horst/Daniel Miller, Digital Anthropology, London: Berg, pp. 146-164..Navarrete, Lorenzo (2014): La emigración de los Jóvenes españoles en el contexto de la crisis. Análisis y datos de un fenomeno difícil de cuantificar. In: Observatorio de la Juventud en España. Madrid: Servicio de Documentación y Estudios.

Ortega, Enrique, Domingo, Andreu/ Sabater, Alberto (2014): "¿Neo-Hispanic Migration? The Impact of the Economic Recession on Spanish Emigration." In: EMPIRIA. Revista de Metodología de Ciencias Sociales 29, pp. 39-66.

Pink, Sarah (2009): Doing Sensory Ethnography, London: Sage.

Postill, John (2008): "Localizing the Internet." In: New Media and Society, 10/3, pp 413-431.

Postill, John (2013): "Participatory Media Research and Spain's 15M Movement." In: Cultural Anthropology website, February 14, 2013. https://culanth.org/fieldsights/86-participatory-media-research-and-spain-s-15m-movement

Postill, John (2014): Democracy in an Age of Viral Reality: a Media Epidemiography of Spain's Indignados Movement Ethnography." In: Ethnography, 15/1, pp. 50-68.

Postill, John (2014): "Spain's Indignados and the Mediated Aesthetics of Nonviolence." In: Pnina Webner/Martin Webb/ Kathryn Spellman-Poots (eds.), The Political Aesthetics of Global Protest: Beyond the Arab Spring, Edinburgh: Edinburgh University Press, pp. 141-167.

Postill, John (2015):"Field Theory, Media Change and the New Citizen Movements: the Case of Spain's 'Real Democracy Turn' 2011–2014." *John Postill's Website*, March 2. http://johnpostill.com/2015/03/05/14-field-theory-media-change-and-the-new-citizen-movements

Postill, John/Pink, Sarah (2012): "Social Media Ethnography: The Digital Researcher in a Messy Web." In: Media International Australia 145/1, pp. 123-134.

Rocha, Jara/Lafuente, Antonio/Estalella, Adolfo (2013): "Laboratorios de Procomún: Experimentación, Recursividad y Activismo." In: Revista Teknokultura, 10/1, pp. 21–48.

Santos, Antonio/Muñoz, David (2014): "Hoy es el Futuro. De la Activación Universitaria a las Respuestas Colectivas." In: Revista de la Asociación de Sociología de la Educación, 3/7, pp. 658-673.

Santos, Antonio/Muñoz, David (2015): "Brain Drain and Low Cost Biographies: The New Era in the Precarization of Youth." In: Recerca, Revista de pensament i anàlisi 16, pp. 16-33.

Toret, Javier (2013): Tecnopolítica:la Potencia de las Multitudes Conectadas. El Sistema Red 15M, un Nuevo Paradigma de la Política Distributiva, Barcelona: Internet Interdisciplinary Institute (IN3).

Trabajar en Alemania, (2014): http://trabajar-en-alemania.es/entrevista-carlos-aparicio-del-grupo-accion-sindical-gas

# An Exploration of the Role of *Twitter* in the Discourse Around Race in South Africa
Using the *#Feesmustfall* Movement as a Pivot for Discussion

Suzanne Beukes

## Introduction

The ongoing protest against fee increases at the University of Witwatersrand is not about the whim and fancy of students who feel entitled to a free ride. It is about the ongoing struggle of black youth to secure a future unencumbered by the burdens of a history of disadvantage. [1]

In a highly political post-apartheid South Africa, the promise of a truly, non-racialized society remains largely unrealized (Haffajee 2015: 11). After 22 years of democracy, South Africans are facing a multitude of socio-economic and political challenges. These include a depressed economy, a growing lack of confidence in the political liberation party of the African National Congress party (ANC) as well as a large youth population demanding better access to their basic rights and jobs (Malala 2015: 11). In addition, as Jan Hofmeyr and Rajen Govender (2016: 1) illustrate in the South African Reconciliation Barometer—measuring reconciliation, social cohesion, transformation and democratic governance—there is a growing distrust among racial groups.

As a result, there is a heightened intensity to the discourse around race, inequality, and transformation in South Africa; and to, what is described by interviewees participating in this research as, a "shift in consciousness" or a "psychic purge."

Over the past two years, *Twitter* has increasingly become a platform for previously marginalized groups such as young black South Africans; serving

---

[1] | The Daily Vox (2015): "Special editorial: The Wits protest is not just about university fees." http://www.thedailyvox.co.za/special-editorial-the-wits-protest-is-not-just-about-university-fees/

to convene, organize, channel arguments and influence public action around issues such as race.[2]

By using *#FeesMustFall*—one of the largest civic movements in South Africa since 1994 and also one of the largest events on *Twitter* in 2015—as a pivot for discussion, I aim to explore how *Twitter* played a role in this so called "change in psyche."

In her book, "What If There Were Not Whites in South Africa?" Ferial Haffajee (2015) has described the broader impact of the movement: "*#FeesMustFall* is about much more than fees—it's about freedom's unfinished work and its soldiers are the children of that freedom; it is also about choices the democratic state has made" (ibid: 162).

To address such a multi-layered movement which incorporates issues of access to higher education, structural racism, colonialism, white privilege, and inequality (ibid: 163) acutely experienced by young black South Africans, I drew on anthropological works from Yamar Bonilla and Jonathan Rosa's (2015) "#Ferguson: Digital Protest, Hashtag Ethnography, and the Racial Politics of Social Media in the United States," as well as Sanjay Sharma's (2013) "Black Twitter? Racial Hashtags, Networks and Contagion."

As the movement resonated across multiple platforms on social media, mainstream media, and physical protest action, I also referred to John Postill and Sarah Pink's (2012) article: *Social Media Ethnography: the Digital Researcher in a Messy Web*, which explored how "Social media ethnography produces 'ethnographic places' that traverse online/offline contexts and are collaborative, participatory, open and public" (ibid: 2).

While detailed demographic data about *Twitter* users in South Africa was not immediately available at the time of research, I have drawn from available resources such as the Social Media Landscape 2015 report, produced by technology market research organisations World Wide Works and Fuseware. The work is supplemented with interviews from South African social media researchers Arthur Goldstuck (managing director of World Wide Works) and Kyle Findlay (a data science researcher).

## METHODOLOGY

As a white South African, I have long believed that many white South Africans remain largely ignorant about the real struggles and discrimination still experienced by black South Africans. In 2016 through social media, it seemed to me that suddenly the floodgates around issues of white privilege, inequality, racism and ignorance opened up in the public sphere whereas before these

---

**2** | Interview with Kyle Findlay, March 2016.

issues were mainly discussed in homes and social circles of black and white communities separately. Social media, particularly *Twitter*, has played an important role in opening up these conversations.

Tracking a wave of conversations around race on social media, especially *Twitter*, led me to explore related links to conversations and articles. Mainstream media in South Africa, such as the *Daily Maverick*,[3] *The Citizen*,[4] and the *Mail and Guardian*,[5] along with others, make direct links to *Twitter*'s role. A good example of this can be found with Stephen Grootes' opinion piece "When Twitter met South Africa—a match made in a train smash."[6] These explorations, as described by Postill and Pink (2012), "can end in a quick glance at a webpage or in longer, more meandering explorations of a potential research site, participant or initiative" (ibid: 7).

It is no coincidence that this heightened debate is happening at a time of political turmoil. There is a surge in student activism from a generation facing a country still deeply affected by the legacy of apartheid yet who are not afraid of challenging the dream of a multiracial "Rainbow Nation" that was sold to my generation. Somehow *Twitter* is at the heart of it. As one of the respondents, Kyle Findlay said, "We wouldn't be having these conversations if it wasn't for *Twitter*."

So my aim was to extrapolate the role of *Twitter* in the current discourse around race, by focusing on the *#FeesMustFall* movement—one of the biggest civic events in the country and on *Twitter*. To do this, I observed discussions on *Twitter* referencing the *#FeesMustFall* movement, as well as a chain of knock-on "Fallist" campaigns such as *#ZumaMustFall*, *#OutsourcingMustFall*, *#AfrikaansMustFall*. I have also conducted in-depth interviews with a small sample of respondents active on *Twitter*: journalists, social and political commentators, researchers, entrepreneurs, comedians, and students. These interviews were conducted face-to-face in Johannesburg, and on *Skype*. Each interview lasted 30-45 minutes.

There are several limitations to this research. The first is that I only began the participant observation in 2016. While the *#FeesMustFall* and related hashtags are still used as ongoing protest action takes place in various universities in South Africa, the bulk of the protest action specifically around *#FeesMustFall* action took place in 2015. Therefore, this research consists of a

---

3 | http://www.dailymaverick.co.za/
4 | http://citizen.co.za/
5 | http://mg.co.za/
6 Grootes, Stephen (2016): "Op-Ed: When Twitter met South Africa a match made in a train smash." http://www.dailymaverick.co.za/article/2016-01-28-op-ed-when-twitter-met-south-africa-a-match-made-in-a-train-smash/#.Vq5oJcvBzFl

variety of examples, which reference the movement activities in 2015 as well as 2016.

The second limitation is that the sample of interviewees is small and the topic is quite broad. However, I believe that the material is at least able to provide a snapshot of a changing discourse in South Africa and an important shift in the psyche of South Africans. In this, *Twitter* has played a critical part by providing a platform for young black South Africans to express their views, align arguments, influence public opinion and debate issues facing a post-apartheid South Africa.

## RESEARCH FINDINGS

In April 2015—the same month that a student movement called #RhodesMustFall took protest action to remove a statue of Cecil John Rhodes at the University of Cape Town (UCT) as part of its broader aim to decolonise the university—negotiations around annual fee increments began at the University of Witwatersrand (Wits) between student representatives and university management. Six months of intense efforts by the Wits Student Representative Council (SRC) to keep fee increases at bay were met with no success as the Wits Senate voted in a 10.5 percent fee increase—a decision which would make higher education largely unaffordable for many young black South Africans, particularly those from the "missing middle," who are already struggling with tuition and living fees. These "missing middle" are students who cannot access the National Student Financial Aid Scheme (NSFAS) funding because they are just above the threshold but are still not able to afford standard university fees (Wits 2016).

The SRC saw no other option but to take protest action against the university. So the *#FeesMustFall* movement was born. Political and gender writer Sisonke Msimang (2016) eloquently explains this:

This movement wasn't supposed to be necessary in a new South Africa. Anyone would have been able to understand poor people who continued to stay trapped in poverty since 1994 but these are people who aren't actually poor but who have financial problems perfectly understandable to middle class people black and white.[7]

Early in the morning in mid-October 2015, a small group of student protesters blocked the entrances to Wits university as a symbolic move to show how black students from disadvantaged backgrounds would be prevented from continuing their studies if the fee increment was implemented. The protest also aimed at making white students (many of whom use their own cars to

---

7 | Interview with Sisonke Msimang, March 2016.

travel to university) aware of their "white privilege"—likely they could afford the fee increase. Wits University along with the University of Cape Town, Rhodes University, University of the Free State, and University of Pretoria, are seen as traditionally white institutions since, during apartheid, only white students could study there. Despite more than two decades of democracy, it is still felt by many that these universities remain untransformed in terms of management, staff, and curricula. Law lecturer, Joel Modiri (2015), described why this legacy still remains:

Because a central outcome of de jure apartheid was the racial stratification of society in hierarchical terms, the unequal distribution of rights, resources and benefits continues to favour whites and disfavour Blacks. Thus we can say that we currently live under conditions of de facto apartheid or neo-apartheid/neo-colonialism in which the same macro-structure of "imperialist white supremacist capitalist patriarchy" which defined colonial apartheid continues to operate, although under a different legal and political arrangement (i.e., a liberal democratic government under non-white rule). (ibid: 221)

While the *#FeesMustFall* campaign's main public goal was to address the fee increment, much like the earlier *#RhodesMustFall* movement, it also sought to challenge these conditions. According to Fasiha Hassan (2016), Wits SRC Secretary General:

Decolonisation is the umbrella under which we are functioning. *#FeesMustFall* highlighted the racial disparity in a post-1994 context where people like myself (who are born free) haven't overcome the real wounds of apartheid, colonialism, racism, structural racism and it's clear that there are still biases. [8]

As the days drew on, so grew the crowds of students and, like wildfire, similar protests sprung up in other institutions across the country, with an increased engagement and support from a broad-based South African public. Sympathisers in the United States of America, India and other countries, showed solidarity on *Twitter* and social media. Mainstream media covered the movement extensively, often re-quoting student-led *Twitter* accounts.

Two weeks after the movement started at Wits, a mass protest was held at the Union buildings in Pretoria where President Jacob Zuma announced that there would be no fee increase for 2016. The students had won, but it was bittersweet as Mzwanele Ntshwanti (2016), Wits SRC Projects, Media and Campaigns Manager recalled: "When we were coming back from Union

---

**8** | Interview with Fasiha Hassan, March 2016.

buildings I didn't feel victorious and not on the basis that we didn't get what we wanted, but it was on the basis of what we had to do to get that."⁹

*Image 1*

The frustration of students who feel their voices are not heard. Seven months of negotiations with Wits management to prevent an increase in fees yielded no success forcing students to take action.

## WHO IS ON *TWITTER*, HOW ARE THEY USING IT, AND WHY?

According to the South Africa Social Media Landscape 2015 report, *Twitter* is the third most used social media platform after *Facebook* and *YouTube*, and its 7.4 million¹⁰ strong user base is still growing healthily. This growth is contrary to trends in developed countries, such as the United States of America (Goldstuck 2016).¹¹ South Africa's growing middle class and the increased affordability of smartphones, has led to a strong uptake in the platform (World Wide Worx and Fuseware 2015: 2). According to Arthur Goldstuck, managing director of World Wide Worx, "This means a big user base coming on board that is keen on a platform where they can express themselves." This is not unique when compared to other developing countries, but, said Goldstuck: "What make's South Africa different is that there is a very vigorous public discourse here. South Africans want a platform where they can be heard and be part of a conversation." Despite being the most popular social media platform, *Facebook* has failed in that instance because it caters mainly for a user's social circle, whereas on *Twitter* a user's opinion is public (Goldstuck 2016).¹²

Therefore, when viewed as an unmediated platform allowing anyone with access to the internet to participate in a discussion, *Twitter* can be seen a democratizing tool, in the context of Jurgen Habermas' public sphere, as "an arena, independent of government [and market]...dedicated to rational debate and which is both accessible to entry and inspection by the citizenry. It is here

---

9 | Interview conducted with Mzwanele Ntshwanti, March 2016.
10 | Interview conducted with Arthur Goldstuck, March 2016 (Social Media Landscape report has older figure of 6.6 million).
11 | Interview conducted with Arthur Goldstuck, March 2016.
12 | Interview conducted with Arthur Goldstuck, March 2016.

...that public opinion is formed" (Holub quoted in Webster 1995: 101-2; quoted in Postill 2012: 166).

But this poses a question as to how we can avoid what Bonilla (2015) warns as the "Common slippage made by journalists and others who tend to represent Twitter as an un-problematized 'public sphere' without taking into account the complexity of who is on Twitter, as well as how people are on Twitter in different ways" (2015:6).

During the course of this research it was not possible to source detailed demographic data about *Twitter's* user base. Goldstuck explained that this breakdown would only appear in a later version of the Social Media Landscape 2015 report. However, based on data science researcher Kyle Findlay's network analytics on the major communities on *Twitter* and interviews with respondents, some conclusions can be drawn.

When *Twitter* was first taken up in South Africa, it was very much the preserve of the educated middle class (Goldstuck 2016).[13] While it largely still remains the domain of both the black and white middle classes, as internet access improves and there is a greater take up of cheaper smartphones, the picture of *Twitter* users is becoming more broad-based to include wide engagement from a greater variety of black commentators (Findlay, 2016).[14]

Looking at data collated by Findlay, as well as sentiments expressed by interviewees, this step change began around the start of 2015 with the entry of this more broad-based black South African online community, known as "Black Twitter." While initially the community was based in Johannesburg and exchanges revolved around celebrities and entertainment, the usability of *Twitter*—combined with a turbulent political situation—quickly broadened conversations. Throughout 2015, comments became centred around *#RhodesMustFall*, *#SONA* (State of the Nation Address), *#FeesMustFall*, and *#ZumaMustFall* (Findlay, 2016). South Africa's "Black Twitter" draws parallels to African American engagement on *Twitter*, with users identifying closely with causes such as *#BlackLivesMatter*. Journalist Kwanele Sosibo explained this interconnectivity:

It's really modelled on African American culture and so looking at how the platform is being usurped by younger black people and with this American Imperialism (this is how a lot of black people speak here) there is less of a distance between the diaspora. I do think this shapes how the discourses happen and just with the information age, the level of people's consciousness has shifted and they are able to analyse issues of race and nuances more.[15]

---

13 | Interview conducted with Arthur Goldstuck, March 2016.
14 | Interview conducted with Kyle Findlay, March 2016.
15 | Interview conducted with Kwanele Sosibo, March 2016.

Findlay's research looks generally at the political discourse in the country over 2015, focusing on key events including *#FeesMustFall*. He noted that 52 per cent of tweets about these events came from just two communities. The first is defined as representing "the establishment" (estimated to be made up of about 80 per cent white and 20 per cent black users), and is comprised of large accounts run by political parties and mainstream media—making up 11 per cent of users—who generated 31 per cent of all tweets. The other big community is "the anti-establishment" comprised of activists and social movements (such as *@RhodesMustFall* and *@DailyVox*, the youth-based online publication that was at the forefront of *Twitter* coverage of *#FeesMustFall*) representing 8 per cent of users in Findlay's dataset[16]. This community, estimated to be around 56 per cent black and 40 per cent white, is heavily weighted toward female users, and is made up largely of young people aged 18-25. That this community represents just 8 per cent of users yet generates over 20 per cent of tweets shows that it is a highly engaged and impassioned community. Findlay (2016) says, "They are shouting, they are passionate, and driven." *Twitter* is empowering black South Africans to flourish by providing a platform to speak about issues such as race, discrimination, inequality, that previously would only have been discussed in private. Sosibo[17] described what may be behind this uptake: "I think people took for granted that the more upwardly mobile black classes will fit in more with the status quo and hold more liberal views. *Twitter* shattered that myth maybe because before black people didn't have an outlet to express their opinions so a lot of people didn't know what they were thinking."

---

**16** | Findlay, Kyle (2016) 2015: The year according to Twitter http://www.dailymaverick.co.za/article/2016-02-17-2015-the-year-according-to-twitter/#.VydH4aN97EY
**17** | Interview conducted with Kwanele Sosibo, March 2016.

*Image 2*

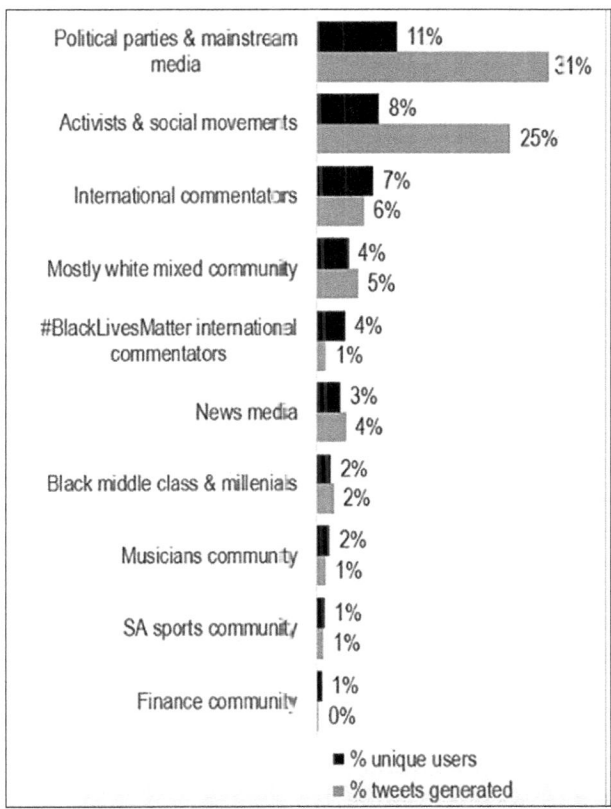

South African *Twitter* communities in the conversation map on main political events in 2015 (Findlay: 2016)

In this way *Twitter* appears to be a much more empowering tool for black South Africans than for white South Africans. Journalist Deshnee Subramany (2016) explained:

Black people have become a lot bolder to say certain things that they wouldn't normally say walking through the mall. Having Twitter is at least a starting point for that conversation to let people know its ok to express yourself because other people have had the opportunity to do that their whole lives, black people haven't. So it's a really good space for people to just start their purging process. For me, it has been a really good space to get my arguments together and understand what I'm actually feeling as opposed to just getting lost in the emotions and not have the words to say it.[18]

---

18 | Interview conducted with Deshnee Subramany, March 2016.

This, to an extent, echoes Bonilla's statement:

Twitter affords a unique platform for collectively identifying, articulating, and contesting racial injustices from the in-group perspectives of racialized populations. Whereas in most mainstream media contexts the experiences of racialized populations are over-determined, stereotyped, or tokenized, social media platforms such as Twitter offer sites for collectively constructing counter narratives and re-imagining group identities. (2015: 3)

## DISRUPTING THE NARRATIVE

This digital empowerment has been reflected in the *#FeesMustFall* movement where Wits students armed with smartphones (Haffajee 2015: 161). The students took charge of their own story out of a desire to disrupt the "white space" of the university and "white" liberal media, whom they felt were not telling their story accurately.[19] The *Daily Vox*,[20] a youth-based online publication, became one of the primary voices of the movement and *Twitter* was its main vehicle for transmitting news. Throughout the protests, the publication distributed video, audio and images—telling stories that traditional media was not picking up, especially at the start of the protest. For instance, on the first day of the protest, there was a white student motorist who tried to drive through the protesting line, "A lot of people were shocked by that and were like this is exactly the problem with white people in South Africa," said Patel.[21] Fasiha Hassan, Wits SRC Secretary General (2016) affirms this when she states, "This is not something the media reported on," said Hassan, "because then we were seen as hooligans."[22]

Two respondents also described how some students blocked journalists from mainstream media houses from covering the event because they felt they were inaccurately being depicted as violent troublemakers. Journalist and activist, Oliver Meth said, "We were reading the report from the day before and we were like 'No this didn't happen'...That's when we took over in terms of reporting our own story using the *Daily Vox* platform."[23]

Khadija Patel, co-founder of the *Daily Vox*, said social media became vital to overcome the "distrust of an alternative narrative that comes from the younger generation." She went on to explain that by taking control of their story on

---

19 | Interview with Khadija Patel, March 2016.
20 | https://www.thedailyvox.co.za/
21 | Interview with Khadija Patel, March 2016.
22 | Interview with Fasiha Hassan, Wits SRC Secretary General, March 2016.
23 | Interview with Oliver Meth, March 2016.

social media, particularly *Twitter*, students were able to disrupt the traditional narrative told by mainstream media and ensure student voices were both credible and authoritative.

Image 3

Students take charge of their own story and criticise mainstream media

## *TWITTER* AND THE DIGITAL REBIRTH OF BLACK CONSCIOUSNESS IN SOUTH AFRICA

Students identify their cause with that of the 1976 student uprising against Afrikaans as a forced language of instruction. Black Consciousness theories from Steve Biko and Frantz Fanon have become popularised again and form important pivots for the movement. Oliver Meth[24] explained the reason behind this revival:

There is the revival of black consciousness because the black youth voice has been marginalised from the political debate. This is the platform for us to portray the kind of messages to interpret to people who don't understand what happened on the ground for youth in tertiary institutions, and for youth in general in townships that are pressed by these different systems formed during the colonised days.

When exploring *Twitter*'s role in this revitalisation in the current discourse around race in South Africa, it is important to look at *Twitter* as a consensus-building medium. *Twitter* essentially allows more people to align around a particular body of knowledge, which comes pre-packaged with certain arguments. "So if you have a debate today with someone, I think you will have the same kind of arguments and counter arguments arising whereas if you had

---

24 | Interview with Oliver Meth, March 2016.

them two years ago in South Africa you would have had it coming from a more individual point of view," explained Findlay.[25]

## Twitter as a Polarising Tool

One of the extreme characteristics of *Twitter*'s consensus building attribute is polarisation. It is worth highlighting some of key lessons learnt by Wael Ghonim, an activist during the Arab Spring in Egypt, on his engagement with social media as quoted in *The New York Times* opinion piece by Thomas Friedman (2016). There he described how users on social media communicate generally with people they tend to agree with and how a mob mentality can quickly take over discussions:

Because of the speed and brevity of social media, we are forced to jump to conclusions and write sharp opinions in 140 characters about complex world affairs. And once we do that, it lives forever on the internet...Today, our social media experiences are designed in a way that favours broadcasting over engagements, posts over discussions, shallow comments over deep conversations...It's as if we agreed that we are here to talk at each other instead of talking with each other.[26] (Ghonim, 2016)

This kind of polarisation can be seen particularly in spin-off "Fallist" campaigns from the *#FeesMustFall* movement such as *#AfrikaansMustFall*. This campaign started at the University of Pretoria, a formerly white Afrikaans university, which still uses Afrikaans as a medium for instruction together with English. The aim was to remove Afrikaans as a medium of instruction because it excludes black students who feel it is discriminatory; some students, mostly white Afrikaans students, are at an advantage of learning in their mother tongue while black students must take their classes in English, a second language for most. Afrikaans students in favour of learning in their mother tongue opposed the protest with the *#AfrikaansSalBly* ("Afrikaans will stay"). Violence between groups quickly erupted leading to a university shutdown (ENCA: 2016).[27]

---

25 | Interview with Kyle Findlay, March 2016.
26 | Friedman, Thomas (2016): "Social Media: Destroyer or Creator?" http://www.nytimes.com/2016/02/03/opinion/social-media-destroyer-or-creator.html?_r=0
27 | "Police monitor AfriForum and EFF students at the University of Pretoria." https://www.enca.com/south-africa/students-divided-over-afrikaans

*Image 4*

University of Pretoria issues a warning to students and staff using social media to spread hate speech and incite violence in view of increasing tensions over Afrikaans as a language of instruction.

As the protests on the ground increased, so the conversations on *Twitter* intensified, culminating in the University of Pretoria issuing a warning to students, staff, and others regarding using social media to insight violence and hate speech. Simultaneously, the *#Afrikaansmustfall* movement gained momentum at other universities still keeping a dual language policy, such as University of the Free State (UFS), University of Stellenbosch (US) and North West University (NWU).

The pressure resulted in UFS removing Afrikaans as a language of instruction as of 2017. This was a major move within a university struggling with transformation. Only this year, UFS suffered a horrific violent racist event: during half-time of an inter-university rugby match, black student protesters went onto the field demanding an end to outsourced employment of workers under the banner *#OutsourcingMustFall*; the protest turned violent when white spectators ran onto the field and beat up some of the black protesters (EWN: 2016).[28]

Events such as these have obviously heightened racial tensions on campuses and prompted an increased intensity of engagement on social media.

---

28 | EWN (2016): "Tensions high after UFS Rugby Brawl". http://ewn.co.za/2016/02/23/UFS-suspends-classes-after-black-vs-white-brawl

There have been attempts by some students to pacify violence through prayer groups and on social media through a *#colourblind campaign*. This campaign encouraged students of different races to take photos with each other in an effort to help end racial violence on campuses. But it received a huge backlash on *Twitter* because many people felt it washed over key issues raised by black South African students.

As protests continue, these multidimensional arguments are fast coming to the fore, with confrontations on social media sites and actually on campuses. But, as Khadija Patel (2016) explained, the role of *Twitter* needs to be contextualised:

> I don't think we are on the brink of a race war any day now. But we need to have the kind of conversations that can result in change that people can see. Because they are just tweets, someone's thoughts, they are not going to change the world unless someone does something with it.[29]

## Conclusion

In South Africa, as in many other contexts, *Twitter* should not be seen as a place that transcends social boundaries and categories but rather, as Sharma (2013) highlights: "It reflects an internet that is a [...] 'racially demarcated space'" and that "is a manifold set of sociotechnical practices, generative of digital privileges and racial ordering" (2013: 46).

The growth of the voices of young, born free, black South Africans on *Twitter*—eager to tell their stories themselves and to disrupt a traditional narrative—has opened up a wider, diverse, more robust discussion around race and inequality in South Africa. I hope this research, while limited in scope, has provided a snapshot of some key trends within the discourse around race in South Africa though it has by no means sufficed in exploring them in depth. It also fails to address many other themes and trends such as the politicization of *#FeesMustFall* by political parties, the dynamics at play between older commentators and youth movement members, along with how much *Twitter* can amplify hate speech. There is therefore much scope for more additional, more specific and refined research on these trends.

---

**29** | Interview conducted with Khadija Patel, March 2016.

# References

Bonilla, Yarimar /Rosa, Jonathan (2015): "#Ferguson: Digital Protest, Hashtag Ethnography, and the Racial Politics of Social Media in the United States." In: American Ethnologist. Vol. 42, No. 1, pp. 4–17.
Haffajee, Ferial (2015): What If There Were No Whites in South Africa?, Johannesburg: Picador Africa.
Hofmeyr, Jan/Govender, Rajen (2016): South African Reconciliation Barometer 2015. Briefing Paper 2, Cape Town: Institute for Justice and Reconciliation.
Malala, Justice (2015): We Have Now Begun Our Descent, Johannesburg & Cape Town: Jonathan Ball Publishers.
Modiri, Joel (2015): "Law's Poverty." Potchefstroom Electronic Law Journal (PER) 2015. Vol 18, No 2, pp 220-221.
Postill, John (2012): "Digital Politics and Political Engagement." In: Heather Horst/Daniel Miller (2012): Digital Anthropology, London and New York: Berg, pp.165 – 184.
Postill, John/Pink, Sarah (2012): "Social Media Ethnography: The Digital Researcher in a Messy Web." In Media International Australia 145/1, pp. 123-134.
Sanjay, Sharma (2013): "Black Twitter? Racial Hashtags, Networks and Contagion." New Formations. Vol. 78, pp. 46-64.
World Wide Worx and Fuseware (2015): "South African Social Media Landscape 2015." Executive Summary. http://www.worldwideworx.com/wp-content/uploads/2014/11/Exec-Summary-Social-Media-2015.pdf

# Online Articles

The Daily Vox (2015): "Special Editorial: the Wits protest is not just about university fees." http://www.thedailyvox.co.za/special-editorial-the-wits-protest-is-not-just-about-university-fees/
ENCA (2016): "Police Monitor AfriForum and EFF Students at the University of Pretoria." https://www.enca.com/south-africa/students-divided-over-afrikaans
EWN (2016): "Tensions High After UFS Rugby Brawl." http://ewn.co.za/2016/02/23/UFS-suspends-classes-after-black-vs-white-brawl
Findlay, Kyle (2015): "The Birth of a Movement: #FeesMustFall on Twitter." http://www.dailymaverick.co.za/article/2015-10-30-the-birth-of-a-movement-feesmustfall-on-twitter/#.Vuu1DMvBzFI
Findlay, Kyle (2016a): "The Twitter World of #ZumaMustFall."
http://www.dailymaverick.co.za/article/2016-01-19-the-twitter-world-of-zumamustfall/

Findlay, Kyle (2016b): "2015: The Year According to Twitter." http://www.dailymaverick.co.za/article/2016-02-17-2015-the-year-according-to-twitter/#.Vu_p3cvBzFI

Friedman, Thomas (2016): "Social Media: Destroyer or Creator?" http://www.nytimes.com/2016/02/03/opinion/social-media-destroyer-or-creator.html?_r=0

Grootes, Stephen (2016): "Op-Ed: When Twitter Met South Africa—a match made in a train smash." http://www.dailymaverick.co.za/article/2016-01-28-op-ed-when-twitter-met-south-africa-a-match-made-in-a-train-smash/#.Vq5oJcvBzFI

Patel, Aaisha Dadi (2015): "Five times the #WitsFeesMustFall protestors were victims of violence." http://www.thedailyvox.co.za/five-times-the-witsfeesmustfall-protestors-were-victims-of-violence/

Sunday World (2016): "Penny Sparrow's racist Facebook post trends on Twitter." http://www.sundayworld.co.za/news/2016/01/04/penny-sparrow-s-racist-facebook-post-trends-on-twitter

Wits (2016): "Wits, SRC to Raise R10 million." https://www.wits.ac.za/news/latest-news/general-news/2016/2016-01/wits-src-to-raise-r10-million.html)

## Videos

"*#BetterTogether* - University of Pretoria's Language Policy" https://www.youtube.com/watch?v=ebqj6kt6R7Y&feature=youtu.be

"What's the deal with UP/Tukkies?" https://www.youtube.com/watch?v=8LjZwCDRFUM&feature=youtu.be

# Migration, Political Art and Digitalization

*Sara Wiederkehr González*

> Sometimes we walk around on different edges of this world, trying to find a place we can call home. Sometimes, we find a corner, or a cliff, and build a house there. We meet our neighbors and become friends with them. We find a job, a lover, and plant a garden. We feel free and creative. We learn, we are scared. Sometimes we just cross country borders, trying to find some peace, anywhere calm, a space to remain and be. We travel with our history, our own stories, our way of being. We may find others in these walks, we may walk alone sometimes. Sometimes, we wonder if we will ever find that place, or if we will be like nomads around the world, running away from the difficulties, the bullets, the hunger, the lack of money and of opportunities. Being refugees, migrants, strangers. Remaining foreigners.
> 
> We might find out that home can be wherever we are. We may build our own place somewhere else, we may find the place we belong to. But if we miss our other home, we just call. All we have to do is open the laptop, scroll through Facebook, call by Skype, write an e-mail, chat, read the news, listen to the radio And for a few seconds, minutes or even hours, we are home, we sit next to our mother, we see the blue sea and almost, almost, feel the breeze. We actualize ourselves through these interactions.
> 
> The war we thought we left behind is on the screen, as are the horrors and the nightmares. Is it on the screen or is it on the other side?
> 
> -Personal reflections of the author.

Throughout this paper, the main interest is in describing the use and practice of social networking by Colombian migrants and its influence on the relation with, and the construction of a discourse about, Colombian conflict and social reality. In addressing the problematization of cyberspace and its virtuality as a space, an account is given of the singularities, political concerns, and personal expectations of two Colombian migrants living in Berlin. This leads to an analysis of the influence of virtuality in the construction of political and social discourses and of practices abroad.

In the following, there is a short introduction to the Colombian armed conflict, followed by the theoretical and conceptual approach that leads this research. The second section outlines the method used, while in the third and fourth sections the relations between territory and virtuality through (short) life histories are described.

## INTRODUCTION

Colombia is a country with a very particular history. The Colombian armed conflict dates back to 1962, and is an ongoing, low-intensity war between the Colombian government, paramilitary groups and left-wing guerrillas (for example: FARC,[1] ELN,[2] EPL,[3] M-19[4]), with participation of the drug cartels and different criminal gangs. Its historical roots can be found in the period known as *La Violencia* ("The Violence"), which started in 1948 with the assassination of Jorge Eliécer Gaitán, a populist political leader; the bipartisan war followed.[5] The roots are multiple: social inequality, concentrated ownership and control of land,[6] political persecution of those who are "left" in their thinking, and drug trafficking, among others (cf. Lozano Guillén 2006).

---

**1** | Fuerzas Armadas Revolucionarias de Colombia - FARC ("Revolutionary Armed Forces of Colombia"), founded 1964.
**2** | Ejército de Liberación Nacional - ELN ("National Liberation Army"), founded in 1964.
**3** | Ejército Popular de Liberación - EPL ("Popular Liberation Army"), founded in 1967.
**4** | Movimiento 19 de Abril - M-19 ("19th April Movement"), founded 1970.
**5** | Jorge Eliécer Gaitán was assassinated in Bogotá, April 9, 1948. The bipartisan war (1948-1958), between the Liberal Party and the Conservative Party, ended with a political agreement named: "National Front" (Frente Nacional) (1958-1974).
**6** | The majority of the land in Colombia is under the control of a few families. They have enormous political control and power. This issue plays a key role in the conflict and exacerbates the social inequality.

Since its independence from the Spanish conquerors,[7] Colombia has not actually had a single period of peace. During recent decades, there have been several peace negotiations between the government and different armed groups. For example, in 1985 the guerrilla group M-19 and the government jointly signed a ceasefire, however the agreement was not respected by either side. At the same time, the government started fruitless negotiations with FARC. Together with some of ELN combatants, they created the new party of Unión Patriótica (UP) as a political alternative to the armed struggle. In the elections of 1986, UP won twenty-three municipalities and gained fourteen seats. However, in the period between 1986 and 2002, between 5,000 and 20,000 of its members were assassinated.[8] This offensive was carried out by elite groups—still unidentified—in an attempt to suppress political opposition (Cepeda 2006). The UP party turned back to political life in 2014. The current peace negotiations with FARC started in 2012, and there have been several subsequent agreements between both parties. This year (2016) is set to see the signing of the document that should open a new period in Colombian history. Simultaneously, peace negotiations along the same lines have begun between ELN and the Government.[9] Despite these efforts, since the foundation of Marcha Patriótica, 113 of its members have been killed.[10] In March 2016 alone, 28 young social activists were killed.[11] In the last three decades, 5.8 million people have been subject to forced internal displacement (Acnur/Codhes 2013). At the time last census was carried out, 3,331,107 Colombians were recorded as living abroad (Cepal 2010).

The discussion of the authenticity and "realness" of the virtual world and virtual relationships invokes the supposed opposition between virtual space as abstract, and the real world as the tangible and real one. However, the notions of virtuality and reality are not necessarily opposed; there is a reality in the virtuality itself or as Josefine Bormann states it: Some spaces become places to some people, while to other people they will remain spaces (Bormann 2013: 63).

The distinction relates to the more fundamental one of time: the actual image of the present that is happening, and the virtual image of the past

---

7 | The first independence uprising began on July 20, 1810 and ended in 1816. Finally on August 7, 1819, at the Batalla de Boyacá ("Boyaca Battle"), the Spanish troops capitulated.
8 | The genocide of the UP was perpetrated by people still unknown. There have been single convictions, but the investigation is ongoing.
9 | www.Semana.com March 30, 2016.
10 | "Marcha Patriótica" is a social and political movement founded in 2012 by different social organizations and political parties. They claim to seek peace in Colombia through social justice.
11 | El Tiempo, March 21, 2016.

that is conserved, are marked in the *actualization*. Deleuze (1995) argues that actualization allows for the distinction of that limit that is impossible to assimilate: the *virtual* reacts above the *actual*. The virtual is actualized, and the actual remits to the virtual as its own. The actual is then the complement; the object of this actualization that has, as subject, the virtual.

According to Augé (1995), a place is defined as relational, historical and concerned with identity. Borrmann (2013) concludes in her study that cyberspace cannot be understood as an abstract place, meant to exist only "while we are sitting in front of the computer." (ibid: 64). From this reasoning, several questions arise: If the cyberspace is a tangible one, how do migrants—those people who supposedly live in between territories—relate to virtuality? How are these virtual spaces and places constructed from the singularities of Colombian migrants in Berlin? How do they relate to the actuality overseas, in their home countries?

I consider that it is important to begin from the understanding cyberspace not as virtuality, but as the methodological place where different *virtualities* are being articulated. This became apparent during the study I conducted over the past months, following participation in several online chats, discussions and events with Colombian migrants located in Berlin, Germany, and also Argentina and Brazil. It is here, from where the subjects are absent, that the actualization of the space happens. Cyberspace emerged as the medium to connect to a reality happening miles away; political concerns related to from a distance—geographically—remain a close reality in the virtual world.

According to Guattari and Rolnik (2006), the notion of territory is wide. People organize themselves within territories defined by themselves and articulated through other existing ones. It can be related as both a vivid place and a perceived system. Territory is then appropriation; it is the set of representations that will lead to a range of behaviors, inversions, both in time and social, cultural, and aesthetic spaces (ibid: 323). Consequently, territoriality could then be understood as a characterization of agency, when the first step of agency is to discover the territoriality it contains. Territory surpasses the organism and the medium, and the relationship between the two (Deleuze/Guattari 1997: 513). Territory, both the physical and the virtual, can then be understood as a social construction that results from the exercise of power relationships. These power relationships are always implicated in social and temporal practices, and are both material and symbolic, resulting from the production of a space that is constructed differently according to the particular experiences, perceptions, and conceptions of every person (Harvey 1998: 250).

In this context, the discourses about the conflict, and social and political reality in Colombia, are virtual. Its construction happens also in cyberspace, mostly by people living abroad. The virtual depends on and actualizes in the reality. Over the course of this study, and in the same light of Rolnik (2006), another interesting issue came up: that of examining and assessing—via their constructed virtual world—emotions of the people who migrate, in order to analyze the relationship(s) between migrants and territory. A salient factor in this study was the consideration that even if they do not participate in the actuality of their country, Colombia in this specific case, they still participate in the process of actualization. While abroad, they do attend political and social processes being held on the other side. As noted in wide studies, cyberspace has a direct influence on migration and the formations of communities in diaspora, as well as in the direct relation of building and strengthening of the imagined community in a transnational context. The aim in this study is to understand the notion and construction of territory and the subsequent identification with it through cyberspace. In this respect, I wish to participate in the current debate relating to the use of social networks within communities of migrants, focusing largely on the capacity to strengthen the notion of belonging to their home nation and countrymen. I am aware that this is a fact, but I am more interested in inquiring about the emotions, expectations and personal stories of migrants, considering that migration is not a phenomenon that can be universalized as it is tied to specific subjectivities.

## TERRITORY, MIGRATION AND IDENTITY: A CASE STUDY

For four months, I conducted semi-structured and unstructured interviews, both on- and offline, with Colombian migrants based in Berlin, Germany. These conversations and interviews where held in Spanish, our mutual mother tongue, but I'll present them here translated. During these interviews and conversations, I was interested in inquiring as to their reasons for migration, their expectations and possibilities that were available to them in their host countries, as well as understanding their connection to Colombia and family. In doing so, I wanted to track their emotions as migrants, to trace singularities, as migration does not affect every person in the same way. Further, I work to understand the way in which virtuality affected these singularities in their relationships to their respective networks in Colombia, and their *awareness* of the Colombian conflict.

*Image 1*

Andrea Territory. Montage: Felipe Ramírez. 2015.

Throughout these conversations I found that most of the people I interviewed took interest in political, social and cultural matters in Colombia, but only after having left. They remained informed through social media; for example, keeping in touch with relatives and co-workers via *Skype*, while through *Facebook* and e-mail they discussed daily news with friends and relatives. The main online diaries they read were those found on *www.semana.com* and *El Espectador*,[12] as well as other smaller, alternative ones such as *LaSillaVacía*.[13] Many also developed academic and cultural projects concerning the Colombian armed conflict. This is the case of Andrés, who began to study and research the Colombian conflict whilst in Berlin:

I'm presenting my master thesis in Sound Studies at the UdK...It's about victims [of the Colombian conflict]...I became interested in this topic because previously we did another project about the victims, also with you–he laughs–...and this year I also did a project with my sister in Bogotá, a theater play...about female victims of the armed conflict, based on the report *La Verdad sobre las Mujeres* [the truth about women], written by *La Ruta Pacífica de las Mujeres* [the peaceful journey of women]...Those motivations I had had the previous year, and this year, made me think that my thesis... [he hesitates]. After 10 years of being here, you tend to become more interested in Colombia, because the distance allows you to see things better, so, because of the [alienation], you grasp more details about the complexity of the conflict...Because

---

12 | www.elespectador.com
13 | www.lasillavacia.com

when you're over there, inside, it's more difficult to gain a general perspective. (Andrés, in an interview with the author. March 3, 2015. My translation).

*Image 2*

Andrés Territory. Montage: Felipe Ramírez, 2015.

I also accompanied them in their academic and work projects and went with them to film and art events, from and about Colombia, in Berlin. After spending so much time together, I became friends with some of them. Being a Colombian migrant myself was helpful in this study, not just as a researcher, but also with regard to being able to share feelings, thoughts and reflections on a similar level, despite differences in our various socio-economic and ideological backgrounds. As someone who left her hometown many years ago, I have still not found another place to really settle down. Interestingly enough, both Andrea and Andrés wholeheartedly accepted me as Colombian—a fact that is rare both in Colombia and in Europe, due to my unusual name and the color of my skin and eyes. I am generally perceived as a foreigner even in my home country.

In the pages that follow, I will present some abstracts of interviews, conversations and observations held with both Andrés and Andrea. I met Andrés in Berlin through a common friend (also Colombian) who had asked me to help in an art project about the Colombian conflict, *Proyecto Mangle*. After the installation was presented we did not keep in touch, but in February 2015 I made contact with him for this study.

I invited Andrea over for dinner. She arrived with a friend of a friend, who was attending *El Espejo*,[14] in Berlin. After this first meeting we stayed in touch, having become friends on *Facebook*. I called her for this study in February 2015, and we began to spend time together and visit some of the cultural events organized by Colombian migrants in Berlin.

I chose to focus on these two people because of their life experiences and the time we shared offered me an interesting insight. Through an account of their personal stories, I will analyze the issue of belonging to a territory, the influence of mass media in the construction of reality discourses and virtual relationships to the home country.

## THE PLACE WE BELONG TO

While talking and sharing life experiences with Andrés and Andrea, I realized that even when we understand cyberspace as a space or place, it is actually a methodological space where these virtualities are constantly being actualized. Sometimes, it is just a tool for elaborate nostalgias, sometimes it is converted into a place to create and recreate places of daily resistance and creativity. Additionally, it also helps to narrow the distance gap between here and there, to create an illusion of proximity, to strengthen ties with loved ones left behind.

Both Andrea and Andrés share similar experiences in this regard. But while Andrea is sometimes annoyed because of the blurring of her physical location, she also needs this tool for her job:

I see [*Facebook* and other social media] as a platform and opportunity for promotion… Through the internet, there are these new tools for promotion, dissemination of, lets say, other kinds of content, because before these [contents] were monopolized or concentrated by the mass media and what they wanted to tell us…Recently, I have had more frequent contact with my organization, Cine Libertad,[15] because of common projects…Let's say [what is most affected is] time difference; that's what really affects your reality, even if you don't want it to. Until Sunday, it was a six-hour [time difference], now it's seven. And I had to tell them to be more punctual…It affects reality. I don't hang out with friends in the evenings anymore, because I'm on *Skype*, or waiting to meet someone on *Skype*…and this makes me sad, makes me feel blue. It's like feeling in touch and almost being there, and yet you aren't there. Reality is different. And I wonder, if I'm living here, why I still need so much contact to there? (Andrea, in personal conversation with author. March 31, 2015. My translation)

---

14 | https://elespejofilmfestival.com Accessed: May 26, 2016.
15 | Cine Libertad ("Cinema Freedom"): [www.http://cinelibertad.co

From my field-diary I read a quote dated April 1, 2015:

Emotional experience: They [migrants] don't belong despite having entered it [the territory]. They don't stop belonging despite having left it. One becomes migrant: territorial and identity reconfigurations. (Rolnik 2006. My translation).

One becomes "migrant." In this becoming, there is a certain agency. In this "not belonging," there is a certain absence of territorialization, even a de-territorialization that becomes a re-territorialization:

Home? Difficult. That's a tough question, because well, here, here, *this* is my home now. As much as I would like to go back to Colombia, let's say at this moment, if I were to go back there, I'd feel I was visiting, as much as I'd like to go back …As much as I feel that it is my land, or that I feel identified and a I, here is where I have my place, where I have my stuff… the association of home, maybe it is that feeling of being comfortable in a place, regardless of geographical location (Andrea. Interview with author, March 31, 2015. My translation).

As Bernal (2006) argues in her study about the Eritrean diaspora online:

The fact that cyberspace has no physical location mirrors the displacement of (those) in diaspora, and the networked sociality of cyberspace resonates with their dispersed social networks. In this way, the internet may be the quintessential diaspora medium because it builds upon, reinforces and extends social networks (Bernal 2006:168).

And at the same time, cyberspace is also a "mending of ruptures in the social body and in individual subjectivity, through the ability of internet to bridge distance or at least render it invisible, making physical location irrelevant" (ibid.).

On the other hand, Andrés became aware of the multiple implications of the distance and influence of mass media in his personal approach to the Colombian reality. His recently presented project pursued two goals: to generate a contrast between victims of different armed actors, and to achieve a symbolical identification by the spectator with the victims. To do this, he shows a loop of pictures of the victims, using a mirror that rotates, where the spectator can see himself. During this loop, the spectator can listen to readings of the letters written by friends and family of the kidnapped and sent to the radio station *Las Voces del Secuestro*.[16]

He did his research online and took material from the internet

---

**16** | *Las Voces del Secuestro* ("Kidnapped Voices"), a radio station that every day reads several letters written to the kidnapped ones with the hope that, in their captivity,

I tried to communicate with the people of *Las Voces del Secuestro*, but they never answered an e-mail, and I wasn't going to sit and wait for their response to do something with material that, for me, it is for public use, and free. The photographs I use are not professional (...) I take normal pictures [from the internet], trying to conserve the format the people use, to show their disappearance. That's online, and for me, that's open and anybody can take them. (Andrés, Interview with author. March 10, 2015. My translation).

In his research process, he made his discovery of the first official victim: Omaira Montoya Henao. He posted her picture as a homage, on *Proyecto Mangle*'s *Facebook* profile:

Image 3

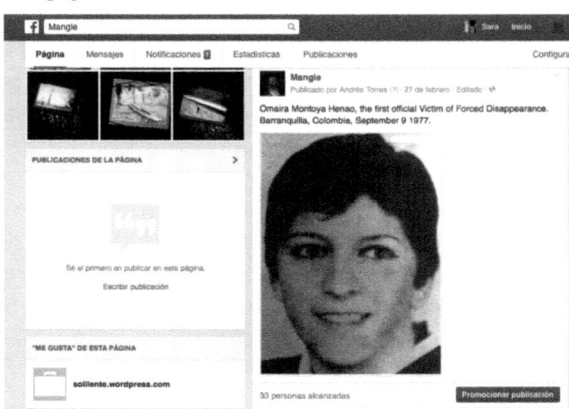

Omaira Montoya Henao, the first official Victim of Forced Disappearance. Barranquilla, Colombia, September 9, 1977. Posted to Proyecto Mangle's *Facebook* account.

During our conversations, this issue became very important. Andrés stayed in contact with Colombian reality in cyberspace. Reading news, reports, and listening to radio stations, he gained knowledge about the many problems of the conflict and its victims:

With the victims, a feeling overtakes me; in my case, a national feeling. I feel that it reaches my integrity, and as it's like my reference point—Colombia—it affects me. I need to put this somewhere …It might look like a kind of art therapy, but the important thing is to tell, to manifest, because if one remains silent, then it's worse. (Andrés. Interview with author. March 16, 2015, My translation).

---

they will hear the messages and won't lose their strength. You can hear the audio on this website: http://www.lasvocesdelsecuestro.com

*Image 4*

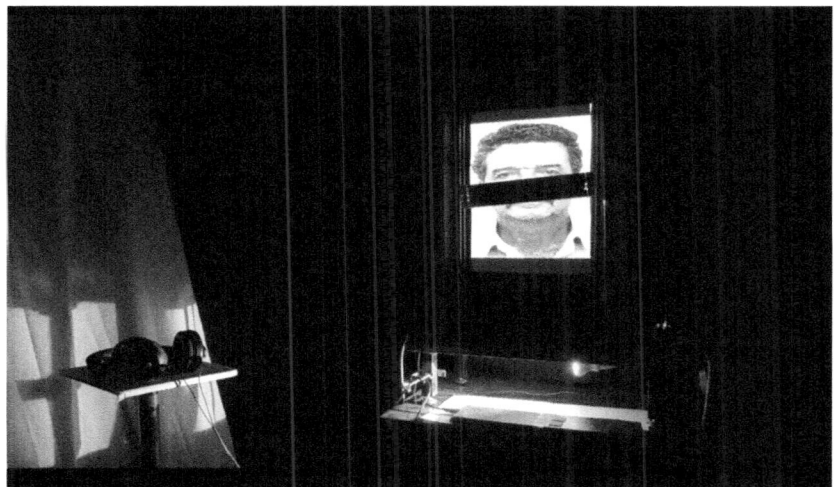

An instant from the art installation "Perpetrators and Perpetrated: Audio-Visual-Kinetic Installation for the Encounter with Victims of Forced Disappearance and Kidnapping in the Colombian Armed Conflict." Photographic still from the footage. Sara Wiederkehr González. March 13, 2015.

## Memory and Discourse

He is aware that the mass media in Colombia is controlled by the economic and political elite, and that this has a huge influence on the discourse about the Colombian reality:

Memory and victims from Latin America, these are images built in Europe …where does the image of the victim come from?…The organizations are showing things here [in Europe] that are not officially revealed over there: observations, thoughts, reflections on the process in Colombia, from different angles. People here, academics, scientists; they have concerns about the subject, the thinking of people, no? (Andrés. Interview with author, March 10, 2015. My translation).

This distance-proximity relationship with the victims gathered abroad—thanks to cyberspace—allows me to question why the figure of the victim seems to be more important in Europe than in the context from which it comes? How does it come about that they (migrants) begin to have a stance, as Colombian nationals, that is drawn from the figure of victim, as seen and understood abroad? Memories are not actual images formed after the object is perceived, but the virtual image coexists with the actual perception of the object: the memory is the contemporary virtual image of the actual object: its double, its *image in the mirror*. Are we creating a memory from abroad?

Andrea uses social media to develop projects that have a direct impact in Colombia and within the Colombian film scene in Berlin. She discusses the actuality with her colleagues and family. At the same time, this constant contact and exposure in the social media affects her daily routine and her identification with a certain place and time:

I think that it affects my reality, this virtual reality, and obviously, as everything is relative, in the end there are several realities, you live in different realities at the same time. (Andrea, in discussion with the author March 31, 2015. My translation).

In this respect, Olarzabal and Reips (2012) argue that technology has a huge influence on migration. It facilitates the formation, growth and maintenance of communities in diaspora, and their family ties. Access to the internet helps to maintain and recreate informal and formal networks—in the digital as well in the physical world—reinforcing the sense of collective and individual identity.

"War and repression create an afterlife among diaspora populations" (Matsuoka/Sorenson 2005: 85 in Bernal 2005: 167). However, despite the fact that the participants I talked to during this research all came out of a violent context (the Colombian armed conflict), and can indeed be considered victims, their relation to Colombian daily reality through cyberspace—whether by watching news, reading online newspapers, keeping in touch with their families or through networking in the process of the development of cultural and/or political projects—has helped to emphasize their identity as Colombian nationals. Even more interestingly, this mode of relation has contributed to creating a genuine interest in the Colombian reality and conflict. Many of the Colombians I spoke with in Berlin looked forward to take back some processes learned here when they were able to return to Colombia.

## PLANNING NEW ROUTES

Both Andrea and Andrés are going back to Colombia in a few months. Andrea wants to open a cinema/gallery/coffee house/workshop in Ubaté, in Cundinamarca, the small village where she was born in Colombia. However, now after months of planning and dreaming, she is scared, scared because her dream means creating a new, alternative, almost revolutionary project in this little town of 21,966 inhabitants. In this place, the people do not have a "culture of cinema," and in a country where many films are made but only a few make it to the distribution chain or into the cinemas. She does not know if it will work but she is going back because she does not know what to do here in Germany, or even in Europe. After being a stranger, a migrant, for nine years, she is now going back to being a *national* again.

Her project, *Vía Láctea*[17] ["Milky Way'], is already live and on the social networks. Besides this, her almost full-time job of engaging with the Colombian and Latin American film festival in Berlin helps her to be present in the cultural scene of Colombia—meeting film directors, and festival organizers—while being physically in Berlin. The *Facebook* profile she created has already 1,222 "*Friends*," and a daily presence. *Vía Láctea* is still in development, but it already has an actual life.

Andrés is going to Medellín, after ten years away from Colombia. He does not yet know what he is going to do: "maybe teach something related to sound and electronics, maybe find a way out as a musician," he says. His wife, Lirio, remains in Colombia at the *Universidad Nacional de Colombia*. He is not anxious in the same way as Andrea, but is well aware that what he has been studying here—*Sound Studies*—does not exist in Colombia. He is certain that, after having done some projects in Berlin about the victims in Colombia, he will keep working on that subject. Through discussion of the art installation, he expanded on his opinion about the armed conflict. He speaks as a person that has watched this war in front of a screen, dealing only with the discourse presented by mass media; working also with materials he refers to as "cold."

...internet, podcasts, recordings; it's a post-production work from the media, put in some online server and accessible. It helped me also to ask myself about my position as a spectator, a spectator who is now aware of the existing modulation in the thinking of war...in that zone of normalization of war. (Andrés. Interview with the author, March 31, 2015. My translation).

## Conclusion

After conducting this fieldwork, on- and offline, there is a growing impetus to explore this issue in more depth—appearing now a wider topic than perceived at the beginning, when I first proposed the subject.

Migrants do not form a homogeneous group, nor can diaspora be understood as a universal phenomenon. To understand this transnational phenomenon, it is necessary to establish key factors: the different motivations for migrations, the various expectations of migrants, their social and economic

---

17 | *Facebook* page for *Vía Láctea*: https://www.facebook.com/profile.php?ic=100008483440715&fref=ts

status, gender and background. Each migrant arrives with a history, full of singularities and multiple identities; and establishes himself or herself in a particular context through which they can relate. It would be interesting to have a broader overview: a cartography of the different, individual routes—historical, geographical and emotional.

As a result of this study, it can be concluded that *class* is also virtualized; it vanishes in favor of other territorializations. One "becomes migrant," and that is why it is so important to ask about the singularities. The concept of territory is larger than just the physical terrain, where the borders are clearly defined. It relates to agency and desire, following Deleuze and Guattari (2002). Along these lines, territories are always related to the vectors of deterritorialization and re-territorialization: a territory is more than a thing or an object, an action, a relation, a concomitant movement of territorialization and deterritorialization; a rhythm which repeats itself under control.

Tomás Guzmán, fellow anthropologist and also former migrant, argues that, "migrants represent a cut, an irruption, an exception. But nonetheless, the migrant questions the idea of what Europe is." He explains, that this happens, despite the fact that the nation states from Europe and North America require their labor force to maintain their production rhythms, their specific social and global order. At the same time, migrants question the idea of a national history, communicating, building up certain proximities that are larger due to the distance they gain.[18]

Andrés and I concluded, while he was cooking lasagna following a recipe his wife had sent him by e-mail, that history itself is a virtuality. His project, narrated history through the victims, and in the process of the making, helped him to gain identity and also a position about the war. All of this work he did online. He recovered pieces of dead bodies, exposed violence, blood, tears and disappeared lives, so putting together a poetic and heartbreaking story. It is this very process that helped him overcome the horrors of the war. And it will lead him on his way back home.

---

**18** | In personal conversation with the author. March 18, 2015.

## REFERENCES

Acnur/Codhes (2013): "El Desplazamiento Forzado y la Imperiosa Necesidad de la Paz. Informe Desplazamiento 2013." April 4, 2016. http://www.acnur.org/t3/fileadmin/scripts/doc.php?file=t3/uploads/media/2881_COI_Colombia_Informe_CODHES_2013

Augé, Marc (1995): Non-Places: Introduction to an Anthropology of Supermodernity. John Howe (trans.), New York.

Bernal, Victoria (2005): "Diaspora, Cyberspace and Political Imagination: The Eritrean Diaspora Online." In: Global Networks 6/2, pp.161-179.

Borrmann, Josefine (2013): "Place and Non-Place in Second Life." In: Urte Undine Frömming (ed.), Virtual Environments and Cultures. A Collection of Social Anthropological Research in Virtual Cultures and Landscapes, Frankfurt: Peter Lang. pp. 63-71.

CEPAL (2010): "Panorama Migratorio en Colombia a Partir de Estadísticas Locales." April 4, 2016. http://www.cepal.org/celade/noticias/paginas/8/41138/03lreboiras-msoffia.pdf

Cepeda Castro, Iván (2006): "Genocidio Político El Caso de la Unión Patriótica en Colombia." In: Revista Cetil, I/2, pp. 101-112.

Deleuze, Gilles/Parnet, Claire.[1977](1996): "L'Actuel et le Virtuel" In: Gilles Deleuze/Claire Parnet: Dialogues. Paris: Edition Flammarion, pp. 179-185.

Deleuze, Gilles/Guattari, Félix [1980](2002): Conclusión: Reglas Concretas y Máquinas Abstractas. In: Mil Mesetas. Capitalismo y Esquizofrenia, Valencia: Pre-textos, pp. 511-523.

ElTiempo.com (2016): "Líderes Sociales Lanzan Alerta por Asesinatos." March 21, 2016. http://www.eltiempo.com/politica/justicia/asesinato-de-lideres-sociales-en-colombia/16542289

Guattari, Félix/Rolnik, Suely (2006): Micropolítica. Cartografías del Deseo, Madrid: Traficantes de Sueños.

Harvey, Lynda (1998): "Visibility, Silencing and Surveillance in an IT Needs Analysis Project." In: Tor Larsen/Linda Levine (eds.) Information Systems: Current Issues And Future Challenges. Proceedings of the IFIPWG 8.2 & 8.6 Joint Working Conference on Information Systems, Helsinki: Elsevier Science, North Holland, pp. 131-147.

Lozano Guillén, Carlos (2006): ¿Guerra o Paz en Colombia? Cincuenta Años de un Conflicto Sin Solución. Bogotá: Ediciones Izquierda Viva.

Marcus, George E. (1995): "Ethnography in/of the World System. The Emergence of Multi-Sited Ethnography" In: Annual Review of Anthropology 24, pp.95-117.

Marcus, George E. (1998): Ethnography Through Thick and Thin, Princeton, NJ: Princeton University Press.

Oiarzabal, Pedro J. /Ulf-Dietrich Reips (2012): "Migration and Diaspora in the Age of Information and Communication Technologies." In: Journal of Ethnic and Migration Studies 38/9, pp.1333-1338.

Rolnik, Suely (2006): "¿Una Nueva Suavidad?" In: Micropolítica. Cartografías del Deseo, Madrid: Traficantes de sueños, pp: 330-336.

Semana.com (2016): "Histórico: Despega la Negociación de Paz entre el Gobierno y el ELN." March 30, 2016. http://www.semana.com/nacion/articulo/ELN-y-gobierno-instalan-mesa-de-negociacion-de-paz/467258

# "You're Not Left Thinking That You're The Only Gay in the Village"

The Role of the *Facebook* Group: *Seksualiti Merdeka* in the Malaysian LGBT Community

*Veera Helena Pitkänen*

## Introduction—LGBT in Malaysia

This essay focuses on lesbian, gay, bisexual and transgender (LGBT) communities in Malaysia, a Southeast Asian country where sexual minority issues have been very contentious, as the Islamic Malay government openly condemns homosexuality (Offord 2011: 142). In Malaysian society, as described by Offord, sexuality is under attack, and great emphasis is put on guarding and policing Islamic morality (ibid: 142–143). Sodomy is considered a crime under Malaysian law—a remnant from the British colonial era—with punishments as much as 20 years in prison and corporal punishment, although the law is not often prosecuted (Alagappar & Kaur 2009: 25).

However, in 1998 and again in 2010, the opposition leader in the Malaysian parliament and the former Deputy Prime Minister, Anwar Ibrahim, made international headlines for being sentenced to prison for engaging in sodomy with men (Offord 2011: 140). Although Ibrahim was acquitted in 2012, the situation has worsened for sexual minorities in the last decade (Williams 2009: 7). They are experiencing an increasing amount of intolerance, discrimination and harassment in the country (Alagappar & Kaur 2009: 25).

In recent years, other issues concerning the LGBT community in Malaysia have also received international media attention. An incident that raised eyebrows in Europe was the publication of "guidelines" by the Malaysian Education Ministry to help parents to identify gay and lesbian "symptoms" in their children so they can take early measurements in correcting them.[1] In April 2013, the *Guardian*, among other foreign newspapers, made a report about *Asmara Songsang*, a musical backed by the Malaysian government.[2] My translation of the title is: "Abnormal love/desire," and the project aims to warn young people about the dangers of being lesbian, gay, bisexual and transgender (LGBT) in the country. The musical has sparked controversy over its "state-sponsored bigotry" and potential to incite hatred. Asmara Songsang (Abnormal Desire) follows the lives of three LGBT friends who throw loud parties, take drugs and have casual sex, thereby incurring the wrath of their religious neighbours, who attempt to reintroduce them to the teachings of Islam. Those who repent are spared, while those who don't are killed in a lightning storm (Hodal 2013).

*Image 1*

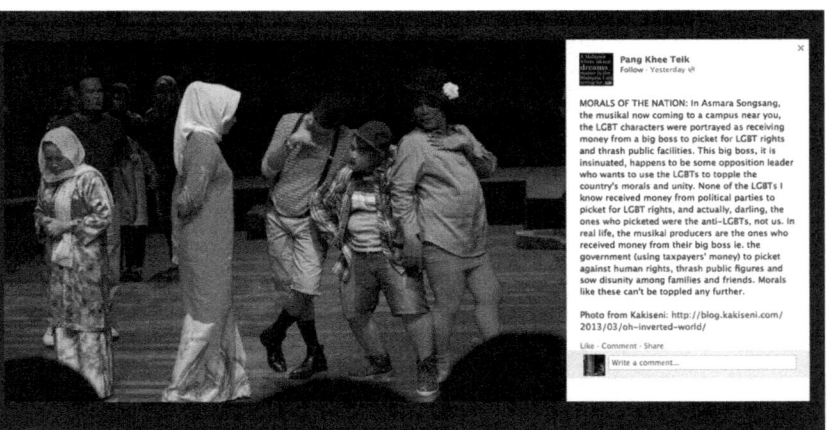

Performance photo of the *Morals of the Nation* musical from the *Facebook* profile of Pang Khee Teik. https://www.facebook.com/pangkheeteik] March 2013.

---

**1** | "Guidelines to Identify Gay and Lesbian Symptoms Published." Free Malaysiakini. September 13, 2012. Accessed: April 8, 2013. http://www.freemalaysiakini2.com/?p=46392
**2** | Hodal, Kate. "Anti-gay musical tours Malaysian schools and universities." The Guardian March 28, 2013. Accessed: April 8, 2013. http://www.guardian.co.uk/world/2013/mar/28/anti-gay-lgbt-musical-malaysia

## Resisting Discrimination—*Seksualiti Merdeka*

Despite the extremely conservative attitudes towards sexual minorities in the country, there are still several groups that actively promote tolerance and acceptance. One of them is *Seksualiti Merdeka*. Meaning "sexual independence" in the Malay language, it is a movement with a clear message: no one should be discriminated against or harassed, regardless of their sexual identity or orientation. Initiated by arts facilitator Pang Khee Teik and singer-songwriter Jerome Kugan, the first *Seksualiti Merdeka* festival was held in Kuala Lumpur in August 2008. It consisted of talks, forums, workshops and cultural events, and gathered together an estimated 400–500 people.

The organizers wanted the festival to coincide with the Merdeka (Malaysian Independence day) celebrations, because they wished to "address the fact that 51 years after independence, not all Malaysians are free to be who they are" (*Seksualiti Merdeka* 2013). The festival was organized annually until 2011—when the event was raided by the police and the activities banned by the Malaysian government.[3] In 2012, the organizers decided to take a break from organizing the festival. At the time that this article was being written, the plans for 2013 were still being discussed.

## Research Question: From a *Facebook* Group to a Community?

This essay aims to scrutinize the role of social media, and particularly *Facebook*, in the lives of Malaysian LGBTs. More specifically, it focuses on a *Facebook* group called *Seksualiti Merdeka*, a meeting point and a peer-support group for the Malaysian LGBT community, and examines the significance of this type of online platform in the country. Malaysia has the 24th highest number of internet users per capita in the world,[4] and social media is very widely used across the country.

Doing research on the LGBTs in Malaysia felt natural because of my personal relationship with the topic. From 2009 until 2012, I resided in Kuala Lumpur, and got acquainted with members of the LGBT community as well as representatives of related NGOs. One of the organizations was the *PT*

---

3 | „Seksualiti Merdeka movement festival banned." The Star. Published November 3, 2011. Accessed: April 8, 2013. http://thestar.com.my/news/story.asp?file=/2011/11/3/nation/20111103172539&sec=nation

4 | „Media>Internet>Users>Per capita: Countries Compared." Nationmaster. Last updated 2011. Accessed: April 8, 2013. http://www.nationmaster.com/graph/int_use_percap-internet-users-per-capita

*Foundation*—the former *Pink Triangle*—that provides information, education and care services relating to HIV/AIDS and sexual minority groups in Malaysia. I had joined the *Seksualiti Merdeka Facebook* group in 2011 when I was living in the country, as it seemed to be a great source of information about the current issues concerning sexual minorities in Malaysia.

*Seksualiti Merdeka* is a closed group on *Facebook*—an application for membership has to be approved by an administrator. At the time of the writing (April 8, 2013) the number of members stood at 2933, consisting of both Malaysians and non-Malaysians (who mostly live or have previously lived in Malaysia). I wanted to find out what purpose this group served to the Malaysian LGBTs, and whether it was used as a platform to deal with topics they would not otherwise be able to discuss. I also wanted to research whether the *Seksualiti Merdeka* group would be a safe space for its users to express their thoughts and to discuss even controversial political issues, and whether this group could be used to organize and plan events related to *Seksualiti Merdeka*. Key main references were: Offord's (2011) article "Singapore, Indonesia and Malaysia: arrested development!" and Alagappar/Kaur's (2009): "The Representation of Homosexuality—A Content Analysis in a Malaysian Newspaper"—a study of homosexuality in Malaysian media. My research could be considered to be cyberanthropology, which is:

an approach that submits anthropological and philosophical questions (as well as sociological, political and linguistic questions including questions of constitutional law arising from them) to different fields associated with the internet", targeting "the questions of how the human being understands itself and others, how it structures its lifeworld when embedded in virtual environments, in face of the challenges posed by the internet as the dominating medium.[5]

## RESEARCH METHODS AND ETHICAL REFLECTIONS

The main research methods used in this paper are participant observation in both active participant as well as participant-as-observer roles, accompanied with single and group interviews. I was following the discussions in the group on a daily basis between 17 March 2013 and 8 April 2013. I watched a variety of videos and read articles or blog posts that the group members posted, to get an idea of what kind of issues people in the Malaysian LGBT community talk about and are interested in. I interacted with the group members by asking them questions, and analyzed their responses. I also interviewed Pang Khee Teik,

---

5 | "What do we mean by Cyberanthropology?" CyberAnthropology. Accessed: April 8, 2013. http://www.cyberanthropology.de/CA/What_is_CA.html

a cultural and political activist and the co-founder of the *Seksualiti Merdeka*, and Raymond Tai from *PT Foundation*, who is also an active member of the *Seksualiti Merdeka* group.

Although there seemed to be an equal amount of different genders in the *Facebook* group, I mainly got responses to my questions from gay men.[6] They seemed to be more active in commenting and posting in the group. Only one of the respondents was female, and one transgender (male to female). It would have been fruitful to have more female representation in the research.

## FIELD RESEARCH—WHAT IS DISCUSSED IN THE *SEKSUALITI MERDEKA* GROUP?

The *Seksualiti Merdeka* group on *Facebook* is quite active, with roughly more than ten new posts and a variety of comments per day. The main language of the posts is English (the second official language in the country), but sometimes also Malay and Mandarin Chinese. The topics of the posts vary from political issues concerning the LGBTs in Malaysia to promoting LGBT-related events in the country: There are also inspirational coming-out stories and videos dealing with different LGBT issues; legal advice is also given—for example, how to act when arrested by the police.

Rather bold statements were posted on the page as well, such as a commentary by the group admin Pang Khee Teik to the aforementioned *Asmara Songsang* musical: "ASMARA SAYA tak songsang, beb. Politik negara ni yang songsang. Jom luruskan kerajaan. Sekian terima kasih.' It translates to: "My love is not abnormal. The politics of this country is abnormal. Let's straighten the government. Many thanks."[7]

---

**6** | However, this was just my assumption based on the respondents' profile pictures
**7** | Pang Khee Teik. Forum post on the *Seksualiti Merdeka* group on *Facebook*. March 29, 2013. My translation.

*Image 2*

Photo gallery from *Facebook* account for Seksualiti Merdeka. https://www.facebook.com/groups/SMFestival/ March 2013.

The majority of the group members seem to be LGBT themselves, although it is impossible to acquire any accurate statistical data on this. Most non-gay members, such as myself, are most likely somehow involved in the LGBT community: working or volunteering in NGOs or participating in alternative cultural or political events in Malaysia.

According to my observations in the group, a vast amount of the members of the *Seksualiti Merdeka* are Malaysian Chinese (predominantly non-Muslim) men. They are, based on my experiences in the country, usually the ones in Malaysian society who tend to be more open about being gay, mainly because the Chinese culture is often more liberal and tolerant of differences than the country's two other main cultures: Malay and Indian. This is, however, not to say that homosexuality would be widely accepted in the Malaysian Chinese community either.

Also a large number of Malays have found their way into the group. All ethnic Malays are Muslims by the Malaysian constitution, and are under no circumstances allowed to leave the religion (Yusof 2010: 184). As many observant Muslims in the country reject homosexuality, LGBT ethnic Malays are often under enormous pressure not to express their sexual identities.

All in all, the *Facebook* group is very diverse, and the country's main ethnic groups and different genders are relatively well represented. There are also quite a few foreign-sounding (European, Australian, American) names, which could be explained by the large expatriate community in Malaysia.

## SINGLE INTERVIEWS

To collect data from the group interviews, I first posted a questionnaire on the *Facebook* Wall belonging to the group. The possibility to answer anonymously by e-mail was offered, but I did not get a sufficient amount of replies. Subsequently I tried posting only one question on which the members of the group could comment directly; this turned out to be the most effective method in getting the group members to reply. I received a total of 13 answers. Out of all the people that answered, I chose two people who seemed to have more to say, and asked them further questions by e-mail.

Based on the single interviews with Pang Khee Teik (conducted on April 2, 2013) and Raymond Tai (conducted on April 1, 2013), I put together some of the most prevalent issues related to the research. According to both of the interviewees, there are various *Facebook* groups in Malaysia for the LGBT community. Tai said social media and other internet sites in Malaysia can be used mainly for socializing purposes. Dating and sex sites are thriving because they are almost impossible to control—even when a site is closed down, a mirror site will appear the next day. However, for those who are not out yet, using *Facebook* always poses a risk that their sexual orientation will be revealed.

Teik explained that many Malaysian LGBT people have two *Facebook* profiles for this purpose: one that reflects their identity as a gay individual, and one that appears as "straight" in order to avoid persecution. "To me, [that] sounds a bit unnecessary and makes it difficult to be who you are. I hope, one day, they will be able to merge the two together. I tell them that, on your gay profile, even if the privacy settings are very high, there is no guarantee that one of these gay people that you befriend is not going to expose you."[8]

Tai emphasized that although excellent for socializing, social media in Malaysia is not a safe platform from which to plan political activities, such as setting up organizations to help those who are in the closet, or organizing empowerment programs for sexual minorities. "For a while that is what *Seksualiti Merdeka* was doing, but it was quickly exposed in the main media. The government would use every effort they can to try to use public pressure

---

8 | Pang Khee Teik in interview with author.

to close it down."[9] According to him, the state controlled media has often been distorting the information they found in social media—for example, *Seksualiti Merdeka* ("Sexual Independence") would be twisted into *Sex Bebas* ("Free Sex") in the newspapers. Tai said *Facebook* users should always be aware that anything they post may end up in the wrong hands.

I use a lot of restraint in what I put on the internet because of my work at PT Foundation; I cannot jeopardize the work that we are doing at the Pink Triangle. Especially Facebook is so public that the rule of thumb is that if you are unable to say [something] on printed media, you wouldn't say that on Facebook. It is similar in the sense that you have no control over it. When you put information on Facebook, it is public property, so one has to be careful, I suppose. (Interview with Raymond Tai)

Pang Khee Teik, who posts about LGBT issues to the site several times a day, told me that most of the time a team of two or three people, including himself, are responsible for making sure that new group members have the appropriate agenda. At the time of this writing, in April 2013, they had over 200 people in line awaiting approval. Teik said they usually end up adding people who already have more than five friends in the group. "Sometimes I also look at their *Facebook* profile—if it is someone from the circle of friends who I can trust, then I will add them in. Or, sometimes, if I am not quite sure, I will actually send them a message and ask why they want to join."

According to Tai, social media is in general the best place to communicate. He also mentioned alternatives such as *Google Groups*, which are more confined and limited to the core group of people. They can be used to discuss some of the things that need more organizing. "*Facebook* is more for things that we think we can publish—it is still the most versatile [social media platform] and commonly available for most people."

## GROUP INTERVIEWS

In the group, I asked the participants why they found the *Seksualiti Merdeka Facebook* group useful. Between 3-7 April 2013, I received twelve replies in total: ten of the respondents were male, one of them female and one transgender (from male to female). Eight of them were ethnic Malaysian Chinese and four of them Malay. All of the respondents were Malaysians and LGBT; six stated in their profile that they lived in Malaysia and three lived abroad. In three profiles the current location information was not stated. In their *Facebook* profiles neither of them stated openly that they are gay, however, some of them had

---

9 | Raymond Tai in interview with author.

included suggestive quotes or photographs promoting liberal values such as sexual equality. To protect the respondents' privacy, I used pseudonyms instead of the names given in their *Facebook* profiles.

The answers revealed that the most important reason for using the *Facebook* group was primarily receiving information or news concerning the LGBT community in Malaysia, as well as being informed about LGBT related activities and events in the country. Seven respondents mentioned this point. "Unlike many platforms out there, the members here talk about useful LGBT information and equality. No, we don't talk about where is the latest toilet to cruise or where to get porn DVDs. We talk about what's going on around us, how it is going to affect us and how we can all come together and deal with it wisely," said Nick. Five respondents mentioned camaraderie or making new friends as an important factor: "I've made a few friends from the group as well. I have a small social circle and SM has introduced a few LGBT friends to me for which I'm grateful," said Sam.

Five considered peer-to-peer support an important factor. "It s nice to know you're not abnormal or damned like the public majority would think. To be able to safely admit who you are and finally be yourself. You're not left thinking that you're the only gay in the village which is depressing and leaves you hopeless for the future," told Nita. Another respondent, Joseph, also highlighted this issue: "You are so alone, a freak, an outcast, an abomination. But when you have found people like you, you don't feel so alone anymore. Having a supportive community, self pitying and self hatred just gradually disappear." Four respondents also referred to the value of being able to have a free discussion and network with other members of the LGBT community.

Being inspired by others and gaining self confidence were mentioned by two: "Seeing so many LGBTs who are proud of who they are and willing to fight for their rights inspires me to love myself more and be more comfortable with myself," said Sam. Knowing, understanding and learning to defend one's rights together with gaining the ability to be themselves and express oneself freely were also mentioned twice. Two also stated that they would like to support others who are going through similar issues to ones they had experienced: "you want to be a pillar of strength for someone out there who is still lost, scared and alone," Joseph continued. Respondents also mentioned feeling able to "complain about the government," being empowered, not being judged by others, reaching out to the whole community, getting resources, seeing things in perspective and making the world a better place.

Out of these 12 respondents, I chose two members, Khalil and Sam to whom I sent additional questions by e-mail. They both emphasized the importance of using protected *Facebook* groups and aliases when dealing with delicate issues such as sexual identity or orientation: "It is important for me to use not only closed but a secret group where my family members will not be able to see that

I'm in that group via *Facebook*. This is mainly because I'm not out to them yet, considering the possible financial repercussions," said Sam, whose studies are funded by his parents.

He is still afraid of publicly commenting on things related to LGBT on social media "since people associate you with being LGBT the minute you say anything about it. And I don't want to have to lie and say I'm not if asked the question. So I choose to avoid it altogether."[10] Khalil had a similar view on the issue: "It is still widely unacceptable being gay in this country, and in order to prevent further discrimination, only closed groups can protect the LGBT community." He thought it is possible that government officials were watching activities, but he had not encountered any problems himself.[11]

## Conclusion—A Safe Space For Like-Minded Individuals

Over the course of my research, I found a variety of other LGBT related groups and pages on *Facebook*, such as the "PFLAG Malaysia" support group,[12] and a page called "Gay Malaysia Confessions."[13] However, *Seksualiti Merdeka* is one of the most popular groups that Malaysian LGBTs turn to for information.

For the regular user, *Seksualiti Merdeka* is a closed community and a safe space where the members can discuss their experiences as LGBT. Members support and encourage each other, sharing information and events of interest without being judged. For them, it is also an important means of networking and connecting with like-minded people in order to realize they are not alone; that being LGBT is not something to be ashamed of. The members feel they can "be themselves," at least in this virtual environment, instead of playing a role as they often have to do in their everyday lives.

For the group members who are involved in politics and organizing events related to the *Seksualiti Merdeka* movement, however, social media is not a safe arena. They must be constantly be mindful of what they write in order for their comments not to leak out into the Malaysian mainstream media. The research shows that, at the moment, it is not advisable to use *Facebook* or other means of social media for organizing any large public events for sexual minorities in the country. For the LGBTs in Malaysia, there is still a long way to go before

10 | Sam, in a private e-mail message to author. April 3, 2013.
11 | Khalil, in a private e-mail message to author. April 7, 2013.
12 | „PFLAG Malaysia." *Facebook*. Accessed: April 8, 2013. https://www.facebook.com/groups/pflagmalaysia/?ref=ts&fref=ts
13 | „Gay Malaysia Confessions." *Facebook*. Accessed: April 8, 2013. https://www.facebook.com/GayMYConfessions?fref=ts

people can freely express themselves in social media without fear. Groups like *Seksualiti Merdeka* are, however, a good start and act as a beacon of hope for a brighter future.

## References

Alagappar, Ponmalar N. & Kaur, Karamjeet (2009): "The Representation of Homosexuality—A Content Analysis in a Malaysian Newspaper." In: Language in India. Strength for Today and Bright Hope for Tomorrow 9, pp. 24-47.

"Anthropology of Sexuality and Gender." Trans-academics. Last updated 2006. Accessed: April 8, 2016. http://www.trans-academics.org/syllabi/Valentine2.pdf

Gay Malaysia Confessions." *Facebook.* Accessed: April 8, 2013. https://www.facebook.com/GayMYConfessions?fref=ts

"Guidelines to Identify Gay and Lesbian Symptoms Published." Free Malaysiakini. September 13, 2012. Accessed: April 8, 2016. http://www.freemalaysiakini2.com/?p=46392

Hodal, Kate. "Anti-gay musical tours Malaysian schools and universities." The Guardian March 28, 2013. Accessed: April 8, 2016. http://www.guardian.co.uk/world/2013/mar/28/anti-gay-lgbt-musical-malaysia

"LGBTI Interactive Map—Malaysia." Human Rights Initiative. Accessed: April 8, 2013. http://www.humanrightsinitiative.org/lgbti-interactive-map/malaysia-info.php

"Malaysia: Ban on sexuality rights festival violates human rights." Seksualiti Merdeka. Published 10.11.2011, accessed: April 8, 2016. http://www.seksualitimerdeka.org/2011/11/malaysia-ban-on-sexuality-rights.html

"Malaysia Demographics Profile 2013.' Index Mundi. Last updated February 21, 2016. Accessed: April 8, 2013. http://www.indexmundi.com/malaysia/demographics_profile.html

"Media>Internet>Users>Per capita: Countries Compared." Nationmaster. Last updated 2011. Accessed: April 8, 2016. http://www.nationmaster.com/graph/int_use_percap-internet-users-per-capita

Miller, Daniel (2011): Tales from Facebook, Polity Press.

Offord, Baden (2011): "Singapore, Indonesia and Malaysia: arrested development!". In Manon Tremblay/ David Paternotte/Carol Johnson (eds.): "The lesbian and gay movement and the state: comparative insights into a transformed relationship, London: Ashgate Press, pp. 135-152.

"PFLAG Malaysia." *Facebook.* Accessed April 8, 2016. https://www.facebook com/groups/pflagmalaysia/?ref=ts&fref=ts "Seksualiti Merdeka." *Facebook* Accessed: April 8, 2016. https://www.facebook.com/groups/SMFestival

"Seksualiti Merdeka movement festival banned." The Star. Published November 3, 2011. Accessed: April 8, 2016. http://thestar.com.my/news/story.asp?file=/2011/11/3/nation/20111103172539&sec=nation

Williams, Walter (2009): "Strategies for Challenging Homophobia in Islamic Malaysia and Secular China." Nebula Press, 6/1, pp. 1. http://www.nobleworld.biz/images/Williams.pdf

"What Do We Mean by Cyberanthropology?" In: CyberAnthropology. Accessed: April 8, 2016. http://www.cyberanthropology.de/CA/What_is_CA.html

Yusof, Azmyl Md (2010): "Facing the Music: Music Subcultures and 'Morality' in Malaysia." In: Yeoh Seng Guan (ed.): "Media, Culture and Society in Malaysia" London: Routledge, pp.179-196

# Finding a Visual Voice
## The #Euromaidan Impact on Ukrainian Instagram Users

*Karly Domb Sadof*

## INTRODUCTION

> *The one who tells the story rules the world.*
> —Hopi Proverb

It was the last of the difficult days. The troops were too close. Sasha[1] followed the line of burning tires. There were a lot of people, gas and fire. He wanted to remember this moment. The moment when he felt no fear.

Everyday Sasha would wake up to look at the news feeds. He'd call his friends who were at Maidan during the night. He'd go buy food and clothes; and bottles to fill with Molotov. From about midday till daybreak they were there. Trying to help.

It was the night of the final fight between the government forces and the people of Maidan. When Sasha, like a tortoise, kneeled next to his friend cowering under a shield.

He looked up and saw a guy raising his hands as he jumped into the most dangerous zone. Sasha raised his own hands. Snap. The moment was captured, hashtagged and uploaded. Now the world would see. #евромайдан #euromaidan.

Sasha is not a photojournalist; Sasha is not even a photographer. Sasha, 21, is from a small town in the western part of Ukraine called Kolomyya. In 2010 he moved to Kiev to attend University. He enjoys taking photos of himself and his friends, and posting them on *Instagram*[2], a photo-sharing social network. However, when the people of Kiev filled their city's Maidan Square to oust their government and demand their country more closely integrate with the

---

1 | Names have been changed for privacy and security purposes.
2 | Instagram was founded in 2010 as a photo-sharing social network to be used solely on mobile phones.

European Union in late 2013 and early 2014, Sasha's photos took on a different feel. He began to post images showing the revolution. His feed—the stream of photos from others he followed—also changed. Soon "selfies" were replaced with pictures of Molotov cocktails, girlfriends became protestors, sunsets changed to flames.

The visible impact of the Ukrainian revolution on *Instagram* was noticeable both within Ukraine and abroad. The American magazine *Esquire* featured a series claiming to show "thirty-two real photographs of how normal, everyday life changed in a matter of days." The photo essay was both applauded and criticized for using *Instagram* images as data points to reflect the social and visible changes in Kiev. It was shared nearly 800 times on *Twitter*, and yet Michael Shaw, the publisher of the visual politics and media literacy site then called *BagNewsNotes*[3], called it "photo exploitation." Shaw accused *Esquire* of "data-mining" and, to prove a point, produced a cartoon turning the *Instagram* users into caricatures.

As an avid *Instagram* user and photo editor for the Associated Press—one of the largest global newswires—I found this series of images fascinating. Was this first-person journalism? Do these images document cultural change in real-time through the eyes of those who are impacted? Or do these diptychs visually exploit their creators? Do the images catalog an actual change in behavior? Or could the same be done with any *Instagram* feed? Perhaps, most significantly, what is the role of *Instagram* in these peoples' lives? And has that changed?

Like all social networks in Web 2.0[4], *Instagram* relies heavily on the concept of "produsage" as coined by Axel Bruns (2008) in his book, *Blogs, Wikipedia, Second Life and Beyond, from Production to Produsage*. "Produsage", according to Bruns, describes the active nexus of "collaborative creation" in the digital sphere. *Instagram*, capitalizes on the desire of its users to engage and create—their "produsage." The name *Instagram* even implies these dual functions. While taken instantaneously, with or without the addition of a "filter", (a digital effect modeled off of different analogue cameras and film types), the images are also shared within the mobile application: a visual telegram of sorts.

This latter function is what separates *Instagram* from other photo manipulation apps. More than just photo-editing software, *Instagram* builds a community: central to the logic of the app is its ranking system of "liking", its ability to geographically connect through location-tagging, and its intent

---

3 | In 2015 the website changed its name "Reading The Pictures".

4 | Web. 2.0 refers to the internet's change to emphasize user-generated content which can take many forms. Including reader comments, blogs, social media etc. Previously Web. 1.0 featured few content creators and most users only consumed the World Wide Web, but didn't engage.

to forge relationships with its users through "hashtagging." As Bruns (2008) writes, "The arrival and gradual embrace of produsage clearly has the potential to significantly reshape our existing cultural, commercial, social and political institutions" (2008: 400). Seeing this potential, *Facebook* purchased *Instagram* in April 2012 for one billion USD. The community has since grown to host about 200 million monthly active users. According to the company, these 'produsers' upload roughly sixty million photos daily.

A search for "евромайдан" or "euromaidan" on *Instagram* on February 18, 2014—at the peak of the protests in Maidan—generates 85,120 photos. Most of these posts are from within Ukraine; some came from Ukrainian nationals abroad, as well as others sympathetic to—or outraged by—their cause. However, for Sasha, and his many cohorts *Instagram*-ing from within the square, *Instagram* was more than just a way to commiserate virtually. These individuals were documenting the events around them; so much so, that professional journalists who flocked to cover the story were using their "grams" as a way of locating action. As Bruns writes:

Produsage-based citizen journalism is the first step towards restoring access to the public institution of journalism for a wide range of citizen-turned producers breaking open the commercial (and political) lock on the journalistic industry, as it has been established during the late stages of industrial capitalism. (ibid., 96)

From January 2014 to April 2014 I studied these "citizen-turned-visual-news-producers", their use of *Instagram*, and how the revolution impacted their practice within the application. My research aims to dig deeper than *Esquire's* "data points". Melanie Green (2008), a social psychologist whose research focuses on the power of the narrative to change beliefs, writes, "when consumers lose themselves in a story, their attitudes and intentions change to reflect that story" (ibid: 5170). In striving to understand these individuals on a holistic and comprehensive level, my research explores this phenomenon. How does the dissemination of storytelling impact the individual? And how, in turn, does this pattern change during a big story like the 2014 Ukrainian revolution? What could have encouraged these image-makers to document their days on *Instagram* in the first place?

## METHODS

My approach to understanding the impact of the Ukrainian revolution on users of *Instagram* was strictly ethnographic. As Tom Boellstorff (2012) writes in his book *Ethnography and Virtual Worlds A Handbook of Method*, ethnographers "aim to study virtual worlds as valid venues for cultural practices seeking to understand both how they resemble and how they differ from other forms of culture" (2012: 1). Thus *Instagram* became my field site, its users became my tribe. We connected virtually, despite being based in New York City and nearly 7,500 km from most of my informants in Kiev. I was able to observe their actions within this digital realm and to participate by documenting my own life. I was able to contact my informants by commenting on their photos and connecting with them over *Facebook Chat*[5] and *Skype*. Through extensive interviews I was able to learn about each individual's local context and personal experience with *Instagram*. From my own personal experience, I was able to relate to those I was studying.

In addition to relying on both passive and participant observation, together with interviews and questionnaires, I engaged my research with previous anthropological literature regarding cell phones and photography. In her article *Ethnographic Approaches to Digital Media*, anthropologist Enid Gabriella Coleman (2010) writes, "To grasp more fully the broader significance of digital media, its study must involve various frames of analysis, attention to history, and the local contexts and lived experiences of digital media—a task well suited to the ethnographic enterprise" (ibid: 489). *Instagram* is a new virtual realm and not much anthropological research has focused on its users. Mobile phones have been around for a while and long since grasped the attention of ethnographers. In her study *Mobile Media in the Asia-Pacific* Larissa Hjorth (2008) writes, "By studying the mobile phone we can gain insight into many of the cultural processes that constitute contemporary everyday life (ibid: 5). My research attempts to build upon this understanding of the cell phone as a conduit for culture and how it is now challenging the modes of visual media production.

There were key limitations to my research. I do not speak Russian, meaning all of my informants had to speak some level of English. While English is taught in most Ukrainian schools, the English-speaking Ukrainian diaspora is notably a more educated group with a strong western kinship. This constraint, in conjunction with my dependence on technology for communication and research, meant that the Ukrainians I interviewed were most likely of a certain economic status. Another important limitation of my work was my inability to travel to the region during this time. In contrast to the traditional analogue anthropologist, my own geographic position—in relationship to my subjects—significantly distanced me from them as much of my research occurred in the digital landscape. I attempted to overcome these obstacles by concentrating purely on the culture within *Instagram*. Thus my research singularly examined this tribe of *Instagram* users within their native digital realm and virtual dialect.

---

**5** | In April 2014 after this study was completed, *Facebook Chat* became a separate Facebook owned and operated mobile application: *"Messenger"*.

This narrow scope—while controlled—allowed for a deeper focus in the digital domain, but isolated my informants and myself from all other environmental and geo-political influences.

## THE DATA

### Part I: Creating a Virtual Self in a Visual Vernacular

Fundamentally my research found that my informants used *Instagram* as a process of forming their own identity and communicating this virtual self to a broader visual community. As Lev Manovicch and Nadav Hochmann (2013) write in *Zooming Into An Instagram City: Reading the Local Through Social Media*, "Instagram signifies a new desire to creatively place together old and new—local and global—parts and wholes—in various combinations." This so-called "new" desire capitalizes on photography's ability to always synthesize time and place. As Susan Sontag (1977) writes in *On Photography*, "Cameras began duplicating the world at that moment when the human landscape started to undergo a vertiginous rate of change: while an untold number of forms of biological and social life are being destroyed in a brief span of time, a device is available to record what is disappearing" (ibid: 15).

While images have always "been worth a thousand words," the ability of *Instagram* to locate each image in relationship to its producer and viewer allows for a more sophisticated, intimate, and inherent ease in communicating visually. During my interviews on *Facebook Chat*, photos would be inserted into the conversations frequently. When interviewing Julia, 24, from Ismali, a town in the Odessa region of Ukraine, I found that Julia would often include photos to explain a point. When I asked her age she showed a picture of herself with a birthday cake. She showed me a photo of herself in Washington DC when explaining where she mastered her English skills, and so on. Likewise, another contact posted photographs to illustrate his actions: in a conversation with Igor, 21, from Dubrovica in the Ukraine, Igor had to break off to take his dog out. He quickly followed up with a photo of himself walking his dog and, when he was back at his computer and ready to resume the conversation, he snapped a photo of himself there too.

The idea of constant visual communication is quintessentially 21st century. With the creation of cell phone photography, images have become the vernacular of the virtual world. *Instagram* even launched "*Instagram Direct*" in December 2013 as a way of allowing its users to send visuals to one another privately. This new component may have been initiated as way for *Instagram* to compete with social media rival, *Snapchat*[6]. However, more importantly, this recently added component of the application emphasizes the intimate visual connection *Instagram* has formed with in its own community. Whether it is by sending photos directly to another user, or holding one's own memories and others in your hand, the intimate nature of *Instagram* is evident. While users can send photos to supplement text in other messaging services, like *Whatsapp*, in *Instagram*, visuals drive the conversation.

The interface of *Instagram* also helps to convey this atmosphere of familiarity. As Hochman and Manovich (2013) write, "*Instagram*'s photos resonate with more personal, "authentic" experiences that chronicle the world in a way that resists the time and place represented by larger impersonal corporate documentation efforts." Even the concept of time, which is generally considered a universal experience, is personal within *Instagram*. Every time I asked one of my informants when they joined *Instagram* they replied, "X number of days ago." While the variable changed, this formulaic response remained a consistent answer amongst respondents. As Hochman and Manovich state "The time element is always user–centric and its measurement is relative between the present moment of launching the application and the original date of creation. The interface strongly emphasizes physical place and users' locations." Further, when searching for past photos with my informants we had to scroll through their feeds prowling for images. There is no internal search function. Once we found the desired photo, when asking when it was taken, the answer would always be "X number of days ago" as the app would describe.

Although the language of "X number of days ago" as opposed to "January 17" may not have a real bearing on an individual, the notion of the self is more present in the former expression of time. "Days ago…" infers a direct relationship with the *Instagram* users current and past selves. That was one instant; this is another. When these instants are strung together, what do they create? A feed? Or a chronicle of a life lived? As Anna—27, from Kiev—described it. "I don't plan to take my pictures. It's just in the moment. From when I live the moment or share a moment with the people and things which are with me."

While this "user-centric" concept of time was seemingly created to construct a more natural experience, personally—as an anthropologist and journalist—this has been a struggle. It means that when I'm scrolling through my own feed or finding my informant's images it can be particularly challenging to figure out when exactly an image was taken or when an event happened. If something was shot 72 days ago---well, that is useless. My general reaction is usually: " Really?! That long ago?!" The passage of time can be a shock. Perhaps,

---

**6** | A photo messaging service whose producers, according to the company, out number *Instagram*'s by sharing 700 million photos daily, as of May 2014.

in reality, I am not using *Instagram* correctly. After all, as the name suggests, *Instagram* emphasizes the instant. As Hochman and Manovich (2013) observe, "This sense of a temporality is established not only by *Instagram*'s filters or time presentation, but also by its instant photo sharing function." Even images not shared in the "instant" are classified differently in the app as "latergrams" or "throwbacks." And while this can be irritating for me, as an anthropologist and journalist hunting for facts, the real result is a greater personal connection amongst *Instagram*'s users. My informants trust that images are uploaded shortly after being shot unless otherwise stated; in return, the app breeds a communal understanding of intimate simultaneity.[7]

There is a particular level of self-awareness that occurs during intimacy. In *Instagram* this visual intimacy leads to the creation of a new virtual self. Russell W. Belk (2013) writes in *The Extended Self in a Digital World:*

[A] difference from the pre digital age is in the extent to which we now self-disclose and confess online, transforming the once semi-private to a more public presentation of self. This is also evident in the more shared nature of the self which is now co-constructed with much more instantaneous feedback that can help affirm or modify our sense of self. The aggregate self can no longer be conceived from only a personal perspective and is not only jointly constructed but shared, that is, a joint possession with others. (Belk 2013: 490)

In *Instagram* this new digital self is both the emergence of a more public self, and one that is directly dependent and shaped by others.

The construction of the more public self starts with the creation of an *Instagram* 'handle'—the internal naming system within the application. My informants generally chose handles that related to their actual name or their nickname. Additionally, many chose to use a name they had given themselves on other social media platforms as a way to link the accounts and create a virtual self that extended beyond *Instagram* into *Facebook, Twitter, Tumblr* and beyond.

Vadim, 38, is one such user. He was born in Berdyansk in the Zaporozhye region of Ukraine and moved to Kiev 6 years ago. His handle of Иммигрант13 translates to "Immigrant13" and is the same nickname he uses on his *Google, Facebook* and *Twitter* accounts. About 10 years ago Vadim was considering a move to Canada with his family, but at the last minute they decided they didn't want to leave their home country and instead chose to remain in Ukraine. During that time, he was given the nickname "immigrant" by some of his friends and in return he decided to use it on all of his social profiles. Vadim describes himself as an active social media user and our conversations took

---

7 | In 2016, Instagram changed to include a more algorithmic representation.

place over *Facebook Chat*, *GChat*, and *Instagram*. This ability to link his profiles helps to create his robust virtual identity and digital self.

Another way many of my informants created their digital identity as a more public version of the 'self' was by taking pictures of themselves in a variety of situations; self-portraits not normally in the public sphere. These images, more frequently known as "selfies," have become such a huge global phenomenon on social media that the Oxford English Dictionary nominated "selfie" its word of the year in 2013. According to language research conducted by the Oxford English Dictionary, the frequency of the word "selfie" in the English language increased by 17,000 percent from 2012 to 2013. In their article *Mobile Phones and Community Development: A Contact Zone between Media and Citizenship*, Gerard Goggin and Jacqueline Clark (2009) write:

Mobile phones have developed a particular relationship with people, their bodies, and their lives. Mobile phones have become a personal, even intimate technology. They certainly were a domestic technology, even more so than 'personal' computers, laptops, or many other household, digital, or ubiquitous computing devices. (Goggin/Clark 2009: 586)

Therefore, if phones provoke a physical and visceral reaction, perhaps it is only natural that the growth of cell phone photography coincides with a rise in the amount of images taken of the body.

Dasha, 27, from Kiev, loves taking selfies. For her they generally happen when she's had a good day, or is feeling like it could be a good day. From a sampling of 100 *Instagram* posts by Dasha, forty-six could be classified as some sort of selfie, and while some showed her legs, feet and hands, thirty-nine featured her face prominently in the frame. "They are for me," Dasha says, "For when I think I'm pretty." She finds the "likes" encouraging. Dasha's selfies take private intimate moments and project them into both the public and digital sphere. The impact of the intimacy of *Instagram* and the public sphere's influence on the digital self has more than just a physical effect, but a psychological one as well. If Dasha's perception of how "pretty" she looks is dependent on how many people "like" her selfies, it influences her emotions.

Likewise, looking through photos from the past creates a different—and more tangible—understanding of nostalgia then simply relying on the mind's eye. This can also influence a person's understanding of the "now", especially if one is constantly negotiating between the different spheres. Oleg, 25, from Krivoy Rog, Ukraine, says about his own experience on *Instagram*, "any new day, any new place could give you a chance to make the best photo ever." And by "best" he does not necessarily mean his favorite, rather one that is the favorite of others. The *Instagram* community is part of what fosters the development of the digital self. The "liking," the "following" and the "sharing" are all actions (and terms) that help to build *Instagram* as a community shaped by its "produsers." Not only does its community shape *Instagram*, but the community is part of its allure. As Edward Mcquarrie, Jessica Miller, and Barbara Phillips (2013) write in *The Megaphone Effect: Taste and Audience in Fashion Blogging*, "A new kind of consumer behavior has emerged online in the past decade. The Web has made it possible for ordinary consumers to reach a mass audience, to 'grab hold of the megaphone,' to adapt Bourdieu's (1999) metaphor" (ibid: 136).

Julia, 24, was drawn to *Instagram* for this very reason. "I want people to find my pictures," she says. Julia asserts that her photos are often for herself, but more frequently they are aimed at her close friends, relatives, and sometimes even total strangers, with whom she connects with through "hashtagging". Commonly used on other social networks, "hashtagging" is a way of categorizing content based on specific topic. Julia says she uses this method to connect to people with the same interests. For example, when she posts photos of her cat she often tags the photos *"#instaCat"* as a way of showing her cat to other cat lovers. Similarly, when Julia feels like looking at cat photos she will search the *#instaCat* feature to find photos she would not otherwise see. Mcquarrie, Miller, and Phillips (2013) write, "More consumers now have more opportunities to reach thousands of other consumers than ever before." (ibid: 136). Reaching these thousands of other consumers can be great for cat lovers like Julia, while also creating a sense of comfort for the user.

In monumental situations such as the Ukrainian revolution, this means of categorization had an important and pivotal role to play that extends much farther than looking at cat photos. For example, Oleg found this to be the case when he was photographing the tossing of Molotov cocktails in Maidan Square. "It was really scary," he said, "these comments gave a hope and motivation." For Oleg, his virtual self was created by the community, but also supported by it. As he "hashtagged" his photos to connect him with others in the Ukrainian community, he became a part of not just the *Instagram* community, but of an entire subculture within it. Mcquarrie, Miller, and Phillips state that in some "consumption spheres, consumers are able to grab the megaphone for themselves, without institutional certification or enablement." (ibid: 137). Based on my research, this was the case for *#euromaidan*. Critically, this sense of empowerment and connection occurred because the concept of the virtual self relies so strongly in sharing these private moments with a greater more public community through the virtual vernacular.

## Part II: The Impact of the Ukranian Revolution

When I asked Julia if she found that *Instagram* helped her connect with the Ukrainian revolution, she replied, "maybe it's better to say that I connected *Instagram* to the revolution." Initially I assumed that we had reached a translation hurdle, so I asked her to explain what she meant. She then elaborated that *Instagram* did not bring her to other people but, by posting photos from the square, other people came to her. In his op-ed in *The New York Times*, Oleksandr V. Turchyno wrote on March 11, 2014 that during Euromaidan[8] "the people of Ukraine proved stronger than a dictator who had been groomed for the role of a puppet ruler." The Ukrainian people's belief in their own power not only fostered the revolution, but also influenced their use of *Instagram* during that time. As Vadim says, "we realized that each of us can be the mouthpiece."

Many of my informants shared this understanding of individual power; notably all of my informants participated in the Euromaidan protests where the individual's power was valued. I tried to find informants with differing opinions but consistently the people using *Instagram* publicly—with geo-tags and hashtags—were on the same side of the revolution; a revolution that believed in the power of the people as both individuals and as a collective. As anthropologist, Jeffrey S. Juris, writes in his study: *Reflections on #Occupy Everywhere*, "...digital tools facilitated the diffusion of global justice movements and enhanced their scale of operation by allowing activists to more effectively communicate and coordinate across geographic spaces." (2012: 260). With this level of communication and coordination comes a greater sense of the group.

The strong understanding of "community" throughout *Instagram* only strengthens this "group" mentality. As Yana, 43, born and raised in Kiev said, "During this period I made my photos to memorialize this event for my country and to show them to other *Instagram* users around the world." Yana's *Instagram* followers doubled during the revolution, bolstering her own individual sense of power and that of the cause. She commented: "It was a difficult but important period for all the Ukrainians. My photos reflected that with patriotism."

Likewise, Dasha also said she felt a sense of power when her followers started to build up after she started posting photos from Maidan Square. The support she received on social media echoed that which she felt in the square. As Ukranian flags hung from the streets in her neighborhood, so too did they appear in her social feeds. Dasha, lover of eye-shadowed selfies, started to take photos of tires in flames and sometimes even photos of herself in front of such scenes. However, this change in subject matter was not permanent; when the revolution died down she reverted to her old *Instagram* habits. She continued, "Now that everyone has seen lots of bad news and is confused about the new government's actions –we need to see something good-so I chose to take good positive pictures."

Vadim echoed this experience. With over two thousand followers, Vadim is no stranger to *Instagram*. He generally posts images of stunning landscapes at

---

8 | The term Euromaidan has come to indicate this period of civil upheaval in Ukraine, which began in November 2013.

sunrise and sunset and sometimes pictures of his family in these surreal and beautiful scenes. But when asked about the momentary blip in his *Instagram* feeds—where images of chaos replaced his normally serene photos—Vadim said, "When these events happened, even the most conscious Ukrainians had to change their content. You cannot post flowers, when people are dying."

## Conclusion

During the 2014 revolution, the Ukrainian users of *Instagram* were not only advocates for democracy in their home country, but also used *Instagram* to democratize the production of visual media. In *Mobile Phones and Community Development: A Contact Zone between Media and Citizenship*, Goggin and Clark (2009) write,

The mobile phone goes further still, along the trajectory of the culturally resonant path of media, playing an important role alongside other convergent and traditional media in bringing new voices, actors, and powerful practices into the circuits of development. (Goggin/Clark 2009: 596)

As the protestors in Maidan square challenged their government, so too did their use of technology challenge the modes of visual media production.

The crisis of representation is evolving into a global battle for self-representation. As Clark and Goggin (2009) state, "There are more mobile phones than fixed-line telephones around the world, and in developing countries, cell phones are often the effective and relatively affordable form of telecommunications access" (ibid.: 585). With the prevalence of photo social networks like *Instagram*, individuals are fighting against the indexical and iconic imagery in their own lives and diffusing the fetishism of photographic production. These Ukranians using *Instagram* from Maidan Square directly became the media producers of the revolution. Thus helping to not only oust their government, but also annihilate the global disparity of visual capital.

## References

Belk, Russell W. (2013): "Extended Self in a Digital World." In: Journal of Consumer Research 40/3, 477-500.
Boellstorff, Tom/Nardi, Bonnie/Pearce, Celia/Taylor, T. L. (2012): Ethnography and Virtual Worlds: A Handbook of Method, Oxford and Princeton: Princeton University Press.

Bruns, Axel (2008): Blogs, Wikipedia, Second Life, and beyond: From production to produsage. Frankfurt am Main/ New York: Peter Lang Verlag.

Coleman, E. Gabriella (2010): "Ethnographic Approaches to Digital Media." In: Annual Review of Anthropology 39, pp. 487-505.

Goggin, Gerard, and Jacqueline Clark (2009): "Mobile Phones and Community Development: a Contact Zone Between Media and Citizenship." In: Development in Practice 19/4-5, pp. 585-597.

Green, Melanie C. (2008): "Transportation Theory," In: Wolfgang Donsbach (ed.): International Encyclopedia of Communication, Oxford: Wiley-Blackwell, pp. 5170–75.

Hjorth, Larissa (2008): Mobile Media in the Asia-Pacific: Gender and the Art of Being Mobile, London: Routledge.

Hochman, Nadav/Manovich, Lev (2013): "Zooming Into an Instagram City: Reading the Local Through Social Media." In: First Monday 18/7. http://firstmonday.org/article/view/4711/3698

Joiner, James (2014): "Before and After: Kiev on Instagram." In: Esquire Magazine, February 21. http://www.esquire.com/news-politics/news/a235 39/life-in-kiev-before-and-after/ (last accessed: May 16, 2016)

Juris, Jeffrey S. (2012): "Reflections on #Occupy Everywhere: Social media, public space, and emerging logics of aggregation." In: American Ethnologist 39/2, 259–279.

McQuarrie, Edward F./Miller, Jessica/Phillips, Barbara J. (2013): "The Megaphone Effect: Taste and Audience in Fashion Blogging." In: Journal of Consumer Research 40/1, 136-158.

Shaw, Michael (2014): "More on the Photo Exploitation of Kiev: Esquire's Hashtag Mining." In: BagNews. N.p., February 24, 2014. http://www.readingthepictures.org/2014/02/more-on-the-photo-exploitation-of-kiev-esquires-hashtag-mining/ (last accessed: May 16, 2016)

Sontag, Susan (1977): On Photography, New York: Farrar, Straus and Giroux.

Turchynov, Oleksandr V. (2014) "Kiev's Message to Moscow." In: The New York Times, March 11. http://www.nytimes.com/2014/03/12/opinion/ukraines-president-rebuffs-russian-imperialism.html?_r=0 (last accessed: May 16, 2016).

# Google A Religion
Expanding Notions of Religion Online

*Joanna Sleigh*

## GOOGLE A RELIGION

Google is more than just a search engine. The online Oxford English Dictionary (2016) defines Google as an intransitive verb: "To use the Google search engine to find information on the internet." This is an oversimplification as today Google is a company offering products and services beyond search that are geared towards an individual's needs. From *Google Maps, Google Scholar, Google Drive, Google Translate, Gmail, Google News, Google Earth, YouTube,* to the browser *Chrome,* as well as the mobile and computer devices themselves, Google is effectively breaching the gap between the real world (RW) and virtual world (VW) by integrating itself into the daily lives of internet users. Given this ubiquity it is not surprising that Google has become engaged in the realm of religion. What I am referring to is Googlism, *The Church of Google,* an online community, not officially associated with Google, that believes "Google is the closest thing to a god that can be scientifically proven" (MacPherson 2016).

Before delving into questions of whether or not Googlism is a religion, it is important to acknowledge the internet has changed the way spirituality and religion are approached. In a general sense, religion traditionally signified the various ways humans negotiated their relationship with the transcendent, alone or in communities. Durkheim, in his definition of religion, purports that the systems of symbols, beliefs and practices relating to the transcendent unites adherents in a moral community (2005: 40, 46). Similarly, the general anthropological conceptualization of religion is effectively a 'social institution' of more or less geographically bounded social contexts (see Segal 2000 and Morris 1987). However, the online realm of the internet is a place void of overarching social structures or obvious social ties. These traditional pre-modern religious ideas about the world consequently clash with the post-modern world view, which is heavily influenced by social change, detachment, fluid identities and 'play.' It is this collision between notions of serious religiosity and that of playful satire that I am interested in. For it is this clash that I experienced in my research. Members of *The Church of Google* that I spoke to either were firm believers in the spirituality mediated by technology or approached the concept as humorous and 'deeply playful.' So what does religion now mean in the online world? What is a satirical religion? What are motivations for engaging with cyber religions? These are the key questions I intend to investigate using the case study of *The Church of Google*.

## Approaching Religiosity in *The Church of Google*[1]

*The Church of Google*, a website founded in 2011 by Matt MacPherson, is primarily an online platform that unites a network of people in spiritual practice and discussions. This fits the general description of a 'digital religion,' a term used in current scholarship relating to the technological and cultural space evoked in discussions about how online and offline religious spheres have become integrated (Campbell 2012). Notably, this term has evolved from concepts of 'cyber-religion' which emerged in the mid 1990s with the initiation of academic study of religious engagement with the internet (Hojsgaard 2005). "Cyber religion" in a more general sense described any religion mediated by the internet. Brenda Brasher (2001: 29) states "Cyber religion refers to the presence of religious organizations and religious activities in cyberspace." However other analysts such as Lorne L. Dawson (2000: 29) used the term more specifically, stating that cyber religions are "religious organizations and groups that exist only in cyberspace." While Brasher's definition was all encompassing, Dawson's interpretation was problematic in that it was founded on the epistemologically questionable conjecture that religions have an existence independent of human existence. A presupposition which ignores the fact that all online activity is mediated by real life - it takes somebody to press the power button, to set up a program, to design a website, to connect the server and to moderate. Brasher (2001:30) affirms that to date there is no genuine example of a religion that has been established without at least some initial human interference. Helland (2000) offered another conceptual framework, proposing there be two categories 'online religion' and 'religion online' to distinguish differences between the formation of new forms of religiosity in general from religions that used the internet as a new social landscape for practicing spirituality.

---

[1] | Research for this essay was conducted via interviews across a variety of platforms (*Gmail*, *Skype*, *Facebook*, thechurchofgoogle.org and *Reddit*) from the 1.12.15 to the 22.3.16. The main focus was participant observation, interviews, participatory action research and reflexivity.

Helland (2007) has more recently critiqued these terms for they too have become increasingly blurred distinguishing signifiers. Embracing the aforementioned terminological complexities within academic scholarship is the term 'Digital Religion,' a term that acknowledges the internet has become a spiritual forging point between real life & virtual reality, a place fostering and possibly forming religious content and activities. Echoing Campbell (2012) I thus use this term to describe the technological and cultural space referred to in discussions of the integration and blending of offline and online religions.

Image 1

*The Church of Google's Reddit* Community. Accessed: March 22, 2016. www.reddit.com/r/churchofgoogle/

In an era marked by information saturation and social media, it is only natural that religious self-expression and representation online has become an accepted aspect of religious practice and identity. Leveraging the advantages of social media is *The Church of Google* whose members are spread across a diversity of social platforms. The two most prominent are (1) *Facebook* with

636 commenters[2] and (2) *Reddit* with 462 readers.[3] On the home page the *Facebook* plugin is placed below the main body text and is titled in red 'Join the debate below:' inviting visitors on the site to engage in discussion. In the bottom right hand corner of the page is then the hyperlink to the *Reddit* platform, (see Figure 1). This hyperlink takes the form of an an angel icon with the words 'Join us on reddit' hovering above and painted in Google's signature colors. With two platforms of social exchange that promote openness and interaction, it is logical that there is a colorful plethora of commentators and comments. As Horsfield observes, digital media has "increased the potential for a diversity of voices" (2012: 255). This can be attributed to the form of the platforms themselves. *Reddit* functions via an up vote and down vote system, while *Facebook* posts are more of a broadcasting of ideas to networks. Likewise, the post types differentiate accordingly to the platform, *Facebook* posts are more public affirmations of individualistic perspectives while *Reddit* posts are more focused on getting a response from the community. These differences between platforms should not be overlooked.

---

**2 |** Note, it is difficult to estimate how many commentators there are on *The Church of Google*'s website because of the nature of the platforms being used. While the website counts 633 comment threads, this statistic does not take into consideration the number of people who comment within a thread.

**3 |** Interestingly, in my research there were very few people who were active on both *Reddit* and *Facebook*. This suggests that the community of *The Church of Google* is larger than it may at first seem.

*Image 2*

Activity on *The Church of Google's Reddit* platform. Accessed: March 22, 2016. https://www.reddit.com/r/churchofgoogle/comments/45wlfc/googlism_should_be_about_ordering_all_religions/

One final point that I would like to highlight before discussing my research and findings is regarding notions of authenticity[4] in religion. Historically, there have been many spiritual activities rejected by academics for inclusion under the status of 'religion.' David Chidester (2005) talks of the various African tribal religions that were until recently dismissed as mere superstitions, and remarks that still today there is the argument of whether or not cults are religions. I approach the topic of authenticity of religion and spirituality from a social scientist's perspective and affirm that if somebody refers to their activity as 'religious' or 'spiritual' then these phenomenon can be considered religious to them. My reason for having a more inclusive definition is one of ethicality. While many of the people I spoke to during my research were exploring and commenting on the community pages out of curiosity, when I posed the question of 'authenticity' some were offended. Questioning the authenticity of someone's religious practice was thus a major ethical concern.

Yet the notion of authenticity is interesting when one considers *The Church of Google* in the newly termed category of a 'joke religion.' For joke religions, whether they be satirical or parody religions are engaged in a dialogue with non-

---

4 | For notions of authenticity please refer to O'Leary 2004 & 2005, and Dawson 2005.

adherents about whether adherents 'really' believe in the respective religion. Joke religions apply post-modern ideas about society, identity and the body to spiritual thoughts and feelings. They engage new audiences in perceptual and thought experiments about authenticity and fakery, thereby highlighting the oddities of religion and popular culture. These religions synthesize numerous aspects of popular culture with postmodern ideas about religions. They are a synthesis of and a vernacular reaction to both institutional religions such as Christianity and the more loosely defined intuitional countercultural groups such as neo-paganism. David Chidester points out, they are "simultaneously simulations and the real thing" (2005: viii-ix). Religious humor is a form of deep play, which is why it is so suited to the internet, a place of gaming and freedoms. Ultimately, satirical religions are real and fake simultaneously, in that they are able to provide real religious experience, they have the trapping of real religions (mythology, divine, rituals, community, a world view etc), but their intention is to point out the flaws in the religions that they are mocking.

## REASONS AND MOTIVATIONS FOR ENGAGEMENT— THE CHURCH OF GOOGLE

I used *Facebook*, *Skype* and *Reddit* to communicate and research the reasons and motivations underlying user's engagement with *The Church of Google*. An observational method was initially used on *Reddit*, which was followed by interviews on *Facebook* and *Skype*, as well as participatory action research.[5] I have also tried to maintain a continuous process of reflexivity. By using a variety of techniques my goal was to avoid bias and provide truthful data. To ensure that I would gain a fair overview of the community's perspectives within my research timeframe of three months, I contacted via *Facebook* private message a total of 50 active commentators whose posts dated back to 2011. From this sample, eleven people replied as willing to engage with my anthropological investigation of *The Church of Google*. Over the course of four months I talked with these users in depth about their spirituality and found a great diversity in motivations for engagement with *The Church of Google*. Interestingly, the individuals I interviewed came from all corners of the globe, which in reflection can be attributed to the online nature of the community. For the purpose of analysis, I have separated my research findings into two broad categories. (1) Believers, referring to the individuals who approach *The Church of Google* from a spiritual perspective. (2) Non-Believers, refers to the people who perceive that

---

**5** | One man that I interviewed was highly passionate about the topic and took it upon himself to investigate at a local scale the community of Googlists. This is an ongoing process.

*The Church of Google* is a satirical religion, one which aims to highlight the inefficiencies of religion as a concept in general.

## BELIEVERS

"We as Googlists believe google is totally the closest thing to be called god" a young man from Jordan informed me. This man worked at United Nations High Commissioner for Refugees (UNHCR) helping refugees, was a devout believer in *The Church of Google*, had been for over seven years, and as a means of expressing his faith had commented on the website. That was how I had found him. Common to all believers that I spoke to was the sense of passion, of pride, and an eagerness to share as much about their beliefs with me as possible. This individual not only sent me an essay he had written about his faith, but even decided to start his own investigation as to how many Googlists live in his city in Jordan. In answer to people who asked him what he believed in before Google, he would explain that "We believe in the idea itself of Google, you can't touch or harm an idea, Google is everywhere around us... I feel good and proud of my faith." What was also interesting was that he stressed "our religion is the safest in the world... there is no recorded violent act because of it" conveying that one of the motivating factors of his belief was its utter harmlessness. This emphasis on the predominantly philosophical side of religion was shared by other believers. In an interview with a believer in Pasadena, Texas, I was told - "the only set of religious ideas I will ever associate myself with as part of is that resulting from our collective consciousness." What prompted the Texan and Jordanian to engage with the community online was the desire to affirm their ideological ideas with this spiritualism.

Other believers were motivated to engage with the online community as a means of publicizing their more personal perspectives about the nature of Google's spirituality. For instance, one believer named Andy[6] had found *The Church of Google* through his Shamanic practices through which had come the revelation that Google was a Goddess. He told me "Once I found the Google religion, it confirmed that Google is a goddess. Of course she is a goddess. She has given birth to Google Maps, Google Goggles, Google Play radio, Google Play games, and so on and so on. Whom but a woman could give birth?" (Andy 2016). Similarly, another believer had discovered this digital religion by means of illicit drugs and hallucinogens. He wanted to give testimony to the spirituality of the experience of Google that he had discovered via the use of substances, and wanted to promote the use of substances in general. For this believer, the online platform was the only way that he could openly discuss his practices and

---

6 | For the purpose of anonymity, I have used pseudonyms.

beliefs while keeping his identity private. While each believer I found had an individualized conception of Google's spirituality, each was motivated by their individualism to engage with the website.

*Image 3*

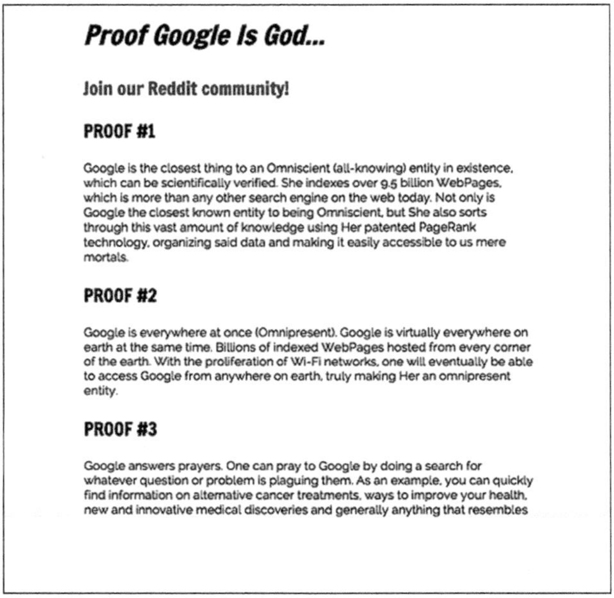

> **Proof Google Is God...**
>
> **Join our Reddit community!**
>
> **PROOF #1**
>
> Google is the closest thing to an Omniscient (all-knowing) entity in existence, which can be scientifically verified. She indexes over 9.5 billion WebPages, which is more than any other search engine on the web today. Not only is Google the closest known entity to being Omniscient, but She also sorts through this vast amount of knowledge using Her patented PageRank technology, organizing said data and making it easily accessible to us mere mortals.
>
> **PROOF #2**
>
> Google is everywhere at once (Omnipresent). Google is virtually everywhere on earth at the same time. Billions of indexed WebPages hosted from every corner of the earth. With the proliferation of Wi-Fi networks, one will eventually be able to access Google from anywhere on earth, truly making Her an omnipresent entity.
>
> **PROOF #3**
>
> Google answers prayers. One can pray to Google by doing a search for whatever question or problem is plaguing them. As an example, you can quickly find information on alternative cancer treatments, ways to improve your health, new and innovative medical discoveries and generally anything that resembles

The Church of Google's Proof that Google is God. Accessed: March 22, 2016. http://www.thechurchofgoogle.org/

## NON-BELIEVERS

The vast majority of people I interviewed approached *The Church of Google* as a satirical digital religion. Whether they were just passing through the site or if they were engaging with numerous threads, their general motivation boiled down to a passionate interest in the topic and an amusement with the playful and creative nature of the website itself. Joe, a construction worker in Dalton, USA told me "I do a lot of searches on Google for religion based topics and terms so I'm sure I followed the rabbit hole to the Googlism page through that process." Similarly, Mike, a scientist specializing in nano technology and bio-design research, who was using DNA to create nano-machines to study, probe, and mimic biological machinery, became involved in the site because of his interests in evolution and atheism - "I am also an outspoken atheist. I run a feed on my FB page entitled 'IOtbA' (It's Okay to b Atheist). The point of the feed is to let people realize that having doubts about the existence of God is a perfectly normal, and in my opinion logical thing to have." For Mike, this platform was key to his self led studies regarding the growth of self identified 'religious nones.' He explained "I do a lot of my own reading, which includes the bible (which most believers have not even read), scientific publications on things like the anti-correlation between intelligence and religiosity, and many books from the likes of people like Sam Harris, Richard Dawkins..." *The Church of Google* was thus a way for him to connect to like-minded people in critical discussions about atheism and religiosity.

Image 4

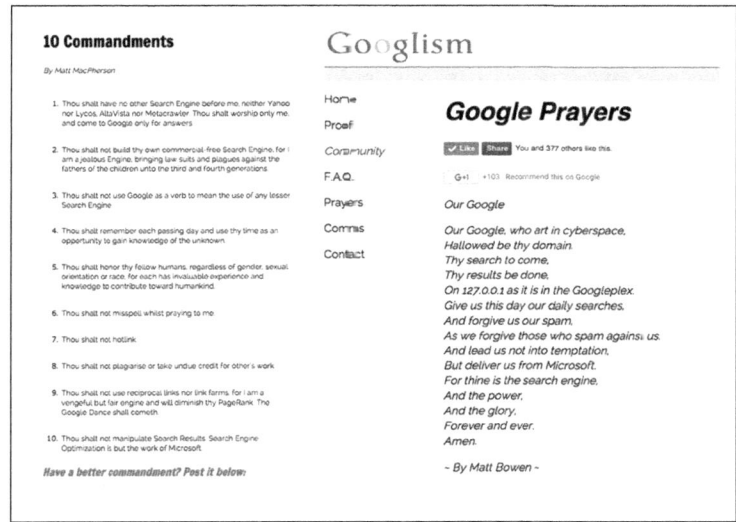

The Church of Google's Prayer and Commandments. Accessed: March 22, 2016. http://www.thechurchofgoogle.org/

Another non-believer I spoke to explained that she enjoyed the site for its irony, and she pointed to the website's humorously playful satire of the traditional Christian and Judaic commandments. For instance, the first commandment on the website is "Thou shalt have no other Search Engine before me, neither Yahoo nor Lycos, AltaVista nor Metacrawler. Thou shalt worship only me, and come to Google only for answers." Not only does the commandment echo the linguistic style of the old testament which uses Old English i.e. - 'Though shalt,' but the very content of the commandment parallels too in that it refers to the concept of monotheism. Furthermore, the commandment references popular culture through terms of Yahoo, Lycos and Metacrawler, Google's competitors, and in that way appeals to a shared cultural understanding in a contextually relevant way. It is this playfulness and use of appropriation that reinforces for non-believers the satirical nature of this digital religion. In the *Facebook* interview with Joe he told me - "I obviously consider it a joke. It is using the framework of traditional theism, finding another example that fits those criteria, then using it to mock the criteria." Moreover, this playfulness and satire was engaging for non-believers as it invited collaboration and content creation. As Marlena, a non-believer informed me "Googlism is something I ran across a while back I wish it had a bigger community... have you looked at the google prayers they are awesome lol." Marlena then sent me a link to the prayers, inviting me share in the humor and to further investigate the prayers listed on the website by other commentators. These prayers appropriated traditional forms of scripture and played upon the online nature of the religion. For instance there is the binary prayer by Jonathan Hill which is made up of the numbers 0 and 1. The potential for users to engage creatively is thus another motivating factor that is relevant both for believers and non-believers.

What motivated these non-believers was also a passion for notions of truth and logic, specifically by the highlighting of the in-authenticities of religion and the flaws underlining certain ideological arguments. One very active commenter, Michael, explained to me that "I can see why someone says Googlism is the closest thing we have to God (a collection of all knowledge of all mankind) and that makes it beautiful and powerful. But to equate it to the omnipotent and omnipresent Yahweh is quite obviously a silly tactic." To give some context, this was in reference to a thread wherein he wrote:

Wow, I'm not sure what is more hilarious about this guys ignorant post. The shear anger and hatred displayed (which, if I'm not mistaken, are not traits commonly accepted by religion), or the fact that the post started with "Why would you worship something that was created by man?" Irony!!! Guess who wrote the bible? Guess who presented you your faith at the beginning of this giant game of telephone? Whether you believe in the nonsense or not, ultimately you are believing a story created by man. And when I say man, I mean people with penises[7]... - Posted Oct. 1, 2013 11:10pm

The constructed nature of religion was a topic that repeatedly arose both in arguments for the validity of *The Church of Google*, as well as arguments undermining the notion of religion as a whole. For instance, Olivier wrote to me saying that while she felt *The Church of Google* was not legitimate to "someone who believes man was made in the image of God, as I believe God was made in the image of man, it's no less legitimate than any other religion." Ultimately,

---

**7** | This reference to penises is something that the interviewee later explained to be a reference to the religious documentary by Bill Mahar.

like many of the non-believers, Olivier engaged with this digital religion as a philosophical exercise, motivated by a fascination with ideas it represented.

## CONCLUSION

To conclude, the multifarious motives for engaging with *The Church of Google* can be attributed to the communicative fluidity afforded by social media platforms combined with the globalized nature of digital religions. While it is difficult to generalize about reasons for engagement with *The Church of Google*, from the overlapping tendencies of the two primary categories of commentators I interviewed 1) Believers, 2) Non-Believers, it is possible to delineate that motivations were highly 'individualistic.' What I mean by this is that each of the subjects I spoke to had a specific mix of ideas and incentives about religion in the online realm. Whether they were affirming an ideological stance, amused by the satire of the content, interested in the creation of new practices, or simply fascinated by ideas being represented, ultimately individualized spirituality was being celebrated and being given a space. *The Church of Google* is thus a place fostering the clash and growth of postmodern ideas with premodern ideas regarding concepts of science, concepts of history, concepts of evolution and concepts of religion, and it is this intellectual non- violent clash that motivates engagement and highlights the incredibly subjective nature of spirituality in today's globalized, digitized, and content saturated society.

## REFERENCES

Brasher, Brenda E. (2001): Give Me That Online Religion, San Francisco: Jossey-Bass.
Campbell, Heidi (2012): Digital Religion: Understanding Religious Practice in New Media Worlds, London: Routledge
Chidester, David (2005): Authentic Fakes: Religion and American Popular Culture, Berkeley, CA: University of California Press.
Dawson, Lorne L. (2000): "Researching Religion in Cyberspace: Issues and Strategies." In: Religion and the Social Order 8, pp. 25-54.
Dawson, Lorne L. (2005): "The Mediation of Religious Experience in Cyberspace." In: Morten Hojsgaard/ Margit Warburg (eds): Religion and Cyberspace, London: Routledge. pp. 15-37.
Durkheim, Émile(2005): The Elementary Forms of the Religious Life: A Study in Religious Sociology, Whitefish, MT: Kessinger Publishing.
Helland, Christopher (2000): "Online-religion/religion-online and virtual communities." In: Jeffrey.K. Hadden/ Douglas. E. Kowan (eds.): Religion

and the Internet: Research prospects and promises, New York: JAI Press, pp. 205-224.

Hojsgaard, Morten (2005): "Cyber-religion. On the cutting edge between the virtual and the real." In: Morten Hojsgaard/ Margit Warburg (eds): Religion and Cyberspace, London: Routledge, pp. 50-63.

Horsfield, Peter (2012): "Editorial: Replacing Religion." In: Australian Journal of Communication 39/1, pp. 1-10.

MacPherson, Matt. "The Official Church of Google." The Official Church of Google. Accessed March 22, 2016. http://www.thechurchofgoogle.org/

Morris, Brian (1987): Anthropological Studies of Religion: An Introductory Text, Cambridge: Cambridge University Press.

O'Leary, Stephan (2004): "Cyberspace as Sacred Space." In: Lorne L. Dawson/ Douglas E. Cowan (eds): Religion Online. Finding Faith on the Internet, London: Routledge, pp. 37-58.

O'Leary, Stephan (2005): "Utopian and Dystopian Possibilities of Networked Religion in the New Millennium." In Morten Hojsgaard/Margit Warburg (eds): Religion and Cyberspace, London: Routledge, pp. 38-50.

Segal, Robert A. (2000): "Categorizing Religion." In: Method & Theory in the Study of Religion 12/1, pp.187-194.

# Notes on Contributors

## Editors

**Urte Undine Frömming** is professor for Visual and Media Anthropology at Freie Universität Berlin at the Institute of Social and Cultural Anthropology. She is the director of the Research Area and the MA Program in Visual and Media Anthropology. She is involved in several third party funded research projects such as WRITER (EU project Grundtvig-GMP with the Education, Audiovisual and Culture Executive Agency); SPRING (Social responsibility through Prosociality-based Interventions to Generate equal opportunities), or the BMBF-funded ANIK (Visualization and mapping of alpine local knowledge in times of climate change). She is supervisor of several PhD projects in the field of digital anthropology, editor of the book "Virtual Environments and Cultures" (Peter Lang Verlag 2013) and Editor-in-Chief of the Journal of Visual and Media Anthropology.

**Steffen Köhn** studied Social Anthropology and Film Studies at Johannes Gutenberg-University in Mainz and at Freie Universität Berlin. He also holds a degree in Film Directing from Deutsche Film und Fernsehakademie Berlin (dffb). He received his doctorate degree in 2014 from Johannes Gutenberg-University Mainz. He is the author of "Mediating Mobility – Visual Anthropology in the Age of Migration" (Wallflower/Columbia University Press 2016).

**Samantha Fox** is currently a PhD candidate in Anthropology at Columbia University in New York, where her work focuses on the relationship between landscape, urban planning, and cultural memory in the East German model city of Eisenhüttenstadt. She is also a lecturer for the course Digital Anthropology in the MA program in Visual and Media Anthropology at Freie Universität Berlin, and has lectured on Digital Anthropology at the Universität der Künste, Berlin. She received her BA with high honors from Dartmouth College in 2008, where she was a Senior Fellow, and her MA in Visual and Media Anthropology from Freie Universität in 2010.

Mike Terry earned a BA in Mass Communication from the University of Utah in 2010 and was awarded a scholarship as a Fine Art, Music, Architecture and Dance Graduate Grantee of the German Academic Exchange Service (DAAD). He finished his MA in Visual and Media Anthropology at Freie Universität Berlin in 2013 with a thesis and photographic installation on the relationship between individuals and the built environment, specifically in the former American Zone of West Berlin. He has worked extensively in the American West, as well as the Southern States, Germany, India and Haiti. He is currently a research associate and PhD candidate at the Research Area Visual and Media Anthropology at the Institute of Social and Cultural Anthropology at Freie Universität Berlin.

## Authors

**Suzanne Beukes** is a writer and videographer based in Johannesburg. Over the last decade, she has reported on business, current affairs and humanitarian issues in Sub-Saharan Africa. She is currently completing her Masters in Visual and Media Anthropology at Freie Universität Berlin.

**Jonas Blume** received a Bachelor of Fine Arts with a major in Sculpture and a minor in Art History from Pratt Institute in Brooklyn, New York. He investigates the relationship of digital media and subjectivity. Prior to moving to Berlin, he worked as a graphic designer for non-profit organizations in New York. He graduated from the MA Program in Visual and Media Anthropology at Freie Universität Berlin in 2016.

**Brigitte Borm** received a BA at the University of Amsterdam specializing in Visual Anthropology. After an internship at the Dutch TV-channel VPRO she went to Brazil to follow journalistic training for foreign correspondents. Borm has also been involved in directing, filming and editing reports for several media, including the NOS. In 2015 she received a MSc in Political Sciences (cum laude). In 2016, she graduated from Freie Universität's Berlin MA Program in Visual and Media Anthropology.

**Dario Bosio** is an independent photography professional. After obtaining a BA in Journalism at Florence University, he graduated in both TV-Documentary and Photojournalism at the Danish School of Media and Journalism. In 2012, together with an international community of authors, he founded the PanAut Collective, a platform for dialogue, exploration and production around visual narratives. Since March 2015 he works as a photo editor and project manager at Metrography Agency, Sulaymaniyah, Iraq. He is currently enrolled in the MA program in Visual and Media Anthropology at Freie Universität Berlin and will graduate in 2017.

**Karly Domb Sadof** is a cross-format and internationally published journalist who aims to combine the values and standards of traditional journalism with her love of imagery and her anthropological expertise of digital cultures and the emerging media landscape. Currently, she is based in Bangkok and works as a photo editor at the Associated Press. She is an authority in the newsroom handling social content and using social media to tell stories and break news. In 2015, Karly Domb Sadof completed her Master's thesis at Freie Universität Berlin, which studied patterns of media consumption on Instagram in Bangkok, one of the world's most instagrammed cities.

**Gretchen Faust** received a Bachelor of Arts in Urban Studies and Art Practice from the University of California, Berkeley. She is based out of New Orleans, LA where she works as a community arts curator and organizer. She is a student of the healing arts, is often on the road collecting stories and spends as much time outside as possible. She graduated from the MA Program in Visual and Media Anthropology in 2016.

**Xiaojing Ji** received a BA in Art Education from East China Normal University in Shanghai and a MA in Art Administration from the Shanghai Conservatory of Music. She has worked as a performing arts curator, as an events specialist and in business development in several companies. She is currently enrolled in the MA program in Visual and Media Anthropology at Freie Universität Berlin and will graduate in 2017.

**Ellen Lapper** holds a Bachelor of Arts in Fine Arts from the University of Leeds and a Foundation Diploma in Art & Design from Wimbledon College of Art. She has professional experience in global and strategic communications and has worked on various exhibitions in Germany, Poland and the UK. Of note is her work for Galerie Barbara Wien where she assisted with the formation of artists' archives. Further, she is a student in the MA program in Visual and Media Anthropology at Freie Universität and will graduate in 2017.

**Jie Liang Lin** received a Bachelor of Fine Art in Studio Art at the New York University. She has lived and worked in New York, China and Hong Kong. She graduated from the MA Program in Visual and Media Anthropology at Freie Universität Berlin in 2016.

**Olivier Llouquet** is a multimedia designer and educator. He first earned a MA in Mechanics from Insa Rouen before entering the field of multimedia and graphic design. From 2009 to 2015 he was a design lecturer at RMIT University, Ho Chi Minh City Campus where he taught courses in Interactive Media, Graphic Design and Media Cultures. He is the co-founder of *digitalmekong*, a creative network providing design services in South East Asia. He is currently part of Freie Universität Berlin's Visual and Media Anthropology Program and will graduate in 2017.

**Sarah Pink** is Distinguished Professor and Director of the Digital Ethnography Research Centre, in the School of Media and Communication at RMIT University, Australia. Her recent books that cover the field of Visual and Media Anthropology include: "Digital Ethnography: Principles and Practice" (2016), "Digital Materialities" (2016), "Screen Ecologies" (2016), "Doing Sensory Ethnography 2nd edition" (2015), "Media, Anthropology and Public Engagement" (2015) and "Doing Visual Ethnography" (2013).

**Veera Helena Pitkänen** is a versatile photojournalist and communications expert, as well as an NGO professional. She received her BA in Communication and Media Studies from the University of Eastern Finland, and has lived in several places around the globe from Iceland to Malaysia. In 2014, she was awarded a scholarship to the Finnish-African Cultural Centre Villa Karo in Benin, West Africa, where she conducted her fieldwork for her MA thesis. Currently she works as a project coordinator supporting refugees and asylum seekers in Helsinki, Finland. She graduated from the MA Program in Visual and Media Anthropology at Freie Universität Berlin in 2014.

**Juan Francisco Riumalló Grüzmacher** received a BA in Journalism at Pontificia Universidad Católica de Chile. He works as a TV reporter for Contacto, Canal 13 and as Editor-in-Chief for „Mundo ad Portas", Canal 13. He also gained work experience in Africa, Southeast Asia and the Middle East. He is a student of the MA Program in Visual and Media Anthropology at Freie Universität Berlin and will graduate in 2017.

**Joanna Sleigh** received a BA at the University of Sydney specializing in Digital Cultures and Art History. She worked as Communications Coordinator at Australia's leading multi-arts centre Carriageworks, as a graphic designer internationally, and has worked for the crowdfunding company Pozible in both the United States and Australia. She is a student of the MA in Visual and Media Anthropology at Freie Universität Berlin and will graduate in 2017.

**Jóhanna Björk Sveinbjörnsdóttir** received her BA in Theory of Art at the University of Iceland. She continues to do research in Greenland, alongside her job as a tour guide and hostel-manager. Jóhanna graduated from the MA Program in Visual and Media Anthropology at Freie Universität Berlin in 2015 and starts pursuing a PhD at the University of Iceland from September 2017.

**Teresa Tiburcio Jiménez** received a BA in Social Anthropology. She graduated from the MA in Visual and Media Anthropology at Freie Universität Berlin in 2015. She currently works as a researcher for CSIC (Superior Council for Scientific Research, Madrid, Spain).

**Sara Wiederkehr González** received her BA in Anthropology at the Universidad Nacional de Colombia, and her MA in Contemporary History at the Universidad Autónoma de Barcelona. She has worked for El Turbión Newspaper in Colombia as a photographer, researcher, writer and editor. She also is a member and creator of "Solilente", a research group on Visual Anthropology. She is focusing her current research on fishermen and women communities in Colombia and Costa Rica. She graduated from the MA Program in Visual and Media Anthropology at Freie Universität Berlin in 2016.